TEXT BOOK OF PHARMACEUTICAL ANALYSIS

[According to latest syllabus of B. Pharm – I semester of Pharmacy Council of India]

Dr. Prince Prashant Sharma
Assistant Professor
Faculty of Pharmaceutical Sciences,
Gurukula Kangri Deemed to be University
Haridwar, Uttarakhand

Dr. Kapil Kumar Goel
Assistant Professor
Faculty of Pharmaceutical Sciences,
Gurukula Kangri Deemed to be University
Haridwar, Uttarakhand

Mr. Rajendra Yadav
Assistant Professor
Faculty of Pharmaceutical Sciences,
Gurukula Kangri Deemed to Be University
Haridwar, Uttarakhand

Dr. Priyanka Tyagi
Assistant Professor
Department of Chemistry,
Dhanauri PG College,
Dhanauri, Haridwar, Uttarakhand

TEXT BOOK OF PHARMACEUTICAL ANALYSIS

NOTION PRESS

PREFACE

The authors feel great pleasure in presenting the first edition of the book **"Text Book of Pharmaceutical Analysis"** for graduate and post graduate students. The present book on **Text Book of Pharmaceutical Analysis** has been written according to the syllabus of B. Pharm – I semester of Pharmacy Council of India and covers full course of the subject.

THE SALIENT FEATURES OF THE BOOK ARE:-

- *Easy to understand style of writing* which makes the book a self-study material.
- *Each new concept has been introduced through day-today problem of interest* to the students which makes the subject matter interesting.
- *The language of the book, on the whole, is lucid and easy to understand.*
- Wherever needed *neatly labeled figures have been drawn.*

The authors hope that the students, teachers and other readers will find the book interesting and to the point covering the course. We hope that the students will receive the book warmly.

I express a sincere thank you to the Management of Faculty of Pharmaceutical Sciences, Gurukula Kangri Deemed to be University and Department of Chemistry, Dhanauri PG College, for their support during the writing of this book.

Every effort is made to keep the book error free. The author will gratefully acknowledge the suggestions to improve the book to make it more useful.

Wishing our readers success in examination and life ahead. The authors feel that their efforts will be fully rewarded if the book serves the purpose for which it is written.

TEXT BOOK OF PHARMACEUTICAL ANALYSIS

CONTENTS

CHAPTER – 1

PHARMACEUTICAL ANALYSIS

INTRODUCTION:

Pharmaceutical analysis is a crucial field within the pharmaceutical sciences, focusing on the qualitative and quantitative analysis of drugs and pharmaceutical formulations. It ensures the safety, efficacy, and quality of pharmaceutical products. Here is a detailed introduction to pharmaceutical analysis:

1. Definition and Importance

Pharmaceutical analysis involves the identification, quantification, and purification of a substance, determination of its structure, and elucidation of its chemical properties. It plays a pivotal role in drug development and manufacturing by ensuring that pharmaceutical products meet regulatory standards.

2. Objectives of Pharmaceutical Analysis

a. **Quality Control**: Ensuring that drugs meet required standards for safety, efficacy, and quality.

b. **Regulatory Compliance**: Adhering to guidelines set by regulatory agencies like the FDA, EMA, and other national bodies.

c. **Drug Development**: Supporting the formulation and development of new drugs.

d. **Stability Testing**: Determining the shelf life and stability of drugs under various environmental conditions.

e. **Identification and Quantification**: Identifying the active pharmaceutical ingredients (APIs) and measuring their concentrations in formulations.

3. Types of Pharmaceutical Analysis

A. Qualitative Analysis

a. **Identification Tests**: Confirming the presence of specific drugs or excipients in a sample.

b. **Structural Elucidation**: Using techniques like NMR, IR, and mass spectrometry to determine the molecular structure of a compound.

B. Quantitative Analysis

a. **Assay Methods**: Measuring the amount of API in a drug formulation.

b. **Content Uniformity**: Ensuring uniform distribution of the API within a batch of tablets or capsules.

c. **Impurity Profiling**: Detecting and quantifying impurities and degradation products.

4. Analytical Techniques

A. Classical Methods

a. **Titrimetric Methods**: Involves acid-base, redox, and complexometric titrations.

b. **Gravimetric Methods**: Measuring the mass of an analyte or its derivative.

B. Instrumental Methods

a. **Spectroscopy**:

i. **UV-Visible Spectroscopy**: Used for analyzing compounds that absorb light in the UV-visible region.

ii. **Infrared (IR) Spectroscopy**: Identifies functional groups in molecules.

iii. **Nuclear Magnetic Resonance (NMR) Spectroscopy**: Provides detailed information about the structure, dynamics, reaction state, and chemical environment of molecules.

iv. **Mass Spectrometry (MS)**: Identifies compounds based on their mass-to-charge ratio.

b. **Chromatography**:

i. **High-Performance Liquid Chromatography (HPLC)**: Separates, identifies, and quantifies components in a mixture.

ii. **Gas Chromatography (GC)**: Used for volatile and semi-volatile compounds.

iii. **Thin Layer Chromatography (TLC)**: Used for quick and efficient separation and identification of compounds.

c. **Electrochemical Methods**:

i. **Potentiometry**: Measures the potential of electrochemical cells.

ii. **Voltammetry**: Measures current as a function of an applied voltage.

5. Regulatory Aspects

Pharmaceutical analysis is governed by stringent regulatory requirements. Key guidelines and standards include:

a. **Good Laboratory Practice (GLP)**: Ensures the quality and integrity of non-clinical laboratory studies.

b. **Pharmacopoeias**: Official publications like the USP, BP, and EP provide standards for drug substances and products.

c. **International Conference on Harmonisation (ICH) Guidelines**: Provides guidance on stability testing, validation of analytical methods, and impurities.

6. Analytical Method Validation

Validation of analytical methods is essential to demonstrate that the methods are suitable for their intended purpose. Key parameters include:

a. **Accuracy**: Closeness of the test results to the true value.

b. **Precision**: Repeatability and reproducibility of the results.

c. **Specificity**: Ability to assess the analyte in the presence of other components.

d. **Detection Limit**: The lowest amount of analyte that can be detected.

e. **Quantitation Limit**: The lowest amount of analyte that can be quantitatively determined.
f. **Linearity**: Ability to obtain test results proportional to the concentration of the analyte.
g. **Robustness**: Ability to remain unaffected by small variations in method parameters.

7. Applications of Pharmaceutical Analysis

a. **Drug Discovery and Development**: Analyzing new chemical entities and their pharmacokinetic profiles.
b. **Quality Assurance**: Ensuring consistency and compliance in manufacturing processes.
c. **Clinical Trials**: Monitoring drug levels in biological samples.
d. **Post-Market Surveillance**: Monitoring the quality and stability of marketed products.

SCOPE OF PHARMACEUTICAL ANALYSIS

The scope of pharmaceutical analysis encompasses a broad range of activities essential for the development, manufacturing, and quality assurance of pharmaceutical products. It plays a pivotal role in ensuring that these products are safe, effective, and of high quality. Here is a detailed overview of the scope of pharmaceutical analysis:

1. Drug Development and Formulation

A. Pre-formulation Studies

a. **Characterization of Drug Substances**: Determining physical and chemical properties such as solubility, stability, and polymorphism.
b. **Compatibility Studies**: Assessing interactions between drug substances and excipients.

B. Formulation Development

a. **Selection of Excipients**: Ensuring that excipients are compatible and do not affect the drug's efficacy or stability.

b. **Optimization of Formulation**: Using analytical techniques to optimize the formulation for maximum efficacy and stability.

2. Quality Control and Assurance

A. Raw Material Testing

a. **Identification and Purity**: Confirming the identity and purity of raw materials used in drug formulation.

b. **Microbial Testing**: Ensuring raw materials are free from microbial contamination.

B. In-Process Testing

a. **Uniformity**: Ensuring uniform distribution of active ingredients in the formulation.

b. **Dissolution Testing**: Measuring the rate at which the drug is released from the formulation.

C. Finished Product Testing

a. **Assay**: Quantifying the active pharmaceutical ingredient (API) in the final product.

b. **Impurity Profiling**: Identifying and quantifying impurities and degradation products.

c. **Stability Testing**: Evaluating the stability of the final product under various conditions to determine shelf life.

3. Regulatory Compliance

A. Adherence to Pharmacopoeias

a. **Compliance with Standards**: Ensuring products meet the standards set by pharmacopoeias such as USP, BP, EP, and others.

B. Good Laboratory Practices (GLP)

a. **Standard Operating Procedures (SOPs)**: Implementing SOPs to ensure consistency and reliability in analytical procedures.

b. **Documentation and Record Keeping**: Maintaining thorough documentation for regulatory audits and reviews.

C. Method Validation

a. **Validation Protocols**: Developing and validating analytical methods to ensure they are suitable for their intended purpose.

b. **Regulatory Submissions**: Preparing data for regulatory submissions to agencies like the FDA and EMA.

4. Research and Development

A. New Analytical Techniques

a. **Innovative Methods**: Developing new and improved analytical techniques to enhance the accuracy and efficiency of pharmaceutical analysis.

B. Drug Metabolism and Pharmacokinetics

a. **Bioanalytical Methods**: Analyzing biological samples to study the pharmacokinetics and metabolism of drugs.

5. Clinical Trials

A. Bioavailability and Bioequivalence Studies

a. **Drug Levels in Biological Fluids**: Measuring drug concentrations in blood, plasma, or urine to assess bioavailability and bioequivalence.

B. Safety and Efficacy Monitoring

a. **Therapeutic Drug Monitoring (TDM)**: Ensuring that drug levels remain within therapeutic ranges to avoid toxicity or subtherapeutic dosing.

6. Post-Market Surveillance

A. Quality Monitoring

a. **Batch Testing**: Continuously testing batches of marketed products to ensure ongoing quality and compliance.

b. **Adverse Event Investigation**: Analyzing samples related to adverse events to identify potential issues with the product.

B. Stability Studies

a. **Long-term and Accelerated Stability Testing**: Conducting stability studies to ensure that products remain stable throughout their shelf life.

7. Environmental and Safety Testing

A. Environmental Impact

a. **Waste Analysis**: Analyzing pharmaceutical waste to ensure it does not harm the environment.

b. **Ecotoxicity Studies**: Studying the effects of pharmaceuticals on the environment and ecosystems.

B. Occupational Safety

a. **Exposure Monitoring**: Monitoring the exposure of pharmaceutical workers to ensure a safe working environment.

DIFFERENT TECHNIQUES OF ANALYSIS

Pharmaceutical analysis employs a variety of techniques to ensure the quality, safety, and efficacy of pharmaceutical products. These techniques can be broadly categorized into classical methods and instrumental methods. Here's a detailed look at the different techniques used in pharmaceutical analysis:

1. Classical Methods

A. Titrimetric Methods

a. **Acid-Base Titration**: Used to determine the concentration of acidic or basic drugs. Indicators or pH meters are used to detect the endpoint.

b. **Redox Titration**: Involves oxidation-reduction reactions to determine the concentration of analytes. Common reagents include potassium permanganate and iodine.

c. **Complexometric Titration**: Used for the determination of metal ions using complexing agents like EDTA.

d. **Precipitation Titration**: Involves the formation of a precipitate during the titration process, such as using silver nitrate for chloride ion determination.

B. Gravimetric Methods

a. **Precipitation Gravimetry**: Involves precipitating the analyte as a solid, filtering, drying, and weighing the precipitate to determine its quantity.

b. **Volatilization Gravimetry**: The analyte is converted to a gaseous form and its mass is determined by measuring the mass loss.

2. Instrumental Methods

A. Spectroscopic Techniques

1. Ultraviolet-Visible (UV-Vis) Spectroscopy

a. **Principle**: Based on the absorption of UV or visible light by molecules, leading to electronic transitions.

b. **Applications**: Quantification of drug substances, impurity profiling, and dissolution testing.

2. Infrared (IR) Spectroscopy

a. **Principle**: Measures the absorption of IR radiation by molecules, causing vibrational transitions.

b. **Applications**: Identification of functional groups, structural elucidation, and studying polymorphism.

3. Nuclear Magnetic Resonance (NMR) Spectroscopy

a. **Principle**: Based on the absorption of radiofrequency radiation by nuclei in a magnetic field.

b. **Applications**: Detailed structural elucidation, studying molecular dynamics, and identifying impurities.

4. Mass Spectrometry (MS)

a. **Principle**: Measures the mass-to-charge ratio of ions to identify and quantify molecules.

b. **Applications**: Structural elucidation, impurity profiling, and quantification in complex matrices.

5. Atomic Absorption Spectroscopy (AAS)

a. **Principle**: Measures the absorption of light by free atoms in the gaseous state.

b. **Applications**: Determination of trace metals in pharmaceuticals.

B. Chromatographic Techniques

1. High-Performance Liquid Chromatography (HPLC)

a. **Principle**: Separation based on the differential partitioning of compounds between a mobile phase and a stationary phase.

b. **Applications**: Quantification of APIs, impurity profiling, stability testing, and bioanalytical studies.

2. Gas Chromatography (GC)

a. **Principle**: Separation of volatile compounds based on their distribution between a gaseous mobile phase and a solid or liquid stationary phase.

b. **Applications**: Analysis of volatile and semi-volatile compounds, residual solvent analysis, and environmental monitoring.

3. Thin Layer Chromatography (TLC)

a. **Principle**: Separation based on differential adsorption of compounds on a stationary phase coated on a glass or plastic plate.

b. **Applications**: Qualitative analysis, purity testing, and monitoring reaction progress.

4. High-Performance Thin Layer Chromatography (HPTLC)

a. **Principle**: An advanced form of TLC with higher resolution and sensitivity.

b. **Applications**: Quantitative analysis and quality control.

5. Size-Exclusion Chromatography (SEC)

a. **Principle**: Separation based on the size of molecules as they pass through a porous stationary phase.

b. **Applications**: Analysis of proteins, polymers, and other macromolecules.

C. Electrochemical Techniques

1. Potentiometry

a. **Principle**: Measurement of the potential of an electrochemical cell to determine the concentration of an analyte.

b. **Applications**: pH measurement, ion-selective electrode analysis, and titration endpoints.

2. Voltammetry

a. **Principle**: Measurement of current as a function of an applied potential to study redox behavior of analytes.

b. **Applications**: Trace metal analysis, electroactive drug quantification, and studying redox properties.

3. Polarography

a. **Principle**: A type of voltammetry where the working electrode is a dropping mercury electrode.

b. **Applications**: Analysis of metal ions and organic compounds.

D. Thermal Analysis

1. Differential Scanning Calorimetry (DSC)

a. **Principle**: Measures heat flow associated with phase transitions of a sample.

b. **Applications**: Determination of melting points, crystallinity, and thermal stability.

2. Thermogravimetric Analysis (TGA)

a. **Principle**: Measures the change in weight of a sample as a function of temperature.

b. **Applications**: Analysis of thermal stability, decomposition kinetics, and moisture content.

3. Other Techniques

A. X-ray Diffraction (XRD)

a. **Principle**: Measures the diffraction pattern of X-rays passing through a crystalline sample.

b. **Applications**: Identification of crystalline phases, determination of polymorphism, and studying crystallinity.

B. Capillary Electrophoresis (CE)

a. **Principle**: Separation of analytes based on their size and charge in an electric field.

b. **Applications**: Analysis of small ions, peptides, proteins, and nucleotides.

METHODS OF EXPRESSING CONCENTRATION

In pharmaceutical analysis, accurately expressing the concentration of a substance is critical for ensuring the efficacy and safety of drug formulations. Various methods are used to express concentration, each suited to different types of analysis and requirements. Here's a detailed look at the methods of expressing concentration in pharmaceutical analysis:

1. Percentage Concentrations

A. Weight/Weight Percentage (w/w%)

a. **Definition**: The amount of solute (in grams) present in 100 grams of solution or mixture.

b. **Application**: Commonly used for solid mixtures or ointments.

c. **Example**: A 5% (w/w) ointment contains 5 grams of active ingredient in 100 grams of the total mixture.

B. Weight/Volume Percentage (w/v%)

a. **Definition**: The amount of solute (in grams) present in 100 milliliters of solution.

b. **Application**: Frequently used in solutions, suspensions, and emulsions.

c. **Example**: A 10% (w/v) solution contains 10 grams of solute in 100 milliliters of solution.

C. Volume/Volume Percentage (v/v%)

a. **Definition**: The volume of solute present in 100 milliliters of solution.

b. **Application**: Typically used for liquid-liquid mixtures.

c. **Example**: A 70% (v/v) ethanol solution contains 70 milliliters of ethanol in 100 milliliters of solution.

2. Molarity (M)

a. **Definition**: The number of moles of solute per liter of solution (mol/L).

b. **Application**: Widely used in chemical reactions and titrations.

c. **Example**: A 1 M solution of NaCl contains 1 mole of NaCl dissolved in 1 liter of solution.

3. Molality (m)

a. **Definition**: The number of moles of solute per kilogram of solvent (mol/kg).

b. **Application**: Useful when temperature changes, as molality is independent of temperature.

c. **Example**: A 1 m solution contains 1 mole of solute in 1 kilogram of solvent.

4. Normality (N)

a. **Definition**: The number of equivalents of solute per liter of solution (eq/L).

b. **Application**: Used in acid-base titrations, redox reactions, and precipitation reactions.

c. **Example**: A 1 N solution of HCl contains 1 equivalent (1 mole of H^+ ions) per liter of solution.

5. Mole Fraction (χ)

a. **Definition**: The ratio of the number of moles of solute to the total number of moles of all components in the mixture.

b. **Application**: Used in thermodynamic calculations and colligative properties.

c. **Example**: For a solution containing 1 mole of solute and 9 moles of solvent, the mole fraction of the solute is 0.1.

6. Parts per Million (ppm) and Parts per Billion (ppb)

A. Parts per Million (ppm)

a. **Definition**: The amount of solute present in one million parts of solution.

b. **Application**: Used for trace analysis in environmental and pharmaceutical samples.

c. **Example**: 1 ppm of a solute means 1 milligram of solute in 1 liter of water.

B. Parts per Billion (ppb)

a. **Definition**: The amount of solute present in one billion parts of solution.

b. **Application**: Used for ultra-trace analysis.

c. **Example**: 1 ppb of a solute means 1 microgram of solute in 1 liter of water.

7. Percent Composition

a. **Definition**: The percentage by mass of each element in a compound.

b. **Application**: Used in the analysis of organic compounds to determine their empirical formula.

c. **Example**: The percent composition of water (H_2O) is 11.19% hydrogen and 88.81% oxygen.

8. Pharmacopoeial Units

A. Units per Milliliter (U/mL)

a. **Definition**: The activity of a drug or biological product expressed in units per milliliter.

b. **Application**: Used for biological products like vaccines, hormones, and enzymes.

c. **Example**: Insulin concentration is often expressed in units per milliliter.

B. International Units (IU)

a. **Definition**: A standardized amount of substance agreed upon by international bodies to measure biological activity.

b. **Application**: Used for vitamins, hormones, and other biologically active substances.

c. **Example**: The vitamin D concentration in supplements is commonly expressed in IU.

9. Specific Activity

a. **Definition**: The activity of an enzyme per milligram of total protein (units/mg).
b. **Application**: Used to express the purity and potency of enzyme preparations.
c. **Example**: An enzyme preparation might have a specific activity of 50 units/mg.

10. Osmolarity and Osmolality

A. Osmolarity

a. **Definition**: The number of osmoles of solute per liter of solution (osm/L).
b. **Application**: Used in the formulation of intravenous fluids and parenteral nutrition.
c. **Example**: A solution with 1 osmole of solute per liter has an osmolarity of 1 osm/L.

B. Osmolality

a. **Definition**: The number of osmoles of solute per kilogram of solvent (osm/kg).
b. **Application**: Used in clinical settings to measure the concentration of solutes in body fluids.
c. **Example**: Blood plasma typically has an osmolality of 275-295 mOsm/kg.

PRIMARY AND SECONDARY STANDARDS

In pharmaceutical analysis, standards are crucial for ensuring the accuracy and reliability of analytical results. They are used to calibrate instruments, validate methods, and ensure the quality of pharmaceutical products. Standards can be classified into primary and secondary standards, each with distinct characteristics and applications. Here's a detailed overview:

1. Primary Standards

Definition

Primary standards are highly pure compounds that can be used to prepare solutions of known concentration with high accuracy. These standards are used for the calibration of analytical methods and instruments.

Characteristics

a. **High Purity**: Typically 99.9% or higher.
b. **Stable:** Chemically and physically stable over time.
c. **Non-Hygroscopic**: Do not absorb moisture from the air.
d. **Known Composition**: Their chemical composition and properties are well defined.
e. **High Equivalent Weight**: Reduces the relative error in weighing.
f. **Low Reactivity**: Not prone to degradation or reaction under normal storage conditions.

Applications

a. **Calibration of Instruments**: Used to calibrate analytical instruments such as spectrophotometers, chromatographs, and titrators.
b. **Standardization of Solutions**: Preparing standard solutions for use in titrations and other quantitative analyses.
c. **Reference Material**: Serving as a reference for comparing the results of analytical methods.

Examples

a. **Potassium Dichromate ($K_2Cr_2O_7$)**: Used in redox titrations.
b. **Sodium Chloride (NaCl)**: Used in the preparation of standard solutions for conductivity measurements.
c. **Anhydrous Sodium Carbonate (Na_2CO_3)**: Used in acid-base titrations.
d. **Pure Caffeine**: Used as a standard in UV-visible spectroscopy.

2. Secondary Standards

Definition

Secondary standards are substances whose purity and concentration are determined by comparison with a primary standard. They are used more frequently in routine analysis once they have been standardized.

Characteristics

a. **Less Pure than Primary Standards**: Typically not as pure as primary standards.
b. **Standardized Against Primary Standards**: Their concentration is determined through calibration with a primary standard.
c. **Good Stability**: Generally stable, but not necessarily as stable as primary standards.
d. **Convenience**: Often more readily available and easier to handle in routine laboratory work.

Applications

a. **Routine Analysis**: Used for routine calibration and quality control once standardized.
b. **Method Validation**: Employed in validating analytical methods after initial calibration with primary standards.
c. **Assay of Pharmaceuticals**: Used in the quantitative analysis of pharmaceutical formulations.

Examples

a. **Sodium Hydroxide (NaOH)**: Used in acid-base titrations after standardization with primary standards like potassium hydrogen phthalate.
b. **Hydrochloric Acid (HCl)**: Standardized against primary standards like anhydrous sodium carbonate.
c. **Ethanol**: Used in various pharmaceutical analyses after standardization with a primary standard.

OXALIC ACID

In pharmaceutical analysis, preparing and standardizing solutions of oxalic acid involves several steps to ensure accuracy and reproducibility. Here's a general outline of how you might approach this:

Preparation of Oxalic Acid Solutions:

1. **Molar Solutions (M)**:
    a. **Molar solutions** are prepared to a specific concentration in moles per liter (M).
    b. Calculate the molecular weight of oxalic acid ($H_2C_2O_4$). The molar mass is approximately 90.03 g/mol.
    c. Determine the desired concentration (Molarity, M) of the solution.
    d. Use the formula: Molarity (M)=

$$\frac{\text{Mass of solute (g)}}{\text{Volume of solvent (L)}}.$$

2. **Normal Solutions (N)**:
    a. **Normal solutions** are based on the equivalent weight of the solute.
    b. Oxalic acid is a dibasic acid, so its equivalent weight is half its molecular weight because it can donate two protons (H^+ ions).
    c. Calculate the normality (N) using the formula: Normality (N)=

$$\frac{\text{Weight of solute (g)}}{\text{Equivalent weight (g/equiv)}}.$$

Standardization of Solutions:

1. **Standardization of Molar Oxalic Acid Solution**:
    a. Prepare a primary standard solution of oxalic acid. Potassium hydrogen phthalate (KHP) is commonly used as a primary standard.
    b. Weigh an accurately measured amount of KHP (primary standard) and dissolve it in distilled water.

c. Titrate this solution against the molar solution of oxalic acid using a suitable indicator (phenolphthalein or methyl orange).

d. Calculate the exact concentration of the oxalic acid solution based on the titration results.

2. **Standardization of Normal Oxalic Acid Solution**:

   a. Prepare a standard solution of sodium hydroxide (NaOH) of known concentration.

   b. Titrate the normal oxalic acid solution against the NaOH solution using phenolphthalein as an indicator (as oxalic acid is dibasic and will neutralize two equivalents of base).

   c. Calculate the exact normality of the oxalic acid solution based on the volume of NaOH required.

Safety Considerations:

1. Handle oxalic acid with care as it is toxic and can cause skin irritation and other health issues if mishandled.
2. Use appropriate protective gear such as gloves, goggles, and lab coat when handling oxalic acid and during titrations.

This process ensures that your oxalic acid solutions are accurately prepared and standardized, meeting the stringent requirements of pharmaceutical analysis.

SODIUM HYDROXIDE

In pharmaceutical analysis, sodium hydroxide (NaOH) solutions are commonly used as titrants for the determination of acids and for pH adjustments. Here's how you would typically prepare and standardize various molar and normal solutions of sodium hydroxide:

Preparation of Sodium Hydroxide Solutions:

1. **Molar Solutions (M)**:

   a. **Molar solutions** are prepared to a specific concentration in moles per liter (M).

b. Calculate the molecular weight of sodium hydroxide (NaOH). The molar mass is approximately 40.00 g/mol.
c. Determine the desired concentration (Molarity, M) of the solution.
d. Use the formula: Molarity (M)=

$$\frac{\text{Mass of solute (g)}}{\text{Volume of solvent (L)}}.$$

2. **Normal Solutions (N):**
   a. **Normal solutions** are based on the equivalent weight of the solute.
   b. Sodium hydroxide is monobasic, so its equivalent weight is its molecular weight because it donates one hydroxyl ion (OH^-).
   c. Calculate the normality (N) using the formula: Normality (N)=

$$\frac{\text{Weight of solute (g)}}{\text{Equivalent weight (g/equiv)}}.$$

Standardization of Solutions:

1. **Standardization of Molar Sodium Hydroxide Solution:**
   a. Prepare a primary standard acid solution, such as oxalic acid ($H_2C_2O_4$), which can be accurately weighed and dissolved in distilled water.
   b. Titrate this acid solution against the molar solution of sodium hydroxide using a suitable indicator (phenolphthalein or methyl orange).
   c. Calculate the exact concentration of the sodium hydroxide solution based on the titration results.
2. **Standardization of Normal Sodium Hydroxide Solution:**
   a. Prepare a standard solution of an acid of known concentration, such as hydrochloric acid (HCl).

b. Titrate the normal sodium hydroxide solution against the acid solution using phenolphthalein as an indicator (since sodium hydroxide is monobasic, it neutralizes one equivalent of acid).
c. Calculate the exact normality of the sodium hydroxide solution based on the volume of acid required.

Safety Considerations:

1. Sodium hydroxide is a strong base and can cause severe burns and other health hazards if mishandled.
2. Always handle sodium hydroxide solutions with appropriate precautions, including gloves, goggles, and lab coat.
3. Work in a well-ventilated area to avoid inhalation of vapors.

HYDROCHLORIC ACID

In pharmaceutical analysis, hydrochloric acid (HCl) solutions are commonly used as titrants for the determination of bases and for pH adjustments. Here's a guide on how to prepare and standardize various molar and normal solutions of hydrochloric acid:

Preparation of Hydrochloric Acid Solutions:

1. **Molar Solutions (M)**:
   a. **Molar solutions** are prepared to a specific concentration in moles per liter (M).
   b. Calculate the molecular weight of hydrochloric acid (HCl). The molar mass is approximately 36.46 g/mol (chlorine's atomic weight is 35.45 and hydrogen's is 1.01).
   c. Determine the desired concentration (Molarity, M) of the solution.
   d. Use the formula: Molarity (M)=

$$\frac{\text{Mass of solute (g)}}{\text{Volume of solvent (L)}}.$$

2. **Normal Solutions (N)**:
   a. **Normal solutions** are based on the equivalent weight of the solute.

b. Hydrochloric acid is monobasic, so its equivalent weight is its molecular weight because it donates one hydrogen ion (H^+).

c. Calculate the normality (N) using the formula: Normality (N)=

$$\frac{\text{Weight of solute (g)}}{\text{Equivalent weight (g/equiv)}}.$$

Standardization of Solutions:

1. **Standardization of Molar Hydrochloric Acid Solution**:
   a. Prepare a primary standard base solution, such as sodium carbonate (Na_2CO_3), which can be accurately weighed and dissolved in distilled water.
   b. Titrate this base solution against the molar solution of hydrochloric acid using a suitable indicator (phenolphthalein or methyl orange).
   c. Calculate the exact concentration of the hydrochloric acid solution based on the titration results.
2. **Standardization of Normal Hydrochloric Acid Solution**:
   a. Prepare a standard solution of a base of known concentration, such as sodium hydroxide (NaOH).
   b. Titrate the normal hydrochloric acid solution against the base solution using phenolphthalein as an indicator (since hydrochloric acid is monobasic, it neutralizes one equivalent of base).
   c. Calculate the exact normality of the hydrochloric acid solution based on the volume of base required.

Safety Considerations:

1. Hydrochloric acid is corrosive and can cause burns and irritation. Handle with care and use appropriate personal protective equipment (PPE) including gloves, goggles, and lab coat.
2. Work in a well-ventilated area to avoid inhalation of vapors.

SODIUM THIOSULPHATE

In pharmaceutical analysis, sodium thiosulfate ($Na_2S_2O_3$) solutions are commonly used as titrants for the determination of iodine and in certain oxidation-reduction reactions. Here's how you can prepare and standardize various molar and normal solutions of sodium thiosulfate:

Preparation of Sodium Thiosulfate Solutions:

1. **Molar Solutions (M)**:
    a. **Molar solutions** are prepared to a specific concentration in moles per liter (M).
    b. Calculate the molecular weight of sodium thiosulfate ($Na_2S_2O_3$). The molar mass is approximately 158.11 g/mol.
    c. Determine the desired concentration (Molarity, M) of the solution.
    d. Use the formula: Molarity (M)=

$$\frac{\text{Mass of solute (g)}}{\text{Volume of solvent (L)}}.$$

2. **Normal Solutions (N)**:
    a. **Normal solutions** are based on the equivalent weight of the solute.
    b. Sodium thiosulfate has multiple oxidation states and can act as a reducing agent, so its equivalent weight varies depending on the reaction.
    c. Calculate the normality (N) based on the specific reaction or use, usually determined through standardization against a primary standard solution.

Standardization of Solutions:

1. **Standardization of Molar Sodium Thiosulfate Solution**:
    a. Prepare a primary standard solution of a suitable oxidizing agent, such as potassium iodate (KIO_3) or potassium iodide (KI).
    b. Titrate this solution against the molar solution of sodium thiosulfate using a starch indicator (which detects the endpoint where all iodine has reacted).

c. Calculate the exact concentration of the sodium thiosulfate solution based on the titration results.

2. **Standardization of Normal Sodium Thiosulfate Solution**:
   a. For normal solutions, standardization involves titrating against a primary standard with known concentration, typically iodine solutions.
   b. Prepare a standard solution of iodine (I_2) or an iodide solution (KI) of known concentration.
   c. Titrate the normal sodium thiosulfate solution against the iodine solution using starch as an indicator (the endpoint is when the blue-black color of the starch-iodine complex disappears).
   d. Calculate the exact normality of the sodium thiosulfate solution based on the volume of iodine solution required.

Safety Considerations:

1. Sodium thiosulfate is relatively safe compared to some other chemicals used in titrations, but it's still important to handle it with care.
2. Wear appropriate personal protective equipment (PPE), including gloves and goggles, when handling chemicals.
3. Work in a well-ventilated area to avoid inhaling any vapors.

SULPHURIC ACID

In pharmaceutical analysis, sulphuric acid (H_2SO_4) solutions are used as titrants in acid-base reactions and for pH adjustments. Here's how you can prepare and standardize various molar and normal solutions of sulphuric acid:

Preparation of Sulphuric Acid Solutions:

1. **Molar Solutions (M)**:
   a. **Molar solutions** are prepared to a specific concentration in moles per liter (M).
   b. Calculate the molecular weight of sulphuric acid (H_2SO_4). The molar mass is approximately 98.08 g/mol.
   c. Determine the desired concentration (Molarity, M) of the solution.

d. Use the formula: Molarity (M)=

$$\frac{\text{Mass of solute (g)}}{\text{Volume of solvent (L)}}.$$

2. **Normal Solutions (N)**:
   a. **Normal solutions** are based on the equivalent weight of the solute.
   b. Sulphuric acid is dibasic, so its equivalent weight is half its molecular weight because it can donate two hydrogen ions (H^+).
   c. Calculate the normality (N) using the formula: Normality (N)=

$$\frac{\text{Weight of solute (g)}}{\text{Equivalent weight (g/equiv)}}.$$

Standardization of Solutions:

1. **Standardization of Molar Sulphuric Acid Solution**:
   a. Prepare a primary standard base solution, such as sodium carbonate (Na_2CO_3), which can be accurately weighed and dissolved in distilled water.
   b. Titrate this base solution against the molar solution of sulphuric acid using a suitable indicator (phenolphthalein or methyl orange).
   c. Calculate the exact concentration of the sulphuric acid solution based on the titration results.
2. **Standardization of Normal Sulphuric Acid Solution**:
   a. Prepare a standard solution of a base of known concentration, such as sodium hydroxide (NaOH).
   b. Titrate the normal sulphuric acid solution against the base solution using phenolphthalein as an indicator (since sulphuric acid is dibasic, it neutralizes two equivalents of base).
   c. Calculate the exact normality of the sulphuric acid solution based on the volume of base required.

Safety Considerations:

1. Sulphuric acid is highly corrosive and can cause severe burns and other health hazards if mishandled.
2. Always handle sulphuric acid with extreme caution, wear appropriate PPE including gloves, goggles, and lab coat.
3. Work in a well-ventilated area to avoid inhaling any vapors.

POTASSIUM PERMANGANATE

In pharmaceutical analysis, potassium permanganate ($KMnO_4$) is used as a strong oxidizing agent and is particularly useful in titrations involving reducing agents and for disinfection purposes. Here's how you can prepare and standardize various molar and normal solutions of potassium permanganate:

Preparation of Potassium Permanganate Solutions:

1. **Molar Solutions (M)**:
   a. **Molar solutions** are prepared to a specific concentration in moles per liter (M).
   b. Calculate the molecular weight of potassium permanganate ($KMnO_4$). The molar mass is approximately 158.03 g/mol.
   c. Determine the desired concentration (Molarity, M) of the solution.
   d. Use the formula: Molarity (M)=

$$\frac{\text{Mass of solute (g)}}{\text{Volume of solvent (L)}}.$$

2. **Normal Solutions (N)**:
   a. **Normal solutions** are based on the equivalent weight of the solute.
   b. Potassium permanganate is a strong oxidizing agent, and its equivalent weight is its molecular weight because it can donate one permanganate ion (MnO_4^-).
   c. Calculate the normality (N) using the formula: Normality (N)=

$$\frac{\text{Weight of solute (g)}}{\text{Equivalent weight (g/equiv)}}.$$

Standardization of Solutions:

1. **Standardization of Molar Potassium Permanganate Solution**:
    a. Prepare a primary standard reducing agent solution, such as oxalic acid ($H_2C_2O_4$), which can be accurately weighed and dissolved in distilled water.
    b. Titrate this reducing agent solution against the molar solution of potassium permanganate using a suitable indicator (e.g., phenolphthalein or methyl orange for endpoint detection).
    c. Calculate the exact concentration of the potassium permanganate solution based on the titration results.
2. **Standardization of Normal Potassium Permanganate Solution**:
    a. For normal solutions, standardization involves titrating against a primary standard with known concentration, typically a reducing agent.
    b. Prepare a standard solution of the reducing agent (e.g., oxalic acid) of known concentration.
    c. Titrate the normal potassium permanganate solution against the reducing agent solution using a suitable indicator (the endpoint is typically when the color changes indicating complete oxidation).
    d. Calculate the exact normality of the potassium permanganate solution based on the volume of reducing agent solution required.

Safety Considerations:

1. Potassium permanganate is a strong oxidizing agent and can cause skin irritation and staining. Handle with care and wear appropriate PPE including gloves, goggles, and lab coat.
2. Work in a well-ventilated area to avoid inhaling any vapors.

CERIC AMMONIUM SULPHATE

In pharmaceutical analysis, ceric ammonium sulfate (also known as cerium(IV) ammonium sulfate or $(NH_4)_2Ce(SO_4)_4$) is used as an oxidizing agent in redox titrations. Here's how you can prepare and standardize various molar and normal solutions of ceric ammonium sulfate:

Preparation of Ceric Ammonium Sulfate Solutions:

1. **Molar Solutions (M)**:
   a. **Molar solutions** are prepared to a specific concentration in moles per liter (M).
   b. Calculate the molecular weight of ceric ammonium sulfate $[(NH_4)_2Ce(SO_4)_4]$. The molar mass includes:
      i. Ammonium ion (NH_4^+): Approximately 18.04 g/mol
      ii. Ceric ion (Ce^{4+}): Approximately 140.12 g/mol
      iii. Sulfate ion (SO_4^{2-}): Approximately 96.06 g/mol
   c. Determine the desired concentration (Molarity, M) of the solution.
   d. Use the formula: Molarity (M)= $\frac{\text{Mass of solute (g)}}{\text{Volume of solvent (L)}}$.

2. **Normal Solutions (N)**:
   a. **Normal solutions** are based on the equivalent weight of the ceric ion (Ce^{4+}).
   b. Ceric ammonium sulfate can act as a tetra-positive cation (Ce^{4+}) in redox reactions.
   c. Calculate the normality (N) using the formula: Normality (N)= $\frac{\text{Weight of solute (g)}}{\text{Equivalent weight of } Ce^{4+} \text{ (g/equiv)}}$.

Standardization of Solutions:

1. **Standardization of Molar Ceric Ammonium Sulfate Solution**:
   a. Prepare a primary standard reducing agent solution, such as ferrous ammonium sulfate ($Fe(NH_4)_2(SO_4)_2 \cdot 6H_2O$), which can be accurately weighed and dissolved in distilled water.

b. Titrate this reducing agent solution against the molar solution of ceric ammonium sulfate using a suitable indicator (e.g., ferroin indicator for cerimetric titrations).

c. Calculate the exact concentration of the ceric ammonium sulfate solution based on the titration results.

2. **Standardization of Normal Ceric Ammonium Sulfate Solution**:

   a. For normal solutions, standardization involves titrating against a primary standard with known concentration, typically a reducing agent.

   b. Prepare a standard solution of the reducing agent (e.g., ferrous ammonium sulfate) of known concentration.

   c. Titrate the normal ceric ammonium sulfate solution against the reducing agent solution using a suitable indicator (endpoint determination involves a color change from the reduced to the oxidized form).

   d. Calculate the exact normality of the ceric ammonium sulfate solution based on the volume of reducing agent solution required.

Safety Considerations:

1. Ceric ammonium sulfate is toxic and should be handled with care.
2. Use appropriate personal protective equipment (PPE) including gloves, goggles, and lab coat.
3. Work in a well-ventilated area to avoid inhaling any vapors or dust.

Multiple Choice Questions (MCQs) Based on the Above Context

1. What is the primary function of pharmaceutical analysis?

   A) Marketing pharmaceuticals

   B) Designing drug packaging

   C) Ensuring safety, efficacy, and quality of pharmaceutical products

   D) Pricing of pharmaceutical products

2. Which agency is responsible for regulatory compliance of pharmaceuticals in the United States?

   A) FDA

   B) EMA

   C) WHO

   D) CDC

3. What type of spectroscopy identifies functional groups in molecules?

   A) UV-Visible Spectroscopy

   B) Infrared Spectroscopy

   C) NMR Spectroscopy

   D) Mass Spectrometry

4. In which method are the components separated based on differential partitioning between a mobile phase and a stationary phase?

   A) Gas Chromatography

   B) Potentiometry

   C) Voltammetry

   D) High-Performance Liquid Chromatography

5. What is the principle behind the validation of analytical methods in pharmaceutical analysis?

   A) To prove that methods are unsuitable for their intended purpose

   B) To demonstrate that the methods are suitable for their intended purpose

   C) To comply solely with international shipping regulations

   D) To increase the cost of pharmaceuticals

6. Which of the following is an example of a primary standard?

   A) Sodium chloride

   B) Sodium hydroxide

   C) Potassium dichromate

   D) Ethanol

7. What is the use of IR Spectroscopy in pharmaceutical analysis?
   A) Determining the weight of compounds
   B) Measuring the electrical conductivity of solutions
   C) Identifying functional groups in molecular structures
   D) Separating volatile compounds
8. What type of titration involves oxidation-reduction reactions to determine the concentration of analytes?
   A) Acid-base titration
   B) Redox titration
   C) Complexometric titration
   D) Precipitation titration
9. Which chromatographic technique is used for separating volatile and semi-volatile compounds?
   A) High-Performance Liquid Chromatography
   B) Gas Chromatography
   C) Thin Layer Chromatography
   D) Size-Exclusion Chromatography
10. Which instrumental method measures the mass-to-charge ratio of ions?
   A) UV-Visible Spectroscopy
   B) Infrared Spectroscopy
   C) Mass Spectrometry
   D) Nuclear Magnetic Resonance Spectroscopy
11. What does GLP stand for in the context of pharmaceutical analysis?
   A) Good Legal Practices
   B) Good Laboratory Practices
   C) General Laboratory Procedures
   D) Global Laboratory Protocols
12. What is the purpose of pharmacopoeias in pharmaceutical analysis?
   A) To provide entertainment

B) To regulate drug prices

C) To set standards for drug substances

D) To advertise pharmaceutical products

13. What does molarity measure in the context of solution preparation?

A) The number of ions per liter of solution

B) The number of moles of solute per liter of solution

C) The weight of solute per liter of solution

D) The volume of solute per liter of solution

14. Which is a common use of titrimetric methods in pharmaceutical analysis?

A) Measuring temperature stability of substances

B) Determining concentration of acidic or basic drugs

C) Identifying color properties of substances

D) Calculating the size of particulate matter

15. In what aspect of pharmaceutical analysis is Voltammetry particularly useful?

A) Determining melting points

B) Studying redox properties of analytes

C) Identifying colors in compound mixtures

D) Measuring temperatures

16. Which method is characterized by the separation of compounds based on their size during passage through a porous stationary phase?

A) Gas Chromatography

B) High-Performance Liquid Chromatography

C) Size-Exclusion Chromatography

D) Thin Layer Chromatography

17. What does the term 'potentiometry' refer to in pharmaceutical analysis?

A) A method for determining the potency of a drug

B) A method for measuring potential of an electrochemical cell

C) A process for determining the melting point of a compound

D) A procedure for measuring the volume of a liquid

18. Which is a primary use of Normality in titrations?

A) To measure heat flow in reactions

B) To calculate electrical conductivity

C) To determine equivalents of solute per liter of solution

D) To find the density of solutions

19. What role does the International Conference on Harmonisation (ICH) play in pharmaceutical analysis?

A) Provides entertainment at conferences

B) Provides guidelines on stability testing and validation of methods

C) Organizes pharmaceutical sales conventions

D) Regulates the prices of pharmaceuticals globally

20. What is the significance of measuring the mole fraction in solutions?

A) It helps in thermodynamic calculations and colligative properties

B) It determines the electrical conductivity of the solution

C) It identifies the color properties of the solution

D) It measures the temperature stability of the solution

Short Answer Type Questions (Subjective)

1. What is pharmaceutical analysis and why is it important?
2. List three objectives of pharmaceutical analysis.
3. Define qualitative analysis in the context of pharmaceuticals.
4. What is the role of spectroscopy in pharmaceutical analysis?
5. How does chromatography contribute to the identification of compounds in a sample?
6. Explain the significance of analytical method validation in pharmaceutical analysis.
7. What is Good Laboratory Practice (GLP) and why is it important?
8. How is mass spectrometry used to identify pharmaceutical compounds?

9. Describe the process of impurity profiling in pharmaceutical products.
10. What is the role of stability testing in pharmaceutical analysis?
11. Why are pharmacopoeias important in pharmaceutical analysis?
12. What is the difference between molarity and molality?
13. How do electrochemical methods like potentiometry and voltammetry work?
14. Describe the principle of gas chromatography.
15. Explain the concept of method specificity in analytical validation.
16. What is a primary standard and give an example?
17. Describe how a titrimetric method like acid-base titration is conducted.
18. How does dissolution testing assess the quality of pharmaceutical formulations?
19. Explain the role of therapeutic drug monitoring in clinical trials.
20. What is ecotoxicity testing and why is it conducted?

Long Answer Type Questions (Subjective)

1. Discuss the various phases of drug development and formulation in pharmaceutical analysis.
2. Explain the role and importance of high-performance liquid chromatography (HPLC) in the analysis of pharmaceutical compounds.
3. Describe the process of method validation in pharmaceutical analysis and list the key parameters involved.
4. Detail the significance of regulatory compliance in pharmaceutical analysis and the agencies involved.
5. Explain the process and importance of standardizing solutions using primary and secondary standards in pharmaceutical analysis.
6. Discuss the various applications of spectroscopic techniques like UV-Visible and Infrared (IR) spectroscopy in the identification and analysis of pharmaceutical substances.

7. Describe the procedure for preparing and standardizing a molar solution of sodium hydroxide and its use in pharmaceutical analysis.
8. Explain how stability testing is performed and its significance in determining the shelf life of pharmaceutical products.
9. Discuss the role of environmental and safety testing in the pharmaceutical industry and how it impacts public health.
10. Describe the procedures and safety considerations involved in handling strong oxidizing agents like potassium permanganate in pharmaceutical laboratories.

Answer Key

1. C (Ensuring safety, efficacy, and quality of pharmaceutical products)
2. A (FDA)
3. B (Infrared Spectroscopy)
4. D (High-Performance Liquid Chromatography)
5. B (To demonstrate that the methods are suitable for their intended purpose)
6. C (Potassium dichromate)
7. C (Identifying functional groups in molecular structures)
8. B (Redox titration)
9. B (Gas Chromatography)
10. C (Mass Spectrometry)
11. B (Good Laboratory Practices)
12. C (To set standards for drug substances)
13. B (The number of moles of solute per liter of solution)
14. B (Determining concentration of acidic or basic drugs)
15. B (Studying redox properties of analytes)
16. C (Size-Exclusion Chromatography)
17. B (A method for measuring potential of an electrochemical cell)
18. C (To determine equivalents of solute per liter of solution)

19.B (Provides guidelines on stability testing and validation of methods)

20.A (It helps in thermodynamic calculations and colligative properties)

CHAPTER – 2

ERRORS

INTRODUCTION:

Errors are an inevitable part of human endeavors, particularly in complex fields such as medicine, science, engineering, and everyday life. Understanding errors is crucial to minimizing their impact and improving systems and processes. Here's an introduction to errors, their types, causes, and implications:

What are Errors?

Errors refer to mistakes or deviations from accuracy or correctness. They can occur in various contexts, including:

1. **Measurement Errors:** Discrepancies between measured values and true values.
2. **Human Errors:** Mistakes made by individuals due to oversight, misunderstanding, or lack of knowledge.
3. **Systemic Errors:** Flaws within a system or process that lead to consistent inaccuracies.

Types of Errors

1. **Systematic Errors:**
    a. **Definition:** Consistent, repeatable errors associated with faulty equipment or flawed experimental design.
    b. **Examples:** Calibration errors, environmental changes, instrument bias.
    c. **Characteristics:** These errors can be predicted and corrected once identified.
2. **Random Errors:**
    a. **Definition:** Errors that arise from unpredictable fluctuations in experimental conditions.

b. **Examples:** Variations in temperature, slight changes in measurement technique, human reaction time.
c. **Characteristics:** These errors are unpredictable and vary in magnitude and direction.

3. **Human Errors:**
   a. **Definition:** Errors made by individuals due to various factors such as fatigue, misinterpretation, or lack of knowledge.
   b. **Examples:** Misreading measurements, incorrect data entry, forgetting steps in a procedure.
   c. **Characteristics:** Can be reduced through training, automation, and error-proofing strategies.
4. **Blunders:**
   a. **Definition:** Gross errors typically resulting from human oversight.
   b. **Examples:** Recording wrong units, transposing numbers, miscalculations.
   c. **Characteristics:** Often obvious and can be detected through double-checking and verification processes.

Causes of Errors

1. **Instrumental Factors:**
   a. Faulty or uncalibrated instruments.
   b. Inappropriate selection of tools for the task.
2. **Environmental Factors:**
   a. Changes in temperature, humidity, or pressure.
   b. External noise or vibrations.
3. **Human Factors:**
   a. Inattention or distraction.
   b. Lack of knowledge or experience.
   c. Physical and mental fatigue.
4. **Procedural Factors:**

a. Incomplete or unclear instructions.
b. Poorly designed processes or systems.

Implications of Errors

1. **In Medicine:**
    a. Misdiagnosis or incorrect treatment.
    b. Adverse drug reactions.
    c. Impact on patient safety and outcomes.
2. **In Science and Engineering:**
    a. Inaccurate data and flawed conclusions.
    b. Failed experiments or projects.
    c. Financial loss and resource wastage.
3. **In Everyday Life:**
    a. Financial errors, such as incorrect billing.
    b. Miscommunication and misunderstandings.
    c. Safety hazards in daily activities.

Reducing Errors

1. **Training and Education:**
    a. Regular training programs to enhance skills and knowledge.
    b. Emphasis on attention to detail and double-checking work.
2. **Improved Processes:**
    a. Designing error-proof systems and processes (Poka-Yoke).
    b. Implementing standard operating procedures (SOPs).
3. **Technology and Automation:**
    a. Using advanced technology to reduce human intervention.
    b. Automation of repetitive and error-prone tasks.
4. **Quality Control:**
    a. Regular calibration and maintenance of equipment.
    b. Implementing rigorous quality control measures and audits.

SOURCES OF ERRORS

Understanding the sources of errors is crucial for diagnosing and mitigating them. Here is a detailed exploration of the sources of errors in various contexts:

Sources of Errors

1. Instrumental Errors

a. **Calibration Issues:** Instruments that are not properly calibrated can produce consistently inaccurate results.
b. **Instrument Drift:** Over time, instruments can drift from their original calibration settings.
c. **Wear and Tear:** Physical wear and aging of instruments can affect their precision and accuracy.
d. **Environmental Influence:** External factors like temperature, humidity, and electromagnetic interference can affect instrument performance.
e. **Design Flaws:** Inherent inaccuracies due to poor design or inappropriate selection of instruments for specific tasks.

2. Environmental Errors

a. **Temperature Fluctuations:** Variations in temperature can affect both the measurement process and the instruments.
b. **Humidity and Moisture:** High humidity levels can influence electrical instruments and affect materials being measured.
c. **Vibrations and Noise:** Physical vibrations and acoustic noise can interfere with sensitive measurements.
d. **Lighting Conditions:** In optical measurements, the intensity and wavelength of light can cause errors.

3. Human Errors

a. **Misreading Data:** Incorrectly reading measurement values due to oversight or poor visibility.

b. **Recording Errors:** Mistakes in documenting data, such as transposing numbers or using incorrect units.

c. **Calculation Mistakes:** Errors in performing mathematical operations, especially under pressure or fatigue.

d. **Misinterpretation:** Misunderstanding instructions, data, or procedures due to lack of knowledge or experience.

e. **Inconsistency:** Variation in performance due to human factors like fatigue, stress, or lack of attention.

4. Procedural Errors

a. **Ambiguous Instructions:** Vague or unclear procedures can lead to inconsistent execution.

b. **Improper Techniques:** Incorrect application of techniques due to insufficient training or experience.

c. **Sequence Errors:** Performing steps in the wrong order, which can compromise the integrity of the process.

d. **Incomplete Procedures:** Omitting necessary steps, leading to incomplete or incorrect results.

5. Systemic Errors

a. **Design and Planning Flaws:** Fundamental errors embedded in the design of experiments, systems, or processes.

b. **Process Inconsistencies:** Variations in processes due to lack of standardization or adherence to protocols.

c. **Software Bugs:** Errors in software algorithms or data processing programs that lead to inaccurate results.

d. **Bias:** Systematic favoritism or prejudice in data collection, analysis, or interpretation.

6. Sampling Errors

a. **Non-representative Samples:** Samples that do not accurately reflect the population being studied.

b. **Sample Size:** Too small sample sizes can lead to significant deviations from the true values.
c. **Selection Bias:** Errors introduced by non-random selection of samples.

Examples of Errors in Various Fields

In Medicine:

a. **Diagnosis Errors:** Misinterpretation of diagnostic tests due to faulty equipment or human error.
b. **Medication Errors:** Incorrect dosage or drug administration due to misreading prescriptions or labels.
c. **Surgical Errors:** Mistakes during surgery due to procedural errors or miscommunication among the surgical team.

In Science and Engineering:

a. **Experimental Errors:** Inaccuracies in experimental results due to instrumental, procedural, or environmental factors.
b. **Data Processing Errors:** Errors in data analysis due to software bugs or incorrect application of algorithms.
c. **Manufacturing Errors:** Defects in products due to faulty machinery, improper techniques, or human error.

In Everyday Life:

a. **Financial Errors:** Mistakes in billing, transactions, or financial records due to human error or system glitches.
b. **Communication Errors:** Misunderstandings and misinterpretations in verbal or written communication.
c. **Safety Hazards:** Accidents and injuries due to improper use of equipment, failure to follow safety protocols, or environmental factors.

Mitigating Sources of Errors

1. **Instrumental Mitigation:**
    a. Regular calibration and maintenance of instruments.

b. Using high-quality, well-designed instruments suitable for the specific task.

2. **Environmental Control:**
   a. Maintaining controlled environmental conditions during measurements.
   b. Isolating sensitive instruments from environmental disturbances.
3. **Human Error Reduction:**
   a. Providing thorough training and continuous education.
   b. Implementing double-check systems and standard operating procedures.
   c. Using automation and error-proofing techniques where possible.
4. **Procedural Improvements:**
   a. Developing clear, unambiguous, and detailed procedures.
   b. Standardizing processes and ensuring adherence to protocols.
   c. Regularly reviewing and updating procedures to incorporate best practices.
5. **Systemic Solutions:**
   a. Designing robust systems and processes with built-in error detection and correction mechanisms.
   b. Conducting regular audits and reviews to identify and address systemic issues.
   c. Implementing quality control measures and feedback loops for continuous improvement.

TYPES OF ERRORS

Errors can be broadly classified into different types based on their sources and characteristics. Understanding these types helps in identifying, diagnosing, and correcting them effectively. Here are the main types of errors associated with the sources of errors:

Types of Errors

1. Instrumental Errors

a. **Zero Error:** When an instrument does not start from exactly zero.

b. **Calibration Error:** Errors due to improper calibration of measuring instruments.

c. **Scale Error:** Inaccuracies due to the physical imperfections or wear and tear of the scale or measurement tool.

d. **Instrument Drift:** Gradual change in instrument readings over time due to internal changes in the instrument.

2. Environmental Errors

a. **Temperature Error:** Variations in measurements due to changes in temperature affecting the instruments or the object being measured.

b. **Humidity Error:** Effects of moisture levels on electronic components or materials being measured.

c. **Pressure Error:** Changes in atmospheric pressure affecting sensitive instruments.

d. **Vibration and Noise Error:** Interference from external vibrations or acoustic noise during measurements.

3. Human Errors

a. **Reading Error:** Mistakes made while reading measurements or recording data.

b. **Calculation Error:** Errors in mathematical operations performed manually.

c. **Interpretation Error:** Misunderstanding instructions, data, or results.

d. **Execution Error:** Mistakes in performing tasks or following procedures due to fatigue, distraction, or lack of knowledge.

e. **Recording Error:** Incorrectly documenting data, such as transposing numbers or using wrong units.

4. Procedural Errors

a. **Omission Error:** Skipping necessary steps in a procedure.

b. **Sequence Error:** Performing steps in the wrong order.

c. **Instructional Error:** Errors due to unclear, incomplete, or incorrect instructions.
d. **Technique Error:** Incorrect application of techniques or methods.

5. Systemic Errors

a. **Design Error:** Flaws in the design of experiments, systems, or processes leading to consistent inaccuracies.
b. **Process Error:** Variations or flaws in processes due to lack of standardization or adherence to protocols.
c. **Software Error:** Bugs or flaws in software algorithms or data processing programs.
d. **Bias Error:** Systematic favoritism or prejudice in data collection, analysis, or interpretation.

6. Sampling Errors

a. **Selection Bias:** Non-random selection of samples leading to unrepresentative results.
b. **Non-response Error:** Errors due to lack of response from part of the sample population.
c. **Sample Size Error:** Errors due to too small or too large sample sizes affecting the reliability and validity of results.

Examples of Errors in Various Fields

In Medicine:

a. **Diagnostic Error:** Incorrect diagnosis due to misinterpretation of diagnostic tests or patient data.
b. **Medication Error:** Administering the wrong dosage or medication due to misreading prescriptions or labels.
c. **Surgical Error:** Mistakes during surgery due to procedural errors or miscommunication among the surgical team.

In Science and Engineering:

a. **Experimental Error:** Inaccuracies in experimental results due to instrumental, procedural, or environmental factors.

b. **Data Processing Error:** Errors in data analysis due to software bugs or incorrect application of algorithms.

c. **Manufacturing Error:** Defects in products due to faulty machinery, improper techniques, or human error.

In Everyday Life:

a. **Financial Error:** Mistakes in billing, transactions, or financial records due to human error or system glitches.

b. **Communication Error:** Misunderstandings and misinterpretations in verbal or written communication.

c. **Safety Hazard Error:** Accidents and injuries due to improper use of equipment, failure to follow safety protocols, or environmental factors.

Mitigating Types of Errors

1. **Instrumental Mitigation:**
    a. Regular calibration and maintenance of instruments.
    b. Using high-quality, well-designed instruments suitable for specific tasks.
2. **Environmental Control:**
    a. Maintaining controlled environmental conditions during measurements.
    b. Isolating sensitive instruments from environmental disturbances.
3. **Human Error Reduction:**
    a. Providing thorough training and continuous education.
    b. Implementing double-check systems and standard operating procedures.
    c. Using automation and error-proofing techniques where possible.

4. **Procedural Improvements:**
    a. Developing clear, unambiguous, and detailed procedures.
    b. Standardizing processes and ensuring adherence to protocols.
    c. Regularly reviewing and updating procedures to incorporate best practices.
5. **Systemic Solutions:**
    a. Designing robust systems and processes with built-in error detection and correction mechanisms.
    b. Conducting regular audits and reviews to identify and address systemic issues.
    c. Implementing quality control measures and feedback loops for continuous improvement.

METHODS OF MINIMIZING ERRORS

Minimizing errors involves identifying potential sources of errors and implementing effective strategies to reduce their occurrence. Here are methods to minimize errors associated with different sources:

Methods of Minimizing Errors

1. Instrumental Errors

a. **Regular Calibration:** Frequently calibrate instruments to ensure accuracy and reliability.

b. **Routine Maintenance:** Perform regular maintenance to keep instruments in good working condition.

c. **High-Quality Instruments:** Use well-designed, high-quality instruments suitable for specific tasks.

d. **Environmental Protection:** Shield instruments from environmental factors such as temperature, humidity, and vibrations.

2. Environmental Errors

a. **Controlled Environment:** Maintain stable environmental conditions (temperature, humidity, pressure) during measurements.

b. **Isolation Techniques:** Use isolation techniques to minimize the impact of vibrations and noise.
c. **Monitoring Systems:** Implement monitoring systems to continuously track environmental conditions and alert deviations.
d. **Protective Enclosures:** Use protective enclosures for sensitive instruments to shield them from environmental fluctuations.

3. Human Errors

a. **Training and Education:** Provide comprehensive training and continuous education to enhance skills and knowledge.
b. **Standard Operating Procedures:** Develop and enforce standard operating procedures (SOPs) to ensure consistency.
c. **Double-Check Systems:** Implement double-check systems where another person verifies critical steps and data.
d. **Automation:** Automate repetitive and error-prone tasks to reduce human intervention and errors.
e. **Ergonomic Design:** Design workstations and tools ergonomically to minimize fatigue and improve accuracy.

4. Procedural Errors

a. **Clear Instructions:** Provide clear, unambiguous, and detailed instructions for all procedures.
b. **Standardization:** Standardize processes to ensure consistency and reduce variations.
c. **Checklists:** Use checklists to ensure all steps are followed and nothing is omitted.
d. **Regular Audits:** Conduct regular audits to identify and address procedural deviations and improvements.
e. **Feedback Mechanisms:** Implement feedback mechanisms to continually refine and improve procedures.

5. Systemic Errors

a. **Robust Design:** Design robust systems and processes with built-in error detection and correction mechanisms.

b. **Quality Assurance:** Implement rigorous quality assurance and control measures throughout processes.

c. **Regular Reviews:** Conduct regular reviews and audits to identify systemic issues and make necessary adjustments.

d. **Bias Mitigation:** Use randomization and blinding techniques to reduce bias in data collection and analysis.

e. **Redundancy:** Incorporate redundancy into critical systems to prevent single points of failure.

6. Sampling Errors

a. **Representative Sampling:** Use random sampling techniques to ensure samples accurately represent the population.

b. **Appropriate Sample Size:** Determine and use an appropriate sample size to ensure statistical reliability.

c. **Minimize Non-Response:** Employ strategies to minimize non-response and ensure a high response rate.

d. **Stratified Sampling:** Use stratified sampling to ensure all relevant subgroups are adequately represented.

Examples of Minimizing Errors in Various Fields

In Medicine:

a. **Double-Checking Medications:** Implement double-check systems for medication administration to ensure correct dosage and drug.

b. **Electronic Health Records:** Use electronic health records (EHR) to reduce documentation errors and improve data accuracy.

c. **Standardized Protocols:** Develop standardized protocols for diagnostic tests and treatments to reduce variability.

In Science and Engineering:

a. **Calibration Schedules:** Establish regular calibration schedules for scientific instruments to ensure accuracy.
b. **Controlled Experiments:** Design experiments with controlled variables to minimize environmental impact.
c. **Peer Review:** Use peer review and verification processes to identify and correct experimental errors.

In Everyday Life:

a. **Financial Software:** Use financial management software to reduce errors in billing, transactions, and record-keeping.
b. **Clear Communication:** Practice clear and concise communication to minimize misunderstandings and misinterpretations.
c. **Safety Training:** Provide comprehensive safety training and regular refreshers to reduce accidents and injuries.

Implementing Error Minimization Strategies

1. **Education and Training:**
    a. Invest in continuous education and training programs for all personnel to keep them updated on best practices and new techniques.
2. **Process Improvement:**
    a. Regularly review and refine processes to incorporate new insights and technologies, ensuring continuous improvement.
3. **Technology Integration:**
    a. Integrate advanced technology and automation to reduce human error and enhance precision.
4. **Quality Control:**
    a. Implement stringent quality control measures at every stage to detect and correct errors promptly.
5. **Feedback Loops:**

a. Establish feedback loops to gather input from all stakeholders and use this feedback to drive improvements and minimize errors.

ACCURACY

Accuracy in the context of sources of errors refers to the degree to which the result of a measurement, calculation, or specification conforms to the correct value or a standard. High accuracy means the measured or calculated value is very close to the true or accepted value. Here's an exploration of how accuracy is affected by different sources of errors and how it can be improved:

Accuracy and Sources of Errors

1. Instrumental Errors

a. **Impact on Accuracy:** Instrumental errors can cause measurements to deviate consistently from the true value, leading to systematic inaccuracies.

b. **Improving Accuracy:**

   i. **Calibration:** Regularly calibrate instruments to ensure they provide accurate readings.

   ii. **Maintenance:** Keep instruments in good working condition through regular maintenance.

   iii. **Quality Instruments:** Use high-quality, well-designed instruments that are suitable for the specific task.

2. Environmental Errors

a. **Impact on Accuracy:** Environmental factors like temperature, humidity, and vibrations can cause fluctuations in measurements, reducing accuracy.

b. **Improving Accuracy:**

   i. **Controlled Environment:** Maintain stable environmental conditions during measurements.

   ii. **Environmental Monitoring:** Continuously monitor and control environmental factors.

   iii. **Protective Measures:** Use enclosures or isolation techniques to shield instruments from environmental variations.

3. Human Errors

a. **Impact on Accuracy:** Human errors, such as misreading data or incorrect calculations, can lead to significant inaccuracies.

b. **Improving Accuracy:**

   i. **Training:** Provide thorough training to improve skills and reduce mistakes.

   ii. **Standard Procedures:** Implement standard operating procedures to ensure consistency.

   iii. **Automation:** Automate repetitive tasks to reduce human intervention and errors.

4. Procedural Errors

a. **Impact on Accuracy:** Errors in procedures, such as skipping steps or performing tasks in the wrong order, can compromise the accuracy of results.

b. **Improving Accuracy:**

   i. **Clear Procedures:** Develop clear, detailed, and unambiguous procedures.

   ii. **Checklists:** Use checklists to ensure all steps are followed correctly.

   iii. **Regular Reviews:** Conduct regular reviews and audits to ensure adherence to procedures and identify areas for improvement.

5. Systemic Errors

a. **Impact on Accuracy:** Flaws in the design of systems or processes can lead to consistent inaccuracies.

b. **Improving Accuracy:**

   i. **Robust Design:** Design systems with built-in error detection and correction mechanisms.

   ii. **Quality Control:** Implement rigorous quality control measures to identify and correct systemic issues.

iii. **Continuous Improvement:** Regularly review and refine systems and processes to incorporate best practices.

6. Sampling Errors

a. **Impact on Accuracy:** Non-representative samples and inappropriate sample sizes can lead to inaccurate results that do not reflect the true population.

b. **Improving Accuracy:**

   i. **Random Sampling:** Use random sampling techniques to ensure samples are representative.

   ii. **Adequate Sample Size:** Determine and use appropriate sample sizes to ensure statistical reliability.

   iii. **Stratified Sampling:** Use stratified sampling to ensure all relevant subgroups are adequately represented.

Examples of Improving Accuracy in Various Fields

In Medicine:

1. **Accurate Diagnoses:** Use calibrated diagnostic tools and follow standardized protocols to ensure accurate diagnoses.
2. **Medication Administration:** Implement double-check systems to ensure the correct medication and dosage are administered.
3. **Electronic Health Records:** Use EHRs to accurately document and retrieve patient information.

In Science and Engineering:

1. **Precision Instruments:** Use high-precision instruments and regularly calibrate them to ensure accurate measurements.
2. **Controlled Experiments:** Design experiments with controlled variables to minimize environmental impact on results.
3. **Data Verification:** Implement peer review and verification processes to ensure the accuracy of experimental data.

In Everyday Life:

1. **Accurate Billing:** Use financial management software to reduce errors in billing and transactions.
2. **Clear Communication:** Practice clear and concise communication to minimize misunderstandings.
3. **Safety Protocols:** Follow comprehensive safety protocols to prevent accidents and injuries.

Strategies for Enhancing Accuracy

1. **Education and Training:**
    a. Invest in continuous education and training to keep personnel updated on best practices and new techniques.
2. **Process Improvement:**
    a. Regularly review and refine processes to incorporate new insights and technologies, ensuring continuous improvement.
3. **Technology Integration:**
    a. Integrate advanced technology and automation to enhance precision and reduce human errors.
4. **Quality Control:**
    a. Implement stringent quality control measures at every stage to detect and correct errors promptly.
5. **Feedback Loops:**
    a. Establish feedback loops to gather input from all stakeholders and use this feedback to drive improvements and enhance accuracy.

PRECISION

Precision, in the context of sources of errors, refers to the consistency and repeatability of measurements or results. It is the degree to which repeated measurements under unchanged conditions show the same results. High precision means that the measurements are very close to each other, even if they are not necessarily close to the true value. Here's an exploration of how precision is affected by different sources of errors and how it can be improved:

Precision and Sources of Errors

1. Instrumental Errors

a. **Impact on Precision:** Instrumental errors, such as inconsistencies in the measurement tool, can lead to variations in repeated measurements.

b. **Improving Precision:**

   i. **Regular Calibration:** Regularly calibrate instruments to maintain consistency.

   ii. **High-Quality Instruments:** Use precise, high-quality instruments designed for repeatability.

   iii. **Maintenance:** Perform routine maintenance to ensure instruments remain in optimal condition.

2. Environmental Errors

a. **Impact on Precision:** Fluctuations in environmental conditions, like temperature, humidity, and vibrations, can cause inconsistencies in measurements.

b. **Improving Precision:**

   i. **Controlled Environment:** Maintain stable environmental conditions during measurements.

   ii. **Isolation Techniques:** Use isolation techniques to minimize the impact of external vibrations and noise.

   iii. **Environmental Monitoring:** Implement continuous monitoring systems to detect and correct environmental variations.

3. Human Errors

a. **Impact on Precision:** Human errors, such as inconsistent reading or recording of data, can lead to variability in measurements.

b. **Improving Precision:**

i. **Training:** Provide comprehensive training to improve consistency in performing tasks.
ii. **Standard Procedures:** Implement and follow standard operating procedures to ensure uniformity.
iii. **Automation:** Use automated systems to reduce human intervention and variability.

4. Procedural Errors

a. **Impact on Precision:** Variations in procedures, such as differences in technique or order of operations, can affect the repeatability of results.

b. **Improving Precision:**

i. **Clear Procedures:** Develop and follow clear, detailed procedures.
ii. **Checklists:** Use checklists to ensure all steps are performed consistently.
iii. **Regular Audits:** Conduct regular audits to identify and correct procedural deviations.

5. Systemic Errors

a. **Impact on Precision:** Flaws in the design of systems or processes can lead to systematic variations, affecting precision.

b. **Improving Precision:**

i. **Robust Design:** Design systems and processes with precision in mind, incorporating error detection and correction mechanisms.
ii. **Quality Control:** Implement rigorous quality control measures to ensure consistent processes.
iii. **Continuous Improvement:** Regularly review and refine systems to eliminate sources of variability.

6. Sampling Errors

a. **Impact on Precision:** Variability in sample selection and size can affect the consistency of results.

b. **Improving Precision:**

i. **Consistent Sampling Methods:** Use consistent and standardized sampling methods.

ii. **Adequate Sample Size:** Ensure an adequate sample size to reduce variability.

iii. **Representative Sampling:** Use techniques such as stratified sampling to ensure consistency across different subgroups.

Examples of Improving Precision in Various Fields

In Medicine:

1. **Consistent Diagnostic Tools:** Use standardized and calibrated diagnostic tools to ensure repeatable results.
2. **Standardized Protocols:** Follow standardized treatment protocols to minimize variability in patient outcomes.
3. **Electronic Health Records:** Use EHRs to consistently document patient information and track treatment plans.

In Science and Engineering:

1. **Precision Instruments:** Use high-precision instruments and regularly calibrate them to maintain consistency.
2. **Controlled Experiments:** Design experiments with controlled variables to ensure repeatability.
3. **Data Replication:** Conduct replication studies to confirm the precision of experimental results.

In Everyday Life:

1. **Consistent Financial Records:** Use financial management software to ensure consistent and accurate record-keeping.
2. **Clear Communication:** Establish clear and consistent communication protocols to reduce misunderstandings.
3. **Safety Protocols:** Implement and follow consistent safety protocols to prevent accidents and ensure repeatable safety measures.

Strategies for Enhancing Precision

1. **Education and Training:**
    a. Provide continuous education and training to ensure personnel perform tasks consistently and accurately.
2. **Process Improvement:**
    a. Regularly review and refine processes to eliminate sources of variability and improve consistency.
3. **Technology Integration:**
    a. Integrate advanced technology and automation to reduce human-induced variability and enhance precision.
4. **Quality Control:**
    a. Implement stringent quality control measures to detect and correct inconsistencies in processes and results.
5. **Feedback Loops:**
    a. Establish feedback loops to gather input from all stakeholders and use this feedback to drive improvements in precision.

SIGNIFICANT FIGURES

Significant figures are the digits in a number that contribute to its precision. They include all the non-zero digits, any zeros between them, and any trailing zeros in the decimal part. Understanding and correctly using significant figures is crucial in minimizing and understanding errors, as they directly influence the accuracy and precision of measurements and calculations.

Significant Figures and Sources of Errors

1. Instrumental Errors

a. **Impact on Significant Figures:** Instrument precision limits the number of significant figures that can be accurately reported. For example, a ruler marked to the nearest millimeter cannot accurately measure to the nearest micrometer.

b. **Improving Accuracy with Significant Figures:**

   i. **Instrument Selection:** Choose instruments that provide a suitable number of significant figures for the required measurement precision.

   ii. **Calibration:** Ensure instruments are calibrated to maintain their precision and accuracy, thereby maximizing the number of significant figures.

2. Environmental Errors

a. **Impact on Significant Figures:** Environmental factors such as temperature and humidity can affect the reliability of measurements, potentially altering the significant figures.

b. **Improving Accuracy with Significant Figures:**

   i. **Stable Conditions:** Maintain stable environmental conditions to ensure that measurements reflect the true number of significant figures.

   ii. **Environmental Control:** Use control systems to mitigate the impact of environmental variations on the measurement process.

3. Human Errors

a. **Impact on Significant Figures:** Human errors, such as misreading or improperly recording measurements, can reduce the accuracy and precision of the significant figures reported.

b. **Improving Accuracy with Significant Figures:**

   i. **Training:** Educate individuals on the importance of significant figures and proper measurement techniques.

   ii. **Standard Operating Procedures (SOPs):** Implement SOPs to ensure consistent and accurate recording of significant figures.

4. Procedural Errors

a. **Impact on Significant Figures:** Errors in following procedures, such as incorrect calculations or steps, can lead to inaccurate significant figures in the results.

b. **Improving Accuracy with Significant Figures:**
    i. **Checklists and Protocols:** Use checklists to ensure all steps are correctly followed and significant figures are accurately reported.
    ii. **Verification:** Implement verification steps where calculations and measurements are checked for accuracy in significant figures.

5. Systemic Errors

a. **Impact on Significant Figures:** Flaws in the design of systems or processes can lead to consistent errors in the number of significant figures used or reported.
b. **Improving Accuracy with Significant Figures:**
    i. **Robust Design:** Design systems and processes to minimize systemic errors and ensure accurate reporting of significant figures.
    ii. **Quality Control:** Implement quality control measures to detect and correct systemic errors affecting significant figures.

6. Sampling Errors

a. **Impact on Significant Figures:** Variations in sample selection and size can affect the precision of results and the appropriate number of significant figures.
b. **Improving Accuracy with Significant Figures:**
    i. **Consistent Sampling:** Use consistent sampling methods to ensure that significant figures accurately reflect the population.
    ii. **Adequate Sample Size:** Ensure that sample sizes are large enough to provide reliable results with the appropriate number of significant figures.

Examples of Applying Significant Figures in Various Fields

In Medicine:

a. **Dosage Calculations:** Ensure that medication dosages are calculated and recorded with the correct number of significant figures to avoid errors in administration.

b. **Diagnostic Tools:** Use diagnostic tools that provide results with an appropriate number of significant figures to ensure accurate diagnoses.

In Science and Engineering:

a. **Measurement Precision:** Use instruments that provide the necessary number of significant figures for experimental measurements to ensure accurate results.

b. **Data Reporting:** Report scientific data with the correct number of significant figures to reflect the precision of the measurements accurately.

In Everyday Life:

a. **Financial Transactions:** Ensure financial calculations and records use the correct number of significant figures to avoid errors in billing and transactions.

b. **Construction Measurements:** Use precise measurements with the correct number of significant figures to ensure the accuracy of construction projects.

Strategies for Managing Significant Figures

1. **Education and Training:**
   a. Educate individuals on the importance of significant figures and how to correctly use them in measurements and calculations.
2. **Process Improvement:**
   a. Regularly review and refine processes to ensure that significant figures are accurately maintained throughout measurements and calculations.
3. **Technology Integration:**
   a. Use advanced technology and instruments that provide precise measurements with the appropriate number of significant figures.
4. **Quality Control:**
   a. Implement quality control measures to check and verify the accuracy of significant figures in reported data.
5. **Feedback Loops:**

a. Establish feedback loops to gather input on the accuracy and precision of significant figures and use this feedback to make necessary improvements.

Multiple-choice questions (MCQs):

1. What are systematic errors primarily associated with?
   A) Human mistakes
   B) Faulty equipment or flawed experimental design
   C) Random fluctuations in conditions
   D) All of the above
2. Which type of error is characterized by unpredictability and variation in magnitude and direction?
   A) Systematic errors
   B) Random errors
   C) Human errors
   D) Blunders
3. What is the most effective way to reduce human errors?
   A) Regular training and automation
   B) Using low-quality instruments
   C) Ignoring standard operating procedures
   D) Increasing manual operations
4. Blunders in the context of errors refer to:
   A) Small, often negligible errors
   B) Errors due to unpredictable fluctuations
   C) Gross errors typically resulting from oversight
   D) Errors that are hard to detect
5. Which factor does NOT cause instrumental errors?
   A) Faulty calibration
   B) Environmental changes

C) High-quality equipment

D) Inappropriate tool selection

6. What type of error does high humidity typically cause?

A) Human error

B) Procedural error

C) Instrumental error

D) Environmental error

7. How can systematic errors be addressed?

A) They can be predicted and corrected once identified

B) They are unpredictable and thus cannot be corrected

C) They are always due to human error

D) None of the above

8. Which method is NOT used to minimize errors in measurement?

A) Calibration of instruments

B) Using damaged instruments

C) Training and education

D) Implementing SOPs

9. What type of error is caused by poor design or inappropriate selection of instruments? A) Random error

B) Systemic error

C) Instrumental error

D) Human error

10. Which of the following is a procedural error?

A) Misreading measurements

B) Using faulty instruments

C) Ambiguous instructions

D) Environmental influences

11. How are random errors best characterized?

A) Consistent and repeatable

B) Unpredictable and varying in magnitude

C) Typically resulting from human oversight

D) Always due to poor instrument design

12. What contributes to environmental errors?

A) Regular instrument calibration

B) Variations in temperature or pressure

C) Using high-quality instruments

D) Thorough training programs

13. Which is NOT a typical source of human error?

A) Misinterpretation

B) Fatigue

C) Regular calibration

D) Lack of knowledge

14. What does poka-yoke refer to?

A) A type of systematic error

B) A method to ensure precision in instruments

C) Designing error-proof systems and processes

D) A random error in measurements

15. What are sampling errors often associated with?

A) Environmental influences

B) Instrumental precision

C) Selection and size of the sample

D) Human oversight

16. Which method is effective for minimizing random errors?

A) Using more accurate instruments

B) Increasing the sample size

C) Implementing stringent SOPs

D) All of the above

17. What role does automation play in reducing errors?

A) Increases procedural errors

B) Reduces the chance of human errors

C) Has no impact on errors

D) Leads to more blunders

18. Why are double-check systems used?

A) To increase the speed of processes

B) To reduce human errors by verification

C) They are not effective in error reduction

D) Only useful in financial contexts

19. Which is NOT a characteristic of blunders?

A) Easily detectable

B) Typically gross errors

C) Resulting from oversight

D) Unpredictable and random

20. What is the main purpose of quality control in error management?

A) To ignore minor errors

B) To increase the frequency of errors

C) To detect and correct errors in processes

D) None of the above

Short answer type questions:

1. Define systematic errors and provide an example.
2. What is the main characteristic of random errors?
3. How can human errors typically be reduced?
4. Describe what is meant by a "blunder" in the context of errors.
5. What is the effect of environmental factors on instrumental accuracy?
6. Explain the role of fatigue in human errors.
7. How do procedural factors contribute to errors?
8. What are the implications of errors in medicine?

9. How can training and education reduce errors?
10. Describe the concept of Poka-Yoke.
11. What role does technology play in reducing human errors?
12. How often should equipment be calibrated to reduce errors?
13. What is the main cause of sampling errors?
14. How can systematic errors be identified and corrected?
15. What are some common procedural errors?
16. Give an example of how miscommunication can lead to errors in everyday life.
17. What is the significance of maintaining controlled environmental conditions in error reduction?
18. How can software bugs lead to errors in data processing?
19. What is the benefit of implementing double-check systems?
20. Discuss the impact of incorrect tool selection on measurement accuracy.

Long answer type questions:

1. Discuss how systematic errors can be predicted and corrected in a scientific experiment.
2. Explain the different types of human errors and suggest methods to minimize their occurrence in a healthcare setting.
3. Describe the process of calibration and its importance in maintaining the accuracy of instruments.
4. Analyze the effects of environmental errors on experimental results and propose methods to control such errors.
5. Outline the steps involved in developing and implementing standard operating procedures to minimize procedural errors.
6. Discuss the impact of systemic errors on the reliability of data in research studies and suggest ways to mitigate these errors.

7. Provide a detailed explanation of how sampling errors can affect the outcomes of statistical studies and how they can be minimized.
8. Evaluate the role of technology and automation in reducing errors in the manufacturing industry.
9. Discuss the significance of error-proofing strategies in improving product quality and customer satisfaction.
10. Explain the relationship between error management and quality control in a business environment, and how it can lead to improved operational efficiency.

Answer Key:

1. (B) Faulty equipment or flawed experimental design
2. (B) Random errors
3. (A) Regular training and automation
4. (C) Gross errors typically resulting from oversight
5. (C) High-quality equipment
6. (D) Environmental error
7. (A) They can be predicted and corrected once identified
8. (B) Using damaged instruments
9. (C) Instrumental error
10. (C) Ambiguous instructions
11. (B) Unpredictable and varying in magnitude
12. (B) Variations in temperature or pressure
13. (C) Regular calibration
14. (C) Designing error-proof systems and processes
15. (C) Selection and size of the sample
16. (D) All of the above
17. (B) Reduces the chance of human errors
18. (B) To reduce human errors by verification

19.(D) Unpredictable and random

20.(C) To detect and correct errors in processes

CHAPTER – 3

PHARMACOPOEIA

INTRODUCTION:

A pharmacopoeia is an official publication containing a list of medicinal drugs and their specifications. It provides standards for the identity, purity, strength, and quality of these substances. The primary purpose of a pharmacopoeia is to ensure the consistency and safety of medications.

Key Aspects of a Pharmacopoeia

1. **Historical Background:**
    a. The concept of pharmacopoeias dates back to ancient times. One of the earliest known pharmacopoeias is the "De Materia Medica" by Dioscorides, written in the first century AD.
    b. Modern pharmacopoeias began to emerge in the 16th and 17th centuries. The "London Pharmacopoeia" (1618) and the "Pharmacopoeia of the United States" (USP) (1820) are significant examples.
2. **Types of Pharmacopoeias:**
    a. **National Pharmacopoeias:** These are specific to individual countries, such as the British Pharmacopoeia (BP), United States Pharmacopeia (USP), and Indian Pharmacopoeia (IP).
    b. **International Pharmacopoeias:** These aim to provide a unified standard for multiple countries. The World Health Organization (WHO) publishes the International Pharmacopoeia (Ph. Int.).
3. **Content of a Pharmacopoeia:**
    a. **Monographs:** Detailed descriptions of individual drugs, including their chemical structure, properties, and tests for identity and purity.

b. **General Notices:** Guidelines and standards that apply to all monographs and substances.
c. **Analytical Methods:** Techniques and procedures for testing the quality of drugs, including chromatography, spectrophotometry, and titration.
d. **Specifications for Excipients:** Standards for non-active components used in drug formulations.
e. **Reference Standards:** Established standards for comparison to ensure consistency and quality.

4. **Role and Importance:**
   a. **Quality Assurance:** Ensures that drugs meet specified standards for safety, efficacy, and quality.
   b. **Regulatory Framework:** Provides a basis for regulatory authorities to approve, monitor, and control the manufacture and distribution of drugs.
   c. **Public Health:** Protects public health by ensuring that medications are safe and effective.

5. **Development and Revision:**
   a. Pharmacopoeias are regularly updated to incorporate new scientific knowledge, emerging drugs, and improved analytical techniques.
   b. Revision involves collaboration among scientists, healthcare professionals, and regulatory authorities to ensure that standards remain relevant and accurate.

6. **Global Harmonization:**
   a. Efforts are being made to harmonize pharmacopoeial standards globally to facilitate international trade and ensure consistent quality across borders.

b. Organizations like the International Council for Harmonisation (ICH) and the World Health Organization (WHO) play key roles in this process.

Example of a Monograph Structure:

A typical drug monograph in a pharmacopoeia includes:

1. **Title:** The official name of the drug.
2. **Chemical Structure:** Diagram and molecular formula.
3. **Description:** Physical and chemical properties.
4. **Identification Tests:** Methods to confirm the identity of the drug.
5. **Purity Tests:** Procedures to detect impurities and contaminants.
6. **Assay:** Methods to determine the drug's potency and concentration.
7. **Storage Conditions:** Guidelines for proper storage to maintain drug stability.
8. **Packaging:** Specifications for appropriate packaging materials and methods.

Significance in Pharmacology:

Pharmacopoeias are indispensable in pharmacology as they provide:

1. **Standardization:** Uniform standards for drug quality and safety.
2. **Reference Material:** Authoritative source of information for healthcare professionals.
3. **Regulatory Compliance:** Basis for regulatory approval and quality control in pharmaceutical manufacturing.
4. **Education and Research:** Essential resource for students and researchers in the field of pharmacy and medicine.

HISTORY

The history of pharmacopoeias is rich and spans several centuries, reflecting the evolution of medical science and pharmaceutical practice. Here's a detailed overview of their historical development:

Ancient and Medieval Origins

1. **Ancient Egypt:**

a. The earliest known medicinal texts, such as the Ebers Papyrus (circa 1550 BCE), included descriptions of medicinal plants and treatments. Although not pharmacopoeias in the modern sense, these texts laid the groundwork for future compilations.

2. **Ancient Greece and Rome:**
   a. Hippocrates (460–370 BCE) and his followers documented various treatments and drugs. The "Corpus Hippocraticum" contains early references to medical substances.
   b. Dioscorides' "De Materia Medica" (1st century AD) is one of the most influential early pharmacopoeias. It described around 600 plants, along with animal products and minerals, and their medicinal uses.
3. **Medieval Islamic World:**
   a. Islamic scholars made significant contributions to pharmacology. Works like Avicenna's "Canon of Medicine" and Al-Razi's "Comprehensive Book of Medicine" included extensive sections on drugs and their uses.
4. **Medieval Europe:**
   a. Monastic manuscripts and herbals, such as the "Hortus Sanitatis" (1491), compiled knowledge of medicinal plants and preparations. These works were precursors to formal pharmacopoeias.

Renaissance and Early Modern Period

1. **The Rise of Formal Pharmacopoeias:**
   a. The first official pharmacopoeia, the "Nuovo Receptario," was published in Florence in 1498. Commissioned by the guild of physicians and apothecaries, it aimed to standardize medicinal formulations.
   b. The "London Pharmacopoeia" (1618) was one of the first national pharmacopoeias. It was published by the Royal College of Physicians of London to regulate the quality of medicines.

2. **National Pharmacopoeias:**
    a. The "Pharmacopoeia Augustana" (Augsburg, 1564) and the "Pharmacopoeia Londinensis" (1618) set the stage for other countries to create their own national pharmacopoeias.
    b. The "Pharmacopoeia of the United States" (USP) was first published in 1820, marking a significant milestone in the standardization of medications in the United States.

19th and Early 20th Century

1. **Expansion and Standardization:**
    a. By the 19th century, many countries had developed their own pharmacopoeias. Notable examples include the British Pharmacopoeia (BP) first published in 1864 and the Japanese Pharmacopoeia (JP) in 1886.
    b. These pharmacopoeias provided detailed standards for the preparation and testing of drugs, ensuring consistency and safety.
2. **Pharmacopoeial Conventions:**
    a. The creation of pharmacopoeial conventions, such as the United States Pharmacopeial Convention, helped standardize the development and revision of pharmacopoeias. These organizations brought together experts to update and improve the content of pharmacopoeias.

Mid to Late 20th Century

1. **Global Harmonization:**
    a. The World Health Organization (WHO) established the International Pharmacopoeia (Ph. Int.) in 1951 to provide a unified set of standards for drugs used globally. This effort aimed to harmonize pharmacopoeial standards across different countries.
    b. The European Pharmacopoeia (Ph. Eur.), first published in 1969, aimed to standardize drug quality across Europe. It became a key reference for European Union member states.

2. **Technological Advancements:**
    a. The development of new analytical techniques, such as high-performance liquid chromatography (HPLC) and mass spectrometry, revolutionized the testing and standardization of drugs.
    b. These advancements were incorporated into pharmacopoeias, improving the accuracy and reliability of drug quality assessments.

21st Century and Beyond

1. **Modernization and Digitalization:**
    a. Modern pharmacopoeias have embraced digital platforms, making them more accessible and easier to update. Electronic versions and online databases allow for rapid dissemination of information.
    b. Continuous updates and revisions are necessary to keep pace with advancements in pharmaceutical science and technology.
2. **Global Collaboration:**
    a. Ongoing efforts to harmonize pharmacopoeial standards continue through international organizations and collaborative initiatives. The International Council for Harmonisation (ICH) plays a significant role in this process.
3. **Expanding Scope:**
    a. Modern pharmacopoeias cover not only traditional drugs but also complex biologics, biosimilars, and emerging therapies. They address issues related to drug safety, efficacy, and quality in an increasingly globalized market.

TYPES OF PHARMACOPOEIA

Pharmacopoeias are classified into several types based on their scope, jurisdiction, and purpose. Here is a detailed overview of the different types of pharmacopoeias:

1. National Pharmacopoeias

National pharmacopoeias are developed and maintained by individual countries to ensure the quality, safety, and efficacy of medicines used within their borders. These pharmacopoeias provide legally binding standards for pharmaceuticals.

a. **United States Pharmacopeia (USP):**
    i. First published in 1820, the USP sets standards for medicines, food ingredients, and dietary supplements in the United States.
    ii. It is revised every five years and includes monographs for drug substances, dosage forms, and compounded preparations.

b. **British Pharmacopoeia (BP):**
    i. First published in 1864, the BP is the official pharmacopoeia of the United Kingdom.
    ii. It provides standards for the quality of medicinal substances and is updated annually.

c. **Indian Pharmacopoeia (IP):**
    i. First published in 1955, the IP sets standards for drugs manufactured and marketed in India.
    ii. It is revised periodically to incorporate new drugs and advancements in analytical methods.

d. **Japanese Pharmacopoeia (JP):**
    i. First published in 1886, the JP sets standards for drugs in Japan.
    ii. It is revised every five years and includes monographs for pharmaceuticals, excipients, and medical devices.

2. International Pharmacopoeias

International pharmacopoeias are developed to provide a unified set of standards applicable across multiple countries, facilitating international trade and regulatory harmonization.

a. **International Pharmacopoeia (Ph. Int.):**

   i. Published by the World Health Organization (WHO), the Ph. Int. aims to provide global standards for the quality of medicines.
   ii. It includes monographs for essential medicines and is updated regularly to reflect scientific advancements.

b. **European Pharmacopoeia (Ph. Eur.):**
   i. First published in 1969, the Ph. Eur. sets standards for medicines in the European Union and other member states of the Council of Europe.
   ii. It is updated periodically and includes monographs for active substances, excipients, and dosage forms.

3. Regional Pharmacopoeias

Regional pharmacopoeias are developed to serve specific geographic regions, promoting standardization and quality control within those areas.

a. **African Pharmacopoeia:**
   i. Developed to harmonize the standards for medicines in African countries.
   ii. It aims to improve the quality and safety of pharmaceuticals in the African continent.

b. **Pan American Health Organization (PAHO) Pharmacopoeia:**
   i. Provides standards for medicines used in the Americas.
   ii. It aims to promote public health by ensuring the quality of pharmaceuticals in member countries.

4. Pharmacopoeial Compendia

Pharmacopoeial compendia are comprehensive references that compile standards from various national and international pharmacopoeias. They serve as valuable resources for regulatory authorities, manufacturers, and healthcare professionals.

a. **United States Pharmacopeia–National Formulary (USP-NF):**
   i. A combined publication of the USP and the National Formulary (NF).

ii. It includes monographs for drug substances, dosage forms, and excipients, providing a comprehensive reference for pharmaceutical standards in the United States.

5. Specialized Pharmacopoeias

Specialized pharmacopoeias focus on specific types of drugs or therapeutic areas. They provide detailed standards for particular categories of medicines.

a. **Veterinary Pharmacopoeias:**

i. Provide standards for veterinary medicines, ensuring the quality and safety of drugs used in animals.

ii. Examples include the British Veterinary Pharmacopoeia and the United States Pharmacopoeia–Veterinary Medicine.

b. **Homeopathic Pharmacopoeias:**

i. Provide standards for homeopathic medicines, including preparation methods and quality control measures.

ii. Examples include the Homoeopathic Pharmacopoeia of the United States (HPUS) and the European Pharmacopoeia (Ph. Eur.) monographs for homeopathic preparations.

6. Supplementary Pharmacopoeias

Supplementary pharmacopoeias provide additional standards and guidelines that complement the main pharmacopoeial texts. They address specific aspects of pharmaceutical quality and regulatory requirements.

a. **Pharmaceutical Codex:**

i. Provides supplementary information on pharmaceutical standards, including stability, packaging, and storage of medicines.

ii. It complements the standards set by national pharmacopoeias.

INDIAN PHARMACOPOEIA

The Indian Pharmacopoeia (IP) is an official compendium of standards for pharmaceutical substances, dosage forms, and pharmaceutical excipients used in India. It plays a critical role in ensuring the quality, safety, and efficacy of medicines manufactured and marketed in the country. Here are the key details about the Indian Pharmacopoeia:

History and Development

1. **First Edition:** The Indian Pharmacopoeia was first published in 1955 by the Indian Pharmacopoeia Commission (IPC), under the Ministry of Health and Family Welfare, Government of India.
2. **Revisions:** The IP undergoes periodic revisions to incorporate new drugs, update monographs, and revise standards based on scientific advancements and feedback from stakeholders.
3. **Current Edition:** As of the latest update, the Indian Pharmacopoeia is in its eighth edition (IP 2018). This edition incorporates modern analytical techniques and international standards to align with global practices.

Contents of the Indian Pharmacopoeia

1. **Monographs:**
    a. The IP contains monographs that describe the standards and specifications for pharmaceutical substances (active pharmaceutical ingredients - APIs), dosage forms (finished pharmaceutical products), and pharmaceutical excipients.
    b. Each monograph includes information on the identification, tests for purity, assay (quantitative analysis), and other relevant parameters necessary to ensure the quality of the drug or substance.
2. **General Chapters:**
    a. General chapters in the IP provide guidelines and procedures for analytical methods, quality control tests, and regulatory requirements applicable to pharmaceutical manufacturing and testing.
    b. They cover topics such as validation of analytical procedures, storage conditions, packaging materials, and good manufacturing practices (GMP).

3. **National Formulary of India (NFI):**
    a. The IP includes a section known as the National Formulary of India (NFI), which provides standards and guidelines for pharmaceutical formulations and their preparation.
    b. The NFI complements the monographs by detailing dosage forms, excipients, and specific formulation requirements.

Purpose and Significance

1. **Regulatory Compliance:** The standards set by the Indian Pharmacopoeia are legally enforceable under the Drugs and Cosmetics Act and Rules in India. Compliance with IP standards is mandatory for pharmaceutical manufacturers to obtain drug approvals and licenses.
2. **Quality Assurance:** By providing uniform standards for drug quality and safety, the IP helps ensure that medicines produced in India meet consistent levels of quality and efficacy.
3. **Promotion of Public Health:** The IP contributes to public health by promoting the availability of safe, effective, and quality-assured medicines for healthcare providers and patients.

Revision and Updates

1. **Revision Process:** The IPC regularly reviews and updates the IP to reflect advances in pharmaceutical science, changes in regulatory requirements, and emerging public health concerns.
2. **Expert Committees:** Revisions are carried out by expert committees comprising pharmacists, pharmaceutical scientists, healthcare professionals, and regulatory experts.

International Collaboration

1. **Harmonization:** The IPC collaborates with international organizations, such as the World Health Organization (WHO) and other pharmacopoeial authorities, to harmonize standards and align with global pharmacopoeial practices.

2. **Adoption:** Some IP monographs are aligned with standards from the International Pharmacopoeia (Ph. Int.) and other international pharmacopoeias, facilitating international recognition and acceptance of Indian-manufactured medicines.

U.S.P.

The United States Pharmacopeia (USP) is a comprehensive compendium of quality standards for medicines, dietary supplements, and other healthcare products manufactured and distributed in the United States. It serves as a critical reference for ensuring the quality, safety, and efficacy of pharmaceuticals. Here's an in-depth look at the United States Pharmacopeia (USP):

History and Development

1. **Establishment:** The USP was first published in 1820 by the United States Pharmacopeial Convention (USP Convention), a nonprofit organization composed of volunteer experts in pharmacology, pharmacy, medicine, and related disciplines.
2. **Mission:** The USP Convention's mission is to improve global health through public standards and related programs that help ensure the quality, safety, and benefit of medicines and foods.
3. **Legal Status:** While the USP itself is not a regulatory agency, its standards are recognized and enforceable under the U.S. Food, Drug, and Cosmetic Act and its subsequent revisions. Compliance with USP standards is often required for regulatory approval of pharmaceutical products in the United States.

Contents of the United States Pharmacopeia (USP)

1. **Monographs:**
    a. The USP contains detailed monographs for pharmaceutical substances (active pharmaceutical ingredients - APIs), dosage forms (finished pharmaceutical products), excipients (inactive ingredients), dietary supplements, and compounded preparations.

b. Each monograph specifies the identity, purity, strength, and quality tests required for the substance or product.

2. **General Chapters:**
    a. General chapters in the USP provide guidelines and procedures for analytical methods, quality control tests, and regulatory requirements applicable to pharmaceutical manufacturing and testing.
    b. Topics covered include validation of analytical procedures, microbial limits testing, dissolution testing, and packaging requirements.
3. **Reference Standards:**
    a. The USP maintains a collection of reference standards, which are highly characterized substances or materials used to assess the identity, purity, strength, and quality of pharmaceuticals and dietary supplements.
    b. Reference standards help ensure consistency and accuracy in testing and are essential for validating analytical methods and comparing results across different laboratories.
4. **Dietary Supplements:**
    a. The USP Dietary Supplements Compendium (DSC) provides standards and guidelines for the quality and purity of dietary ingredients and dietary supplements marketed in the United States.
    b. It includes monographs for vitamins, minerals, botanicals, and other dietary ingredients, along with testing methods and specifications.

Purpose and Significance

1. **Quality Assurance:** By setting and promoting standards for drug quality and safety, the USP helps ensure that medicines and dietary supplements distributed in the United States meet consistent levels of quality and efficacy.
2. **Regulatory Compliance:** Compliance with USP standards is mandatory for pharmaceutical manufacturers seeking approval from regulatory agencies

such as the U.S. Food and Drug Administration (FDA). USP standards are also referenced in pharmacopeial regulations in other countries.

3. **Public Health Impact:** The USP contributes to public health by promoting the availability of safe and effective medicines and dietary supplements. It helps healthcare professionals make informed decisions about treatment options and patient care.

Revision and Updates

1. **Continuous Improvement:** The USP undergoes regular revisions and updates to incorporate new drugs, revise existing monographs, and adapt to scientific advancements and changes in regulatory requirements.
2. **Expert Committees:** Revisions are conducted by expert committees comprising pharmacists, pharmaceutical scientists, healthcare professionals, and industry representatives. These committees review scientific data and stakeholder input to ensure the standards remain relevant and up-to-date.

International Collaboration

1. **Global Impact:** The USP collaborates with international pharmacopoeial authorities and regulatory agencies to harmonize standards and promote global public health.
2. **International Recognition:** USP standards are recognized and adopted by pharmacopeial authorities in many countries, facilitating international trade and ensuring consistent quality standards across borders.

EXTRA PHARMACOPOEIA

In the context of pharmacopoeias, the term "Extra Pharmacopoeia" typically refers to additional or supplementary information that may not be included in the main pharmacopoeia but is still relevant to pharmaceutical practice. Here's a detailed look at what "Extra Pharmacopoeia" entails:

Definition and Purpose

Extra Pharmacopoeia refers to supplementary information, guidelines, or standards that complement the main pharmacopoeia. It serves several specific purposes within the realm of pharmaceutical practice and regulation:

Definition

1. **Supplementary Information:**
    a. Extra Pharmacopoeia includes additional content that extends beyond the scope of the main pharmacopoeia. This can encompass detailed guidelines, reference materials, and specialized monographs that provide further insights into specific aspects of pharmaceutical manufacturing, testing, or regulatory compliance.
2. **Comprehensive Coverage:**
    a. While the main pharmacopoeia focuses on essential standards and monographs for pharmaceutical substances, dosage forms, and excipients, Extra Pharmacopoeia fills gaps by offering more detailed guidance on complex formulations, specialized preparations (like veterinary medicines or homeopathic remedies), or emerging areas of pharmaceutical science.

Purpose

1. **Enhanced Guidance and Standards:**
    a. Extra Pharmacopoeia enhances the comprehensiveness of pharmacopoeial standards by providing additional guidelines and reference materials. This helps pharmaceutical manufacturers adhere to best practices and regulatory requirements beyond basic compliance.
2. **Specialized Areas of Practice:**
    a. It addresses specific needs in pharmaceutical practice, such as veterinary medicines, herbal preparations, dietary supplements, and homeopathic remedies. These areas often require unique standards and testing protocols not fully covered in the main pharmacopoeia.

3. **Regulatory Compliance:**
   a. Extra Pharmacopoeia supports regulatory compliance by offering detailed insights into quality control measures, manufacturing processes, stability testing, and packaging requirements. This helps ensure that pharmaceutical products meet stringent quality, safety, and efficacy standards set by regulatory authorities.
4. **Educational Resource:**
   a. It serves as an educational resource for pharmacists, pharmaceutical scientists, and healthcare professionals. Extra Pharmacopoeia provides in-depth information on pharmaceutical formulation, quality assurance practices, and emerging trends in the industry.

Examples and Applications

1. **Pharmaceutical Codex:** Offers comprehensive guidelines on formulation development, stability testing, and pharmaceutical quality control practices.
2. **Veterinary Pharmacopoeias:** Provide standards and monographs specific to animal health products, addressing unique considerations in veterinary medicine.
3. **Homeopathic Pharmacopoeias:** Detail standards for preparation methods, dilutions, and quality control measures specific to homeopathic remedies.
4. **Herbal Pharmacopoeias:** Include standards for botanical identification, extraction methods, purity tests, and safety considerations for herbal products.

Types of Extra Pharmacopoeia

"Extra Pharmacopoeia" encompasses various types of supplementary guidelines, reference materials, and specialized standards that extend beyond the scope of the main pharmacopoeia. These types address specific areas of pharmaceutical practice, formulation, and regulatory requirements. Here's a detailed look at the types of Extra Pharmacopoeia:

1. **Pharmaceutical Codex**
    a. **Definition:** The Pharmaceutical Codex provides supplementary guidelines and standards that complement the main pharmacopoeia. It focuses on detailed information related to pharmaceutical formulation, quality assurance, and regulatory compliance.
    b. **Content:**
        i. **Formulation Development:** Guidelines on developing pharmaceutical formulations, including dosage forms, excipients, and stability testing protocols.
        ii. **Quality Assurance:** Detailed standards for quality control measures, analytical methods, and validation procedures applicable to pharmaceutical manufacturing.
        iii. **Regulatory Guidance:** Information on compliance with regulatory requirements, including good manufacturing practices (GMP) and documentation practices.
2. **Veterinary Pharmacopoeias**
    a. **Purpose:** Veterinary pharmacopoeias provide standards and monographs specific to veterinary medicines and animal health products. They address unique considerations in animal healthcare and regulatory requirements.
    b. **Content:**
        i. **Species-Specific Formulations:** Standards for dosage forms and preparations tailored to different animal species, including companion animals, livestock, and exotic animals.
        ii. **Safety and Efficacy:** Guidelines for assessing the safety, efficacy, and quality of veterinary drugs, ensuring their suitability for use in animals.
        iii. **Regulatory Compliance:** Compliance with veterinary drug regulations and guidelines set by national and international authorities.

3. Homeopathic Pharmacopoeias

a. **Definition:** Homeopathic pharmacopoeias provide standards and monographs for homeopathic remedies, which are regulated differently from conventional pharmaceuticals.

b. **Content:**

   i. **Preparation Methods:** Standards for the preparation, dilution, and potentization of homeopathic substances and remedies.

   ii. **Quality Control:** Guidelines for testing the identity, purity, and potency of homeopathic preparations, often using specialized analytical techniques.

   iii. **Regulatory Requirements:** Compliance with homeopathic medicine regulations and guidelines, including labeling requirements and safety considerations.

4. Herbal Pharmacopoeias

a. **Purpose:** Herbal pharmacopoeias focus on standards and guidelines for botanical medicines and traditional herbal remedies.

b. **Content:**

   i. **Botanical Identification:** Standards for identifying and authenticating botanical species used in herbal preparations.

   ii. **Extraction Methods:** Guidelines for the extraction, purification, and standardization of herbal extracts and active compounds.

   iii. **Safety and Efficacy:** Standards for assessing the safety profile, therapeutic efficacy, and quality control of herbal products.

   iv. **Regulatory Compliance:** Compliance with regulations governing the production, labeling, and marketing of herbal medicines and dietary supplements.

5. National Formularies

a. **Definition:** National Formularies provide standards and guidelines for compounded preparations, excipients, and specialized dosage forms not extensively covered in the main pharmacopoeia.

b. **Content:**

    i. **Compounded Preparations:** Standards for preparing customized dosage forms, such as oral solutions, topical creams, and injectable formulations.

    ii. **Excipients:** Guidelines for the selection, testing, and use of excipients in pharmaceutical formulations.

    iii. **Quality Assurance:** Requirements for maintaining quality and consistency in compounded preparations, including storage conditions and stability testing.

Role and Importance

Extra Pharmacopoeia plays a significant role in enhancing and extending the standards and guidelines provided by traditional pharmacopoeias. Its importance lies in addressing specific areas of pharmaceutical practice, formulation development, and regulatory compliance that may not be fully covered in the main pharmacopoeia. Here's a detailed look at the role and importance of Extra Pharmacopoeia:

Role of Extra Pharmacopoeia

1. **Specialized Guidance:**

    a. Extra Pharmacopoeia offers specialized guidelines and standards tailored to specific areas of pharmaceutical practice, such as veterinary medicines, homeopathic remedies, herbal preparations, and compounded formulations.

    b. It provides detailed methodologies, testing protocols, and regulatory requirements that are crucial for ensuring the quality, safety, and efficacy of specialized pharmaceutical products.

2. **Regulatory Compliance:**
    a. It supports pharmaceutical manufacturers, healthcare professionals, and regulatory authorities in meeting stringent regulatory requirements.
    b. Extra Pharmacopoeia provides additional information and reference materials that help ensure compliance with national and international regulations, including good manufacturing practices (GMP), quality control standards, and documentation requirements.
3. **Enhanced Quality Assurance:**
    a. By offering comprehensive guidelines on formulation development, stability testing, and quality control measures, Extra Pharmacopoeia enhances the quality assurance practices in pharmaceutical manufacturing.
    b. It promotes consistency in product quality, batch-to-batch uniformity, and adherence to established standards throughout the product lifecycle.
4. **Educational Resource:**
    a. Extra Pharmacopoeia serves as an educational resource for pharmacists, pharmaceutical scientists, researchers, and students in the pharmaceutical sciences.
    b. It provides in-depth insights into advanced pharmaceutical technologies, specialized dosage forms, and emerging trends in drug development and manufacturing.
5. **Promotion of Innovation:**
    a. It fosters innovation by providing guidelines and standards for novel pharmaceutical formulations, alternative therapies (e.g., homeopathy, herbal medicines), and personalized medicine approaches.

b. Extra Pharmacopoeia encourages the development of new methodologies and technologies that improve the safety, efficacy, and patient outcomes of pharmaceutical products.

Importance of Extra Pharmacopoeia

1. **Comprehensive Coverage:**
    a. Extra Pharmacopoeia expands the scope of traditional pharmacopoeias by addressing diverse categories of pharmaceutical products and specialized formulations.
    b. It ensures that regulatory standards are applicable to a wide range of therapeutic areas, dosage forms, and patient populations, thereby supporting public health and safety.
2. **Global Harmonization:**
    a. By aligning with international pharmacopoeial standards and guidelines, Extra Pharmacopoeia facilitates global harmonization of pharmaceutical regulations and quality standards.
    b. It promotes consistency in product quality and facilitates the international trade of pharmaceutical products across different regions and markets.
3. **Public Health Impact:**
    a. Extra Pharmacopoeia contributes to public health by promoting the availability of safe, effective, and quality-assured medicines and healthcare products.
    b. It plays a crucial role in ensuring that pharmaceutical products meet established standards for efficacy, safety, and purity, thereby protecting patient health and well-being.
4. **Regulatory Acceptance:**
    a. Extra Pharmacopoeia standards are recognized and adopted by regulatory authorities, pharmaceutical manufacturers, and healthcare professionals worldwide.

b. They provide a benchmark for assessing product quality, conducting regulatory inspections, and facilitating market approvals for pharmaceutical products.

Examples

Examples of Extra Pharmacopoeia encompass a variety of supplementary standards, guidelines, and reference materials that extend beyond the main pharmacopoeia. These examples provide specialized information and regulatory support for specific areas of pharmaceutical practice. Here are detailed examples:

1. Pharmaceutical Codex

a. **Definition:** The Pharmaceutical Codex offers supplementary guidelines and standards that complement traditional pharmacopoeias. It focuses on detailed information related to pharmaceutical formulation, quality assurance, and regulatory compliance.

b. **Examples:**

   i. **Formulation Development:** Detailed guidelines on developing pharmaceutical formulations, including dosage forms (tablets, capsules, injectables), excipients, and stability testing protocols.

   ii. **Quality Assurance:** Standards for quality control measures, analytical methods validation, and documentation practices required for pharmaceutical manufacturing.

   iii. **Regulatory Guidance:** Information on compliance with regulatory requirements, including good manufacturing practices (GMP), pharmacovigilance, and labeling regulations.

2. Veterinary Pharmacopoeias

a. **Purpose:** Veterinary pharmacopoeias provide standards and monographs specific to veterinary medicines and animal health products, ensuring their safety, efficacy, and quality.

b. **Examples:**

   i. **Species-Specific Formulations:** Standards for dosage forms and preparations tailored to different animal species, including companion animals, livestock, and exotic animals.

   ii. **Safety and Efficacy:** Guidelines for evaluating the safety and efficacy of veterinary drugs, including pharmacokinetic studies and residue testing.

   iii. **Regulatory Compliance:** Compliance with veterinary drug regulations set by national and international authorities, ensuring products meet stringent quality standards.

3. Homeopathic Pharmacopoeias

a. **Definition:** Homeopathic pharmacopoeias provide standards and monographs for homeopathic remedies, which are regulated differently from conventional pharmaceuticals.

b. **Examples:**

   i. **Preparation Methods:** Standards for the preparation, dilution, and potentization of homeopathic substances and remedies according to recognized methodologies (e.g., Hahnemannian method).

   ii. **Quality Control:** Guidelines for testing the identity, purity, and potency of homeopathic preparations using specific analytical techniques (e.g., chromatography, spectrophotometry).

   iii. **Regulatory Requirements:** Compliance with homeopathic medicine regulations, including labeling requirements, safety assessments, and pharmacopoeial standards.

4. Herbal Pharmacopoeias

a. **Purpose:** Herbal pharmacopoeias focus on standards and guidelines for botanical medicines and traditional herbal remedies.

b. **Examples:**

i. **Botanical Identification:** Standards for identifying and authenticating botanical species used in herbal preparations, including macroscopic and microscopic characteristics.
ii. **Extraction Methods:** Guidelines for the extraction, purification, and standardization of herbal extracts and active compounds (e.g., bioassays, marker compound analysis).
iii. **Safety and Efficacy:** Standards for evaluating the safety profile, therapeutic efficacy, and quality control of herbal products, including toxicity studies and stability testing.
iv. **Regulatory Compliance:** Compliance with regulations governing the production, labeling, and marketing of herbal medicines and dietary supplements, ensuring consumer safety and product quality.

5. National Formularies

a. **Definition:** National Formularies provide standards and guidelines for compounded preparations, excipients, and specialized dosage forms not extensively covered in the main pharmacopoeia.

b. **Examples:**

i. **Compounded Preparations:** Standards for preparing customized dosage forms (e.g., oral solutions, topical creams, injectable suspensions) in accordance with recognized compounding practices.
ii. **Excipients:** Guidelines for selecting, testing, and using excipients in pharmaceutical formulations to ensure compatibility, stability, and safety.
iii. **Quality Assurance:** Requirements for maintaining quality and consistency in compounded preparations, including documentation of compounding processes, storage conditions, and batch records.

Multiple Choice Questions (MCQs)

1. What was one of the earliest known pharmacopoeias?
   A) De Materia Medica
   B) British Pharmacopoeia
   C) United States Pharmacopeia
   D) International Pharmacopoeia
2. Which pharmacopoeia is published by the World Health Organization?
   A) United States Pharmacopoeia
   B) British Pharmacopoeia
   C) International Pharmacopoeia
   D) Indian Pharmacopoeia
3. What is the primary purpose of a pharmacopoeia?
   A) To regulate pharmaceutical prices
   B) To provide educational resources
   C) To ensure the consistency and safety of medications
   D) To advertise pharmaceutical products
4. What does a drug monograph in a pharmacopoeia typically include?
   A) Advertising strategies
   B) Financial data of pharmaceutical companies
   C) Tests for identity and purity
   D) Political implications of drug manufacturing
5. Which organization plays a key role in the global harmonization of pharmacopoeial standards?
   A) FDA
   B) ICH
   C) WHO
   D) USP
6. What type of pharmacopoeia includes monographs for veterinary medicines?

A) National

B) International

C) Veterinary

D) Specialized

7. When was the first edition of the United States Pharmacopeia published?

A) 1618

B) 1820

C) 1864

D) 1955

8. Which pharmacopoeia is a comprehensive reference for the European Union member states?

A) British Pharmacopoeia

B) United States Pharmacopeia

C) European Pharmacopoeia

D) International Pharmacopoeia

9. What aspect of medicines does the Indian Pharmacopoeia primarily focus on?

A) Taste and color

B) Quality, safety, and efficacy

C) Packaging only

D) Marketing strategies

10. What kind of standards does the International Pharmacopoeia primarily provide?

A) For cosmetic products

B) For essential medicines

C) For surgical equipment

D) For dietary supplements

11. What does a pharmacopoeia typically include?

A) Only the chemical structure of drugs

B) Only the brand names of pharmaceutical companies

C) Monographs and analytical methods

D) Investment guides for pharmaceutical stocks

12. What role does the USP play globally apart from setting standards?

A) Provides healthcare policies

B) Regulates international drug trade

C) Harmonizes standards internationally

D) Directly supervises pharmacies

13. Which pharmacopoeia was first published in 1955?

A) British Pharmacopoeia

B) United States Pharmacopeia

C) International Pharmacopoeia

D) Indian Pharmacopoeia

14. What is the purpose of general chapters in a pharmacopoeia?

A) To provide political commentary

B) To outline regulatory guidelines and analytical methods

C) To list pharmaceutical companies

D) To discuss future pharmaceutical trends

15. Which of these is a focus of the European Pharmacopoeia?

A) European culinary standards

B) Medicines in the European Union

C) European clothing regulations

D) Mobile phone standards in Europe

16. In what year was the first British Pharmacopoeia published?

A) 1618

B) 1820

C) 1864

D) 1955

17. What are reference standards used for in pharmacopoeias?

A) Determining executive salaries in pharmaceutical companies

B) Assessing the identity, purity, strength, and quality of pharmaceuticals

C) Setting the prices of drugs internationally

D) Deciding the location of new pharmacies

18.How often is the United States Pharmacopeia revised?

A) Every 10 years

B) Every 5 years

C) Every year

D) It is not revised

19.What does the 'Extra Pharmacopoeia' typically include?

A) Supplementary information beyond the main pharmacopoeia

B) Entertainment sections for pharmacists

C) Listings of pharmacy schools

D) Maps of pharmaceutical manufacturing locations

20.Which type of pharmacopoeia would include monographs for homeopathic medicines?

A) National Pharmacopoeia

B) International Pharmacopoeia

C) Specialized Pharmacopoeia

D) None of the above

Short Answer Type Questions (Subjective)

1. What is the primary purpose of a pharmacopoeia?
2. Name one of the earliest known pharmacopoeias mentioned in ancient texts.
3. How do modern pharmacopoeias differ from the ancient ones?
4. What type of pharmacopoeia is published by the World Health Organization?
5. What are the main components of a drug monograph in a pharmacopoeia?
6. Describe the role of general notices in a pharmacopoeia.

7. What are reference standards, and why are they important in pharmacopoeias?
8. Explain the significance of the United States Pharmacopeia (USP).
9. What is the purpose of the International Pharmacopoeia?
10. How does the European Pharmacopoeia contribute to drug standardization across Europe?
11. What are the key updates found in the Indian Pharmacopoeia?
12. How are veterinary pharmacopoeias tailored to meet specific needs?
13. Why is global harmonization of pharmacopoeial standards important?
14. Mention a type of pharmacopoeia that provides standards for homeopathic medicines.
15. What role do pharmacopoeias play in public health?
16. How does the 'Extra Pharmacopoeia' supplement the main pharmacopoeia?
17. What information does a pharmaceutical codex provide?
18. How are pharmacopoeias revised to stay current with scientific advancements?
19. Discuss the impact of pharmacopoeias on pharmaceutical manufacturing standards.
20. How do pharmacopoeias influence regulatory compliance in the pharmaceutical industry?

Long Answer Type Questions (Subjective)

1. Discuss the historical development of pharmacopoeias from ancient times to the modern era.
2. Explain how the United States Pharmacopeia (USP) influences global pharmaceutical standards and practices.
3. Describe the process and importance of harmonizing pharmacopoeial standards at the international level.

4. Outline the contents of a typical drug monograph in a pharmacopoeia and explain the purpose of each component.
5. Discuss the role of the International Pharmacopoeia in promoting public health globally.
6. Explain the significance of the European Pharmacopoeia in standardizing drug quality across member states.
7. Describe the role and importance of the 'Extra Pharmacopoeia' in providing specialized pharmaceutical standards.
8. Discuss how pharmacopoeias have adapted to technological advancements in drug testing and quality assurance.
9. Evaluate the impact of pharmacopoeias on ensuring the safety, efficacy, and quality of medicines in the global market.
10. Analyze the challenges and benefits of maintaining up-to-date pharmacopoeias in a rapidly evolving pharmaceutical industry.

Answer Key

1. (A) De Materia Medica
2. (C) International Pharmacopoeia
3. (C) To ensure the consistency and safety of medications
4. (C) Tests for identity and purity
5. (B) ICH
6. (C) Veterinary
7. (B) 1820
8. (C) European Pharmacopoeia
9. (B) Quality, safety, and efficacy
10. (B) For essential medicines
11. (C) Monographs and analytical methods
12. (C) Harmonizes standards internationally
13. (D) Indian Pharmacopoeia

14.(B) To outline regulatory guidelines and analytical methods

15.(B) Medicines in the European Union

16.(C) 1864

17.(B) Assessing the identity, purity, strength, and quality of pharmaceuticals

18.(B) Every 5 years

19.(A) Supplementary information beyond the main pharmacopoeia

20.(C) Specialized Pharmacopoeia

CHAPTER – 4

SOURCES OF IMPURITIES IN MEDICINAL AGENTS

INTRODUCTION:

Impurities in medicinal agents can arise from various sources throughout their production, storage, and usage. Here's a detailed introduction to the sources of impurities in medicinal agents:

1. **Synthetic Impurities**:
    a. **Starting Materials**: Residual impurities from starting materials used in synthesis can carry over into the final product. These impurities may result from incomplete purification or synthesis processes.
    b. **Intermediates**: Impurities formed during intermediate steps of synthesis can persist if not properly removed or purified in subsequent steps.
    c. **By-products**: Chemical reactions can yield unintended by-products, which may be structurally similar to the desired compound but possess different properties or biological activities.
2. **Degradation Products**:
    a. **Hydrolysis**: Exposure to water or moisture can lead to hydrolytic degradation, breaking down the chemical structure of the medicinal agent.
    b. **Oxidation**: Reaction with oxygen in the air can cause oxidative degradation, altering the chemical composition and efficacy of the drug.
    c. **Photolysis**: Exposure to light, especially UV light, can induce photolytic degradation, leading to the formation of impurities.
3. **Environmental Contaminants**:

a. **From Production**: Contaminants introduced during the manufacturing process, such as dust, particles, or residues from equipment or packaging materials.
b. **During Storage**: Improper storage conditions, including temperature extremes, humidity, or exposure to light, can contribute to contamination over time.
c. **During Transportation**: Contaminants can be introduced during transportation if not adequately protected or sealed.

4. **Residual Solvents**:
    a. **Used in Synthesis**: Solvents used during the manufacturing process may remain in trace amounts in the final product, posing potential risks to patient safety.
    b. **Extraction Solvents**: In herbal or natural products, solvents used for extraction can leave behind residues if not properly removed.
5. **Impurities from Packaging Materials**:
    a. **Leachables**: Chemicals from packaging materials can leach into the medicinal agent over time, especially if the packaging is reactive with the drug formulation.
    b. **Inks and Labels**: Printing inks or adhesives used in labels can introduce impurities if they migrate into the product.
6. **Microbial Contamination**:
    a. **During Production**: Improper handling or sanitation practices during manufacturing can lead to microbial contamination.
    b. **During Storage**: Poor storage conditions can promote microbial growth, potentially contaminating the medicinal agent.
7. **Cross-contamination**:
    a. **Shared Equipment**: Equipment used for multiple products or in different stages of manufacturing can lead to cross-contamination if not cleaned thoroughly between uses.

b. **Personnel**: Contamination can occur through contact with personnel, especially if proper hygiene practices are not followed.

8. **Impurities from Excipients**:
    a. **Excipient Purity**: Impurities present in excipients (inactive ingredients) used in the formulation can contribute to impurities in the final medicinal agent.
    b. **Compatibility**: Interaction between the active ingredient and excipients can sometimes lead to the formation of new impurities.

CLASSIFICATION:

1. **Synthetic Impurities**:
    a. **Example**: During the synthesis of a drug substance, residual starting materials such as unreacted reagents or catalysts can remain in the final product. For instance, in the synthesis of Ibuprofen, unreacted acetic acid or acetic anhydride can be residual impurities if not adequately removed.
2. **Degradation Impurities**:
    a. **Example**: Hydrolytic degradation can occur in drugs like Captopril, where exposure to moisture or water during storage or manufacturing can lead to the formation of impurities such as Captopril disulfide.
    b. **Example**: Oxidative degradation in drugs like Ascorbic Acid (Vitamin C), where exposure to air or light causes oxidation, leading to the formation of dehydroascorbic acid as an impurity.
3. **Environmental Contaminants**:
    a. **Example**: Contaminants from the production environment, such as particulates or residues from equipment, can affect drug purity. For example, dust particles from manufacturing equipment could contaminate a batch of Paracetamol tablets.

b. **Example**: Improper storage conditions like high humidity leading to microbial growth can contaminate Ampicillin capsules during storage, affecting their purity.

4. **Residual Solvents**:
   a. **Example**: In the production of Diazepam, residual solvents like dichloromethane or methanol used in the synthesis process can remain in trace amounts if not properly removed during purification.
5. **Impurities from Packaging Materials**:
   a. **Example**: Leaching of plasticizers from PVC (polyvinyl chloride) packaging into liquid formulations like Diazepam injection, leading to contamination with diethylhexyl phthalate (DEHP).
   b. **Example**: Inks and labels used on packaging materials can introduce impurities into medications; for instance, printing inks containing heavy metals could contaminate tablets or capsules.
6. **Microbial Contamination**:
   a. **Example**: Microbial contaminants such as bacteria or fungi can proliferate in improperly sterilized ophthalmic solutions like Tobramycin eye drops, compromising their sterility and safety.
   b. **Example**: Poor handling practices during production can lead to contamination of injectable products like Amoxicillin sodium with bacteria, risking patient health.
7. **Cross-contamination**:
   a. **Example**: Cross-contamination during manufacturing of tablets, where equipment used for multiple products isn't adequately cleaned between batches, leading to traces of one drug contaminating another.
   b. **Example**: Cross-contamination due to inadequate cleaning of utensils and surfaces in a pharmaceutical facility can lead to traces of one active ingredient contaminating another during production.

8. **Impurities from Excipients**:
    a. **Example**: In the formulation of tablets containing Acetaminophen, impurities from inactive ingredients like magnesium stearate or microcrystalline cellulose can affect the purity of the final product.
    b. **Example**: Excipient interactions can lead to impurities in liquid formulations like Diphenhydramine syrup, where preservatives or sweeteners can degrade over time, forming impurities.

APPLICATION:

The application of understanding sources of impurities in medicinal agents is crucial across various stages of pharmaceutical development, production, and regulatory compliance. Here's a detailed exploration of its application:

Development Stage:

During the development stage of medicinal agents, understanding and managing sources of impurities is critical to ensuring the safety, efficacy, and quality of the final product. Here's a detailed exploration of how the knowledge of impurity sources is applied in the development stage:

1. Synthesis and Formulation Design:

a. **Identification of Potential Impurities**:
    i. **Purpose**: Chemists and pharmaceutical scientists identify potential impurities that may arise during the synthesis or formulation of the medicinal agent.
    ii. **Methods**: This involves thorough analysis of reaction mechanisms, potential side reactions, and degradation pathways that could lead to impurity formation.
    iii. **Example**: In the synthesis of a drug like Captopril, understanding that hydrolysis can occur in acidic conditions helps in designing synthetic routes that minimize the formation of impurities like disulfides or dimeric forms.

b. **Selection of Starting Materials and Reagents**:

i. **Purpose**: Choosing high-quality starting materials and reagents that are low in impurities minimizes the risk of contamination in the final product.

ii. **Methods**: Analytical techniques such as spectroscopy and chromatography are used to assess the purity of starting materials before synthesis begins.

iii. **Example**: In the synthesis of Ascorbic Acid, selecting citric acid with minimal impurities ensures that residual solvents or contaminants from the starting material do not carry over into the final product.

2. Process Development:

a. **Optimization of Synthetic Routes**:

i. **Purpose**: Developing efficient synthetic routes that reduce the formation of impurities, by-products, and intermediates.

ii. **Methods**: Chemists modify reaction conditions (e.g., temperature, pH) and catalysts to minimize side reactions and increase yield while reducing impurity formation.

iii. **Example**: Modifying the reaction temperature and solvent in the synthesis of Amoxicillin sodium to prevent degradation and minimize the formation of impurities.

b. **Purification Techniques**:

i. **Purpose**: Implementing effective purification methods to remove impurities generated during synthesis or isolation processes.

ii. **Methods**: Techniques such as recrystallization, chromatography (e.g., HPLC), and filtration are employed to isolate and purify the medicinal agent from impurities.

iii. **Example**: Purifying Captopril through crystallization and filtration to remove residual solvents and unreacted starting materials.

3. **Quality Control Considerations:**

a. **Raw Material Testing**:

i. **Purpose**: Screening raw materials for impurities before use in production to ensure they meet specified purity criteria.

ii. **Methods**: Comprehensive analytical testing using techniques such as NMR spectroscopy, mass spectrometry, and elemental analysis to detect impurities at trace levels.

iii. **Example**: Testing incoming batches of L-cysteine for Captopril synthesis to verify purity and identify potential contaminants.

b. **In-process Monitoring**:

i. **Purpose**: Monitoring impurities during various stages of production to ensure they remain within acceptable limits.

ii. **Methods**: Regular sampling and analysis during synthesis, purification, and formulation stages to detect and control impurities before they exceed regulatory thresholds.

iii. **Example**: Monitoring the formation of degradation products in Ascorbic Acid solutions during production to prevent the accumulation of harmful impurities.

4. **Risk Assessment and Mitigation:**

a. **Identification of Critical Control Points**:

i. **Purpose**: Conducting risk assessments to identify critical points where impurities could potentially enter or accumulate in the manufacturing process.

ii. **Methods**: Utilizing tools such as Failure Mode and Effects Analysis (FMEA) to prioritize control measures and minimize risks associated with impurity formation.

iii. **Example**: Identifying equipment cleaning protocols as critical control points to prevent cross-contamination between different batches of medicinal agents.

b. **Mitigation Strategies**:

   i. **Purpose**: Implementing strategies to mitigate risks associated with impurity formation and contamination throughout the development and production phases.

   ii. **Methods**: Establishing robust cleaning procedures, conducting validation studies, and employing advanced analytical techniques to ensure impurity control.

   iii. **Example**: Implementing stringent environmental monitoring and control measures in manufacturing facilities to minimize particulate contamination in formulations like Tobramycin eye drops.

5. Documentation and Regulatory Compliance:

a. **Impurity Profiling**:

   i. **Purpose**: Providing comprehensive documentation on impurity profiles during drug development and production for regulatory submissions.

   ii. **Methods**: Generating detailed reports that outline impurity identification, characterization, and control strategies to meet regulatory requirements.

   iii. **Example**: Documenting the characterization of degradation products in stability studies of Captopril to demonstrate stability and safety over the product's shelf life.

b. **Regulatory Requirements**:

   i. **Purpose**: Adhering to regulatory limits and guidelines for impurities set by authorities such as FDA, EMA, and ICH to ensure product safety and efficacy.

   ii. **Methods**: Conducting validation studies and performing batch testing to confirm compliance with impurity specifications outlined in pharmacopoeial standards.

iii. **Example**: Ensuring that impurities in Ascorbic Acid formulations meet the specified limits defined in USP or EP monographs for pharmaceutical grade materials.

Production Stage:

During the production stage of medicinal agents, the application of understanding sources of impurities is crucial to ensuring the final product meets high standards of quality, safety, and efficacy. Here's a detailed exploration of how this knowledge is applied:

1. Good Manufacturing Practices (GMP):

a. **Facility Design and Environmental Control**:

i. **Purpose**: Designing production facilities to minimize environmental contaminants and maintain controlled conditions (e.g., temperature, humidity).

ii. **Methods**: Implementing cleanroom technology, HVAC systems, and appropriate air filtration to prevent particulate contamination and airborne impurities.

iii. **Example**: Using HEPA filters and positive pressure in cleanrooms where sterile products like Tobramycin eye drops are manufactured to prevent microbial contamination.

b. **Equipment Cleaning and Maintenance**:

i. **Purpose**: Ensuring equipment used in production is properly cleaned, sanitized, and maintained to prevent cross-contamination and the introduction of impurities.

ii. **Methods**: Establishing validated cleaning procedures (e.g., CIP/SIP systems) and conducting regular equipment inspections to ensure cleanliness and functionality.

iii. **Example**: Cleaning and validating multi-use equipment between batches of Amoxicillin sodium to prevent cross-contamination with other antibiotics.

2. Quality Control (QC):

a. **Raw Material Testing**:

   i. **Purpose**: Screening incoming raw materials for impurities to ensure they meet specified purity criteria before use in production.

   ii. **Methods**: Performing comprehensive analytical testing (e.g., HPLC, GC-MS) to detect and quantify impurities at trace levels in raw materials.

   iii. **Example**: Testing batches of active pharmaceutical ingredients (APIs) like Captopril for residual solvents, heavy metals, and other impurities before formulation.

b. **In-process Monitoring**:

   i. **Purpose**: Continuously monitoring impurity levels during various stages of production to ensure they remain within acceptable limits.

   ii. **Methods**: Sampling and analyzing intermediate products and formulation batches to detect impurities and take corrective actions as necessary.

   iii. **Example**: Monitoring the formation of degradation products and impurities in Ascorbic Acid solutions during mixing, filling, and packaging stages.

c. **Finished Product Testing**:

   i. **Purpose**: Conducting comprehensive testing of finished products to verify impurity profiles and ensure compliance with regulatory standards.

   ii. **Methods**: Conducting assays, dissolution testing, and stability studies to evaluate impurity levels and assess product quality over time.

   iii. **Example**: Testing Tobramycin eye drops for microbial contamination, particulate matter, and chemical impurities before release for distribution and sale.

3. **Packaging and Labeling:**

   a. **Packaging Material Compatibility**:

      i. **Purpose**: Selecting packaging materials that are inert and do not interact with the medicinal agent to prevent leaching of impurities.

      ii. **Methods**: Conducting compatibility studies and using packaging materials certified for pharmaceutical use to ensure product integrity.

      iii. **Example**: Using glass vials or polyethylene containers for Ascorbic Acid formulations to prevent interaction with packaging materials that could introduce impurities.

   b. **Labeling and Traceability**:

      i. **Purpose**: Ensuring accurate labeling to provide information on impurity limits, storage conditions, and batch traceability for regulatory compliance and patient safety.

      ii. **Methods**: Implementing labeling controls and batch numbering systems to facilitate traceability and recall procedures if necessary.

      iii. **Example**: Printing batch numbers and expiration dates on packaging of Amoxicillin sodium tablets to track and manage product distribution and usage.

4. **Regulatory Compliance:**

   a. **Documentation and Reporting**:

      i. **Purpose**: Providing detailed documentation on impurity control measures, testing protocols, and results to regulatory authorities.

      ii. **Methods**: Compiling batch records, validation reports, and stability data to demonstrate adherence to GMP and pharmacopoeial standards.

      iii. **Example**: Submitting a Drug Master File (DMF) or Certificate of Analysis (CoA) to regulatory agencies detailing impurity specifications and control strategies for approval and market authorization.

b. **Audits and Inspections**:

   i. **Purpose**: Undergoing regular audits and inspections by regulatory authorities to ensure compliance with impurity limits and GMP requirements.

   ii. **Methods**: Preparing for and participating in inspections, addressing any findings or non-conformances related to impurity control.

   iii. **Example**: Hosting FDA inspections at manufacturing facilities producing Captopril to verify compliance with USP standards for impurity limits and quality assurance practices.

5. Continuous Improvement:

a. **Process Optimization**:

   i. **Purpose**: Continuously improving production processes and impurity control measures based on data and feedback from quality assessments.

   ii. **Methods**: Implementing corrective and preventive actions (CAPAs) to address deviations and improve impurity management strategies.

   iii. **Example**: Upgrading filtration systems in the production of Ascorbic Acid to enhance removal of particulate impurities and improve product quality.

b. **Training and Development**:

   i. **Purpose**: Training personnel on proper GMP practices, impurity control strategies, and regulatory requirements to ensure consistent adherence and competence.

ii. **Methods**: Providing ongoing training programs and workshops to educate employees on the importance of impurity control and quality assurance.

iii. **Example**: Conducting annual GMP training sessions for production staff involved in manufacturing Amoxicillin sodium to reinforce best practices and regulatory compliance.

Regulatory Compliance:

Regulatory compliance regarding impurities in medicinal agents is critical to ensure patient safety, efficacy, and quality of pharmaceutical products. Here's a detailed exploration of how regulatory compliance is applied in managing impurities:

Understanding Regulatory Requirements:

1. **Guidelines and Standards**:
   a. Regulatory agencies such as the FDA (Food and Drug Administration), EMA (European Medicines Agency), and ICH (International Council for Harmonisation) provide guidelines and standards for impurity limits, testing methods, and control strategies.
   b. Pharmacopoeial standards (e.g., USP, EP) outline specific requirements for impurity profiles and permissible limits in pharmaceutical products.
2. **Impurity Identification and Characterization**:
   a. Manufacturers are required to identify and characterize impurities present in medicinal agents through thorough analytical testing.
   b. This includes understanding the chemical nature, origin, and potential risks associated with each impurity.

Application in Regulatory Compliance:

1. **Documentation and Reporting**:

a. **Impurity Profiling**: Manufacturers must document comprehensive impurity profiles throughout drug development and production.
b. **Validation Studies**: Conducting validation studies to demonstrate control over impurities and adherence to regulatory limits.
c. **Batch Records**: Maintaining detailed batch records that include impurity testing results, manufacturing processes, and controls implemented.

2. **Risk Assessment and Mitigation**:
   a. **Risk Management Plans**: Developing risk assessment plans to identify critical impurities and potential sources of contamination.
   b. **Control Strategies**: Implementing control strategies to minimize impurities, such as optimized manufacturing processes, stringent quality control measures, and validated cleaning procedures.
3. **Quality Control Measures**:
   a. **Raw Material Testing**: Screening raw materials for impurities before use in production to ensure they meet specified purity criteria.
   b. **In-process Monitoring**: Continuously monitoring impurity levels during production to prevent deviations and ensure compliance with regulatory standards.
   c. **Finished Product Testing**: Conducting comprehensive testing of finished products to verify impurity levels and compliance with pharmacopoeial limits.
4. **Validation and Verification**:
   a. **Method Validation**: Validating analytical methods used for impurity testing to ensure accuracy, precision, and reliability of results.
   b. **Process Validation**: Validating manufacturing processes to demonstrate consistency in impurity control and product quality.

5. **Audits and Inspections**:
    a. **Regulatory Inspections**: Being subject to regular inspections by regulatory authorities to assess compliance with GMP (Good Manufacturing Practice) standards and impurity control measures.
    b. **Audit Readiness**: Maintaining readiness for audits by ensuring documentation, records, and processes related to impurity control are readily accessible and up-to-date.
6. **Market Authorization and Post-Marketing Surveillance**:
    a. **Submission Requirements**: Submitting comprehensive data on impurity control as part of regulatory submissions for market authorization (e.g., New Drug Application).
    b. **Post-Marketing Monitoring**: Monitoring impurities in marketed products through pharmacovigilance and post-marketing surveillance to detect any emerging issues or deviations.

Examples of Regulatory Compliance in Practice:

1. **Example 1**: Submitting a Drug Master File (DMF) that includes detailed impurity profiles and control strategies for an active pharmaceutical ingredient (API) like Captopril to regulatory authorities for approval.
2. **Example 2**: Conducting stability studies on Ascorbic Acid formulations to demonstrate that impurity levels remain within acceptable limits throughout their shelf life, as per regulatory requirements.
3. **Example 3**: Implementing CAPA (Corrective and Preventive Action) plans following deviations in impurity levels during production, documented and reported to regulatory agencies to ensure corrective measures are effective.

Safety and Efficacy:

In the context of medicinal agents, ensuring safety and efficacy involves rigorous management of impurities throughout their lifecycle, from development to production and beyond. Here's a detailed exploration of how the application of understanding sources of impurities contributes to safety and efficacy:

Safety Considerations:

1. **Identification and Control of Harmful Impurities**:
    a. **Purpose**: Identifying and controlling impurities that pose potential health risks to patients.
    b. **Methods**: Analytical techniques such as chromatography, spectroscopy, and mass spectrometry are used to detect and quantify impurities, ensuring harmful substances are minimized or eliminated.
    c. **Example**: Detecting and controlling genotoxic impurities in pharmaceuticals, like those found in certain degradation products of APIs, which could potentially cause mutations or cancer.
2. **Microbial Contamination Prevention**:
    a. **Purpose**: Preventing microbial contamination that could lead to infections or adverse reactions in patients.
    b. **Methods**: Implementing sterile manufacturing processes, environmental monitoring, and microbiological testing to ensure medicinal agents are free from harmful microorganisms.
    c. **Example**: Ensuring Tobramycin eye drops are produced under aseptic conditions to prevent bacterial contamination that could harm ocular health.
3. **Allergenic Impurities Management**:
    a. **Purpose**: Managing impurities that could trigger allergic reactions or sensitivities in susceptible individuals.
    b. **Methods**: Assessing potential allergens in raw materials and ensuring thorough cleaning of equipment to prevent cross-contamination.

c. **Example**: Ensuring that excipients used in formulations like Amoxicillin sodium tablets do not contain allergens that could cause adverse reactions in patients with allergies.

Efficacy Considerations:

1. **Maintaining Active Ingredient Purity**:
   a. **Purpose**: Ensuring that the active pharmaceutical ingredient (API) remains pure and effective in delivering therapeutic benefits.
   b. **Methods**: Optimizing synthesis and purification processes to minimize the presence of impurities that could interfere with API efficacy.
   c. **Example**: Controlling degradation impurities in Ascorbic Acid formulations to maintain its potency as a vitamin supplement.
2. **Minimizing Interference with Drug Action**:
   a. **Purpose**: Preventing impurities from altering the pharmacological action or bioavailability of the medicinal agent.
   b. **Methods**: Conducting compatibility studies and assessing potential interactions between impurities and the active ingredients.
   c. **Example**: Ensuring that impurities in Captopril formulations do not affect its ability to inhibit angiotensin-converting enzyme (ACE) for effective blood pressure control.
3. **Stability and Shelf-Life Assurance**:
   a. **Purpose**: Maintaining product stability over time to ensure consistent efficacy throughout its shelf life.
   b. **Methods**: Conducting stability studies under various storage conditions to monitor degradation and impurity formation.
   c. **Example**: Testing the stability of L-Thyroxine formulations to ensure the hormone remains potent and effective until its expiration date.

Risk Mitigation Strategies:

1. **Risk Assessment and Management Plans**:
    a. **Purpose**: Proactively identifying and mitigating risks associated with impurities to safeguard patient safety and maintain product efficacy.
    b. **Methods**: Implementing risk assessment tools (e.g., FMEA) to prioritize impurity control measures and establish robust quality control processes.
    c. **Example**: Developing risk management plans for Mifepristone formulations to address potential impurities that could impact its effectiveness in medical termination of pregnancy.
2. **Continuous Monitoring and Improvement**:
    a. **Purpose**: Continuously monitoring impurity levels and implementing improvements in production processes to enhance safety and efficacy.
    b. **Methods**: Conducting regular reviews of impurity data, feedback from quality assurance measures, and implementing corrective actions as necessary.
    c. **Example**: Using feedback from stability testing of Prednisolone formulations to adjust packaging materials and storage conditions to minimize degradation impurities.

Continuous Improvement:

Continuous improvement in managing sources of impurities in medicinal agents is essential to enhance product quality, safety, and regulatory compliance throughout the drug development and production lifecycle. Here's a detailed exploration of how continuous improvement is applied:

Process Optimization:

1. **Optimizing Synthetic Routes**:

a. **Purpose**: Improving synthetic routes to minimize impurity formation and increase yield.
b. **Methods**: Evaluating alternative reagents, catalysts, and reaction conditions through process optimization studies.
c. **Example**: Modifying the synthesis of Captopril to reduce the formation of impurities like disulfides by adjusting pH and temperature conditions.

2. **Enhancing Purification Techniques**:
   a. **Purpose**: Refining purification methods to effectively remove impurities generated during synthesis or isolation processes.
   b. **Methods**: Implementing advanced purification techniques such as chromatography or crystallization optimization.
   c. **Example**: Upgrading filtration systems in the production of Ascorbic Acid to improve removal of particulate impurities and ensure product quality.

Advanced Analytical Techniques:

1. **Improving Impurity Detection**:
   a. **Purpose**: Enhancing sensitivity and accuracy in detecting impurities at trace levels.
   b. **Methods**: Adopting state-of-the-art analytical instruments (e.g., LC-MS, GC-MS) and developing robust analytical methods.
   c. **Example**: Implementing high-resolution mass spectrometry for precise identification of low-level impurities in Tobramycin eye drops.
2. **Real-Time Monitoring and Control**:
   a. **Purpose**: Implementing continuous monitoring systems to detect deviations in impurity levels during production.
   b. **Methods**: Using process analytical technology (PAT) for real-time monitoring of critical process parameters.

c. **Example**: Installing online spectroscopic systems to monitor reaction kinetics and impurity formation during the synthesis of Amoxicillin sodium.

Quality by Design (QbD):

1. **Risk-Based Approach**:
    a. **Purpose**: Applying risk assessment tools to identify critical impurities and prioritize control measures.
    b. **Methods**: Incorporating QbD principles into product development to design robust processes that inherently minimize impurity risks.
    c. **Example**: Developing control strategies for hydrolysis impurities in Prednisolone formulations based on QbD principles to ensure consistent product quality.
2. **Continuous Validation and Verification**:
    a. **Purpose**: Continuously validating and verifying impurity control measures to ensure effectiveness and compliance.
    b. **Methods**: Conducting ongoing validation studies and periodic reviews of impurity data to assess process robustness.
    c. **Example**: Regularly updating impurity profiles and control strategies for Dexamethasone formulations based on new analytical findings and regulatory guidelines.

Training and Knowledge Sharing:

1. **Employee Training Programs**:
    a. **Purpose**: Educating personnel on best practices for impurity control, GMP standards, and regulatory compliance.
    b. **Methods**: Conducting regular training sessions, workshops, and seminars to enhance skills and awareness.
    c. **Example**: Providing specialized training for production operators on handling specific impurity-related challenges in the manufacture of L-Thyroxine.

2. **Cross-Functional Collaboration**:
    a. **Purpose**: Facilitating collaboration between R&D, manufacturing, quality assurance, and regulatory affairs teams to address impurity-related issues holistically.
    b. **Methods**: Establishing cross-functional teams to review and optimize processes, share insights, and implement continuous improvement initiatives.
    c. **Example**: Collaborating across departments to streamline impurity testing protocols and enhance data sharing for faster decision-making in the production of Hydrocortisone.

Multiple Choice Questions (MCQs)

1. Which of the following is a source of synthetic impurities in medicinal agents?
    A. Starting materials
    B. Environmental contaminants
    C. Microbial contamination
    D. Packaging materials
2. What type of impurity is formed due to exposure to moisture or water?
    A. Oxidative
    B. Hydrolytic
    C. Photolytic
    D. Thermal
3. What can cause oxidative degradation in medicinal agents?
    A. Light exposure
    B. High humidity
    C. Oxygen in the air
    D. Residual solvents

4. Which type of impurity can result from improper storage conditions?
   A. Starting materials
   B. By-products
   C. Environmental contaminants
   D. Residual solvents
5. Residual solvents in medicinal agents can originate from:
   A. Packaging materials
   B. Extraction processes
   C. Microbial contamination
   D. Cross-contamination
6. What is an example of a leachable impurity from packaging materials?
   A. Heavy metals
   B. Plasticizers from PVC
   C. Microbial contamination
   D. Residual solvents
7. How can microbial contamination occur during the production of medicinal agents?
   A. Through the use of unclean equipment
   B. From starting materials
   C. Due to residual solvents
   D. From packaging materials
8. Which of the following can cause cross-contamination in medicinal agents?
   A. Shared equipment
   B. Residual solvents
   C. Photolytic degradation
   D. Leachables
9. Impurities in excipients can affect the purity of which product?
   A. Active pharmaceutical ingredient
   B. Inactive ingredients

C. Starting materials

D. Packaging materials

10. What is a critical control point for minimizing impurity contamination?

A. Labeling

B. Marketing

C. Equipment cleaning

D. Packaging

11. Which regulatory body provides guidelines for impurity limits in pharmaceuticals?

A. WHO

B. FDA

C. EPA

D. USDA

12. What type of impurities can be introduced by improper labeling and packaging?

A. Microbial contamination

B. Photolytic degradation products

C. Inks and adhesives

D. Residual solvents

13. How can environmental contaminants be introduced during storage?

A. Through microbial growth

B. By residual solvents

C. From starting materials

D. By by-products

14. What analytical technique is commonly used to assess impurity profiles?

A. NMR spectroscopy

B. Electrolysis

C. Titration

D. Centrifugation

15. Which impurity can result from the interaction between the active ingredient and excipients?

   A. Microbial contamination

   B. By-products

   C. Environmental contaminants

   D. Residual solvents

16. Which stage involves optimizing synthetic routes to minimize impurity formation?

   A. Development stage

   B. Production stage

   C. Marketing stage

   D. Distribution stage

17. What is an example of a degradation impurity?

   A. Residual solvents

   B. By-products

   C. Hydrolytic degradation products

   D. Environmental contaminants

18. What purpose does risk assessment serve in impurity management?

   A. Identifying critical control points

   B. Marketing

   C. Labeling

   D. Packaging

19. Which of the following helps in real-time monitoring of impurity levels during production?

   A. LC-MS

   B. Centrifugation

   C. Titration

   D. Dissolution testing

20. What is an advantage of continuous improvement in impurity management?

A. Increased marketing

B. Enhanced product quality

C. Reduced production costs

D. Faster regulatory approvals

Short Answer Type Questions (Subjective)

1. What are synthetic impurities in medicinal agents, and how do they arise?
2. Explain how hydrolytic degradation can lead to impurities in medicinal agents.
3. What role does oxidation play in the formation of impurities in medicinal agents?
4. Describe the potential sources of environmental contaminants during the manufacturing process.
5. How can residual solvents become impurities in medicinal agents?
6. Explain how packaging materials can contribute to impurities in medicinal agents.
7. What measures can be taken to prevent microbial contamination during the production of medicinal agents?
8. How does cross-contamination occur in pharmaceutical manufacturing?
9. What are some examples of impurities that can arise from excipients in medicinal formulations?
10. How do regulatory bodies like the FDA and EMA ensure the safety and quality of medicinal agents concerning impurities?
11. Describe the importance of identifying potential impurities during the development stage of a medicinal agent.
12. What are the common methods used to remove impurities during the purification process?
13. How do quality control measures help in managing impurities during the production stage?

14. What is the significance of risk assessment and mitigation in impurity management?
15. How does proper packaging material selection help in minimizing impurities in medicinal agents?
16. Explain the role of in-process monitoring in controlling impurities during pharmaceutical production.
17. How do stability studies help in ensuring the efficacy of medicinal agents over time?
18. What are the key elements of continuous improvement in managing sources of impurities in medicinal agents?
19. How does Quality by Design (QbD) contribute to impurity management in pharmaceutical development?
20. Describe the impact of training and cross-functional collaboration on impurity control in pharmaceutical manufacturing.

Long Answer Type Questions (Subjective)

1. Discuss the various sources of synthetic impurities in medicinal agents and the methods used to control them during the production process.
2. Explain the different types of degradation impurities, providing examples of drugs that are susceptible to each type.
3. Describe the potential environmental contaminants that can affect medicinal agents during production, storage, and transportation. How can these contaminants be controlled?
4. Discuss the impact of residual solvents on the safety and efficacy of medicinal agents. What are the methods used to detect and remove these solvents?
5. Explain how impurities from packaging materials can affect medicinal agents. Provide examples and discuss measures to prevent such contamination.

6. Discuss the various stages in the pharmaceutical development process where impurity management is crucial. How is impurity profiling conducted at each stage?
7. Explain the importance of regulatory compliance in managing impurities in medicinal agents. Discuss the guidelines provided by regulatory bodies and the steps manufacturers must take to comply.
8. Describe the strategies used to maintain the stability and shelf life of medicinal agents by controlling impurities. Provide examples of specific drugs and the measures taken to ensure their stability.
9. Discuss the role of continuous improvement in impurity management in pharmaceutical manufacturing. How do process optimization and advanced analytical techniques contribute to this goal?
10. Explain how cross-contamination can occur in pharmaceutical manufacturing. Discuss the measures that can be implemented to prevent cross-contamination and ensure the purity of medicinal agents.

Answer Key

1. A. Starting materials
2. B. Hydrolytic
3. C. Oxygen in the air
4. C. Environmental contaminants
5. B. Extraction processes
6. B. Plasticizers from PVC
7. A. Through the use of unclean equipment
8. A. Shared equipment
9. A. Active pharmaceutical
10. C. Equipment cleaning
11. B. FDA
12. C. Inks and adhesives

13.A. Through microbial growth

14.A. NMR spectroscopy

15.B. By-products

16.A. Development stage

17.C. Hydrolytic degradation products

18.A. Identifying critical control points

19.A. LC-MS

20.B. Enhanced product quality

CHAPTER – 5

LIMIT TESTS

INTRODUCTION:

Limit tests are analytical techniques used in pharmacopeial and pharmaceutical analysis to detect and quantify impurities or contaminants in drug substances and pharmaceutical formulations. These tests are crucial for ensuring the purity and safety of pharmaceutical products. Here's an introduction to limit tests in detail:

Purpose of Limit Tests:

Limit tests serve several purposes:

1. **Detection of Impurities:** They are primarily used to detect impurities or contaminants present in pharmaceutical substances or formulations.
2. **Safety Assessment:** They help ensure that impurities are present within acceptable limits that do not pose a risk to patient safety.
3. **Quality Control:** Limit tests are part of quality control measures to verify the purity of pharmaceutical products before they are released for distribution.

Key Aspects of Limit Tests:

1. **Threshold Limit:** Each impurity or contaminant has a specified threshold limit, often set by pharmacopeial standards (e.g., USP, BP, EP). This limit defines the maximum acceptable concentration of the impurity in the drug product.
2. **Analytical Techniques:** Various analytical methods can be employed depending on the nature of the impurity. Common techniques include spectrophotometry, chromatography (e.g., HPLC, GC), titration, and gravimetric analysis.

3. **Validation:** The methods used for limit tests must be validated to ensure accuracy, precision, specificity, and robustness.

Steps Involved in Performing Limit Tests:

1. **Sample Preparation:** The pharmaceutical sample is prepared according to specified procedures, ensuring representative sampling and adequate solubility or extraction of impurities.
2. **Analytical Procedure:** The chosen analytical method is applied to quantify the impurity. This may involve calibration with standard solutions of known impurity concentrations.
3. **Comparison with Limits:** The concentration of the impurity in the sample is compared against the specified limit set by pharmacopeial standards.
4. **Reporting and Evaluation:** Results are reported indicating whether the impurity concentration is within acceptable limits. If the impurity exceeds the specified limit, further investigation and corrective actions may be required.

Examples of Limit Tests:

1. **Heavy Metals:** Determination of heavy metals (e.g., lead, arsenic) in pharmaceuticals to ensure compliance with safety standards.
2. **Residual Solvents:** Analysis of residual solvents left from manufacturing processes to ensure they are within safe limits.
3. **Organic Impurities:** Identification and quantification of specific organic impurities that may arise during synthesis or storage of drug substances.

Importance in Regulatory Compliance:

Limit tests are crucial for regulatory compliance in the pharmaceutical industry. Regulatory agencies such as the FDA (Food and Drug Administration) and EMA (European Medicines Agency) require pharmaceutical companies to adhere to stringent limits for impurities to ensure product safety and efficacy.

CHLORIDE

The limit test for chloride is a common analytical procedure used to determine the presence and concentration of chloride ions in pharmaceutical substances and formulations. Chloride ions can be contaminants or impurities that need to be controlled within specified limits to ensure the quality and safety of pharmaceutical products.

Principle:

Limit test of chloride is based on the reaction between silver nitrate and soluble chloride to obtain silver chloride which is insoluble in dilute nitric acid.

$$NaCl + AgNO_3 \xrightarrow{HNO_3} AgCl + NaNO_3$$

The silver chloride produced in the presence of dilute nitric acid makes the solution turbid, the extent of turbidity depends upon the amount of chloride present in the substance is compared with a standard opalescence produced by addition of silver nitrate to a standard solution having a known amount of chloride and the same amount of dilute nitric acid as used in the test solution.

Procedure:

S. No	Test	Standard
1.	Dissolve specific quantity of sample in distilled water and transfer in Nessler cylinder	Take 1 ml of 0.05845% w/v solution of sodium chloride (NaCl)
2.	Add 1 ml of nitric acid	Add 1 ml of nitric acid
3.	Dilute to 50 ml with distilled water.	Dilute to 50 ml with distilled water.
4.	Add 1 ml of silver nitrate solution (5%).	Add 1 ml of silver nitrate solution.
5.	Keep a side for 5 minutes	Keep a side for 5 minutes
6.	Observe for opalescence	Observe for opalescence

Observation: The opalescence produce in sample solution should not be greater than standard solution. If opalescence produces in sample solution is less than the standard solution, the sample will pass the limit test of chloride and visa versa.

Reasoning:

Nitric acid is added in the limit test of chloride to make solution acidic and helps silver chloride precipitate to make solution **turbid** at the end of process.

SULPHATE

The limit test for sulfate is a standard analytical procedure used to detect and quantify sulfate ions (SO_4^{2-}) in pharmaceutical substances and formulations. Sulfate ions can be impurities that need to be controlled within specified limits to ensure the quality and safety of pharmaceutical products.

Principle:

Reaction between barium chloride and soluble sulphate in presence of dilute hydrochloric acid.

Then, the comparison of the turbidity produced by a given amount of the substance is done with a standard turbidity obtained from a known amount of sulphate and same volumes of dilute hydrochloric acid have been added to both the solutions.

$$BaCl_2 + \text{Sulphate} = BaSO_4 + \text{Chloride}$$

$$BaCl_2 + Na_2SO_4 = BaSO_4 + 2NaCl$$

Reasoning:

- Hydrochloric acid helps to make solution acidic.
- Potassium sulphate is used to increase the sensitivity of the test by giving ionic concentration in the reagent.
- Alcohol helps to prevent super saturation and so produces a more uniform opalescence

BARIUM SULPHATE REAGENTS:

S. No	Composition	Used
1.	15 ml of 0.5%$BaCl_2$	Used as precipitating agent
2.	20 ml of sulphate free alcohol	Used to prevent supersaturation
3.	5 ml of 0.01081% w/v Potassium sulphate	Used as seeding agent and to increase the ionic concentration and sensitivity of the test.
4.	Purified water quantity sufficient to 100 ml	Diluent

Observation: The opalescence produce in sample solution should not be greater than standard solution. If opalescence produces in sample solution is less than the standard solution, the sample will pass the limit test of chloride and visa versa.

IRON

The limit test for iron is an analytical procedure used to detect and quantify iron (Fe^{2+} and Fe^{3+}) in pharmaceutical substances and formulations. Iron can be present as an impurity or intentionally added to certain formulations, and its concentration needs to be controlled within specified limits to ensure product quality and safety.

Principle:

Limit test of iron is based on the reaction iron with thioglycollic acid in the presence of ammonical solution and citric acid.

$$2HSCH_2COOH + Fe^{+2} = Fe(HSCH_2COO)_2 + 2H^+$$

Thioglycolic acid   Ferrous thioglycolic acid

A pale pink to deep reddish purple colour is formed due to the formation of ferrous compound. The coloured produced from the specified amount of substance from the test is compared with a standard (ferric ammonium sulphate).

Procedure:

S. No	Test	Standard
1.	Sample +40 ml of water	2 ml of standard solution of iron and dilute 40 ml distilled water
2.	2 ml of 20% w/v (iron free) citric acid	2 ml of 20% w/v (iron free) citric acid
3.	2 drop of thioglycolic acid ; solution mixed	2 drop of thioglycolic acid ; solution mixed
4.	made alkaline with ammonia volume adjusted to 50 ml ;	made alkaline with ammonia volume adjusted to 50 ml ;
5.	allowed to stand and color developed viewed vertically and compared with standard solution	allowed to stand and color developed viewed vertically and compared with standard solution

Observation:

The purple colour produce in sample solution should not be greater than standard solution. If purple colour produces in sample solution is less than the standard solution, the sample will pass the limit test of iron and vice versa.

Reasoning:

1. **Thioglycollic acid**
    - Iron impurities may be present in the trivelant ferric form or in the divelent ferrous form. If it is present in ferric form then thioglycolic acid reduces it to the ferrous form.

- Thioglycolic acid produce purple colour with ferrous ion in the ammonical alkaline medium

2. **Citric acid:**
   - Its prevent precipitation of iron with ammonia. It keeps iron in the solution form even in the presence of ammonia by forming a complex.

   Or

   - Citric acid forms complex with metal cation and helps precipitation of iron by ammonia by forming a complex with it.

3. **Ammonia:**
   - Ammonia is added to make solution alkaline. The pale pink colour is visible only in the alkaline media. The colour is not visible in acidic media as ferrous thioglycolate complex decomposes in high acidic media.

ARSENIC

The limit test for arsenic is a critical analytical procedure used to detect and quantify arsenic (As) in pharmaceutical substances and formulations. Arsenic is a highly toxic element, and its presence in pharmaceuticals must be strictly controlled to ensure product safety and compliance with regulatory standards.

Principle of limit test for Arsenic:

- Arsenic is the conversion of arsenic impurity to arsine gas which passed over $HgCl_2$ paper to form a yellow –brown stain. The intensity of the colour produced by sample is compared with that of the standard.
- Arsenic present as an impurity is first converted to arsenic acid or arsenious acid in the presence of reducing system like $SnCl_2$/HCl.
- The arsine gas is thus produced from arsenious acid in the presence of nascent hydrogen (Which is produced by Zn +HCl)

- The use of KI ensure moderate and constant supply of nascent hydrogen
- The arsine gas reacts with $HgCl_2$ paper to form a yellow brown stain owing to the formation of mercuric arsenide.

$$\underset{\text{Trivalent arsenic}}{As^{3+}} \xrightarrow[SnCl2]{HCl} \underset{\text{Arsenious acid}}{As(OH)_3} \quad (H_3AsO_3)$$

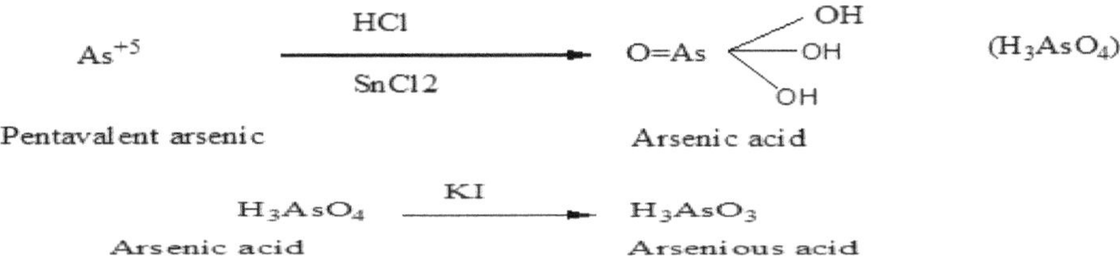

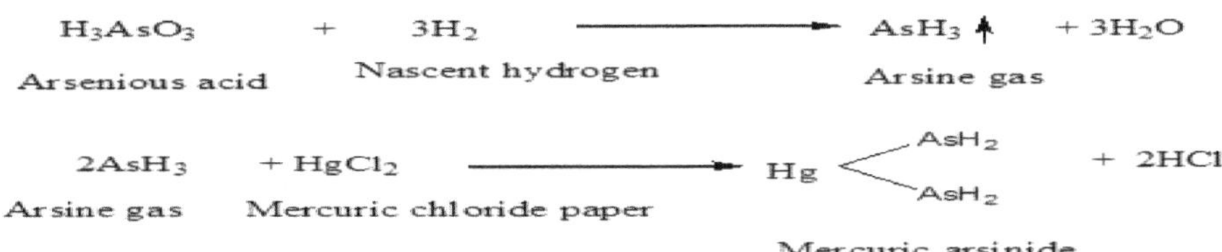

Rupper Bungs
Clip
200 mm Glass Tube
Chloride Paper
Cotton Plug Moistened with Lead Acetate solution
6.5 mm Internal Diameter
2 mm Diameter Hole
120 ml Capacity Bottle

Apparatus for limit test for arsenic

Procedure:

S. No	Test	Standard
1.	The test solution is prepare by dissolving specific amount water and stannated HCl ((arsenic free) and kept in a wide mouthed bottle.	A known amount of dilute arsenic solution in water and stannated HCl ((arsenic free) and kept in a wide mouthed bottle
2.	1 g potassium iodide	1 g potassium iodide
3.	5 ml of stannous chloride acid solution	5 ml of stannous chloride acid solution
4.	10 gm of granulated zinc is added (arsenic free)	10 gm of granulated zinc is added (arsenic free)
5.	Keep the solution aside for 40 minutes	Keep the solution aside for 40 minutes

Observation:

- Stain obtained on mercuric chloride paper is compared with standard solution. Standard stain must be freshly prepared as it fades on keeping.
- Inference: If the stain produced by the test is not deeper than the standard stain, then sample complies with the limit test for Arsenic.

NOTE: If Evaluation hydrogen gas is very slow i.e. if the reaction is very slow, the two apparatus should be warmed to 40^0C by placing these in a warm place or in water bath at 40^0C.

Reasoning:

- Potassium iodide is used because it help in the reduction of pentavelant arsenic acid to trivelent arsenic acid. Potassium iodide is first converted into hydroiodic acid (HI), which helps in this reduction process
- Zinc granulated is used instead of ordinary zinc because evolution of nascent hydrogen is steady and prolonged with granulated zinc.
- Stannous chloride is used for complete evolution of arsine.

- Zinc, potassium iodide and stannous chloride is used as a reducing agent.
- Hydrochloride acid is used to make the solution acidic.
- Lead acetate paper are used to trap any hydrogen sulphide which may be evolved along with arsine.
- Zinc granules usually contain traces of sulphate impurities. These impurities with react with nescent hydrogen forming hydrogen sulphide gas, which coming into contact with $HgCl_2$ paper gives a black stain (HgS). So , to prevent this interference, lead acetate cotton wool is used to drop hydrogen sulphide gas (H_2S) by converting it PbS in the glass tube itself.

$$\underset{\text{Lead acetate}}{Pb(CH_3COO)_2} + \underset{\text{Hydrogen sulphide gas}}{H_2S\uparrow} \longrightarrow \underset{\text{Lead sulphide}}{PbS} + 2CH_3COOH$$

MODIFIED LIMIT TEST FOR CHLORIDE

If the limit tests for sample (colour compound) cannot be done by normal method. Potassium permagnate is decolorized by boiling with ethanol, filter to remove precipitated magnesium dioxide and filtrate is subjected to the test

It is based on the reaction between silver nitrate and soluble chloride to obtain silver chloride which is insoluble in dilute nitric acid.

The silver chloride produced in the presence of dilute nitric acid makes the solution turbid, the extent of turbidity depends upon the amount of chloride present in the substance is compared with a standard opalescence produced by addition of silver nitrate to a standard solution having a known amount of chloride and the same amount of dilute nitric acid as used in the test solution.

If turbidity in test solution has been less than standard turbidity, then the sample passes the limit test.

$$NaCl + AgNO_3 \xrightarrow{HNO_3} AgCl + NaNO_3$$

Reasons:

- Nitric acid is added in the limit test of chloride to make solution acidic and helps silver chloride precipitate to make solution turbid at the end of process.
- This test is not use for immiscible solid.

Requirements:

- A pair of Nessler's cylinder
- Pipettes
- Measuring Cylinder
- Beakers
- Droppers
- Standard Sodium Chloride solution (Dilute 50 ml of 0.08245 g NaCl in 100 ml distilled water)
- Dil. Nitric Acid: dilute 1.06 ml of concentrated nitric acid sufficient distilled water to produce 100 ml.
- Silver nitrate Solution (0.1 M): Dissolve 1.7 gm of silver nitrate to 100 ml of distilled water.
- Ethyl alcohol
- Test sample (Potassium permagnate)

NOTE - The solutions used for this test should be prepared with distilled water

Procedure:

Preparation of test sample ($KMnO_4$): Dissolve 1.5 g in 50 ml of distilled water, heat on a water bath and add gradually 6 ml of ethanol (95%), cool, dilute to 60 ml with distilled water and filter.

S. No	Test sample	Standard
1.	Take 40 ml of the above test solution in Nessler cylinder	Take 10 ml of solution of sodium chloride(250 ppm of

		chloride) in 5 ml of water in Nessler cylinder B
2.	Add 1 ml Dil. Nitric acid	Add 1 ml Dil. Nitric acid
3.	Diluted to 50 ml. with distilled water in Nessler cylinder A	Diluted to 50 ml. with distilled water in Nessler cylinder B
4.	Add 1 ml of 0.1 M Silver Nitrate solution	Add 1 ml of 0.1 M Silver Nitrate solution
5.	Stir with glass rod & kept aside for 5 Minute.	Stir with glass rod & kept aside for 5 Minute.
6.	Observe the opalescence	Observe the opalescence

Modified limit test for sulphate:

From I.P. 1996 onwards, limit test for sulphate has been modified to a great extent. It has done away the requirement of barium sulphate reagent

HEAVY METALS

The limit test for heavy metals is a critical analytical procedure used to detect and quantify toxic heavy metals such as lead (Pb), arsenic (As), cadmium (Cd), mercury (Hg), and others in pharmaceutical substances and formulations. These metals are highly toxic even at low concentrations and must be controlled within strict limits to ensure the safety and quality of pharmaceutical products.

Principle:

It based on the reaction between hydrogen sulphide and heavy metals in an acidic medium to produce the metal sulphides. These remain distributed in a colloidal state and produce brownish colouration. The test solution is compared with a standard prepared using solution of lead nitrate (as Heavy metal).

$$\text{Heavy metal} + H_2S \xrightarrow{\text{Acidic medium}} \text{Sulphides of heavy metals (Brown colour)}$$

$$Pb^{+2} + H_2S \longrightarrow PbS\downarrow + H^+$$

Note: Metals that response to this test are lead, mercury, bismuth, arsenic, antimony, tin, cadmium, silver, copper, and molybdenum. The metallic impurities in substances are expressed as parts of lead per million parts of the substance. The usual limit as per Indian Pharmacopoeia is 20 ppm

Procedure:

As Indian Pharmacopoeia, three methods for the limit test of heavy metals.

Method-A: substance which gives clear colorless solution

S. No	Test sample	Standard
1.	Solution is prepared as per the monograph and 25 ml is transferred in Nessler's cylinder	Take 2 ml of standard lead solution and dilute to 25 ml with water
2.	Adjust the pH between 3 to 4 by adding dilute acetic acid or dilute ammonia solution 'Sp'	Adjust the pH between 3 to 4 by adding dilute acetic acid or dilute ammonia solution
3.	Dilute with water to 35 ml	Dilute with water to 35 ml
4.	Add freshly prepared 10 ml of hydrogen sulphide solution	Add freshly prepared 10 ml of hydrogen sulphide solution
5.	Dilute with water to 50 ml	Dilute with water to 50 ml
6.	Allow to stand for five minutes	Allow to stand for five minutes
7.	View downwards over a white surface	View downwards over a white surface

Observation: The color produce in sample solution should not be greater than standard solution

Method II: Use for the substance which do not give clear colorless solution under the specific condition.

S. No	Test sample	Standard
1.	Weigh specific quantity of test substance, moisten with sulphuric acid and ignite on a low flame till completely charred. Add few drops of nitric acid and heat to 500 °C Allow to cool and add 4 ml of hydrochloric acid and evaporate to dryness. Moisten the residue with 10 ml of hydrochloric acid and digest for two minutes. Neutralize with ammonia solution and make just acid with acetic acid	Take 2 ml of standard lead solution and dilute to 25 ml with water
2.	Adjust the pH between 3 to 4 and filter if necessary	Adjust the pH between 3 to 4 by adding dilute acetic acid 'Sp' or dilute ammonia solution 'Sp'
3.	Dilute with water to 35 ml	Dilute with water to 35 ml
4.	Add freshly prepared 10 ml of hydrogen sulphide solution	Add freshly prepared 10 ml of hydrogen sulphide solution
5.	Dilute with water to 50 ml	Dilute with water to 50 ml
6.	Allow to stand for five minutes	Allow to stand for five

		minutes
7.	View downwards over a white surface	View downwards over a white surface

Observation: The color produce in sample solution should not be greater than standard solution.

Method III: the substance which gives clear colorless solution in sodium hydroxide solution

S. No	**Test sample**	**Standard**
1.	Solution is prepared as per the monograph and 25 ml is transferred in Nessler's cylinder or weigh specific amount of substance and dissolve in 20 ml of water and add 5 ml of dilute sodium hydroxide solution	Take 2 ml of standard lead solution
2.	Make up the volume to 50 ml with water	Add 5 ml of dilute sodium hydroxide solution and make up the volume to 50 ml with water
3.	Add 5 drops of sodium sulphide solution	Add 5 drops of sodium sulphide solution
4.	Mix and set aside for 5 min	Mix and set aside for 5 min
5.	View downwards over a white surface	View downwards over a white surface

LIMIT TEST FOR LEAD

Principle:

It is the reaction between lead and dithizone (Diphenylthiocarbazone) to form a complex. A chloroform solution of dithizone is prepared, which can extract led from alkaline aqueous solution as lead dithiozone complex (red in colour). The original colour of dithizone in chloroform is green while the lead-dithizonate complex is violet in colour. The intensity of the violet colour of the complex depending upon the quantity of lead present in the solution is compared with standard colour produced by standard solution.

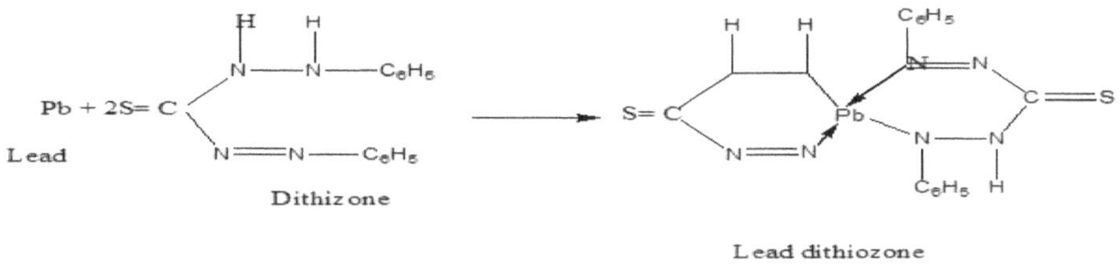

Pb + 2S= C (NH–NH–C_6H_5)(N=N–C_6H_5) ⟶ Lead dithiozone

Lead   Dithizone   Lead dithiozone

Requirements:

- A pair of Nesslers cylinder
- Pipettes
- Measuring Cylinder
- Beakers
- Dropper
- Glass rods
- Ammonium citrate
- Potassium cyanide
- Hydroxylamine hydrochloride
- Phenol red
- Dithizone
- Ammonia solution.

NOTE - The solutions used for this test should be prepared with distilled water.

S	Test sample	Standard
1.	A known quantity of sample	A standard lead solution is

	solution is transferred in a separating funnel	prepared equivalent to the amount of lead permitted in the sample under examination
2.	Add 6ml of ammonium citrate	Add 6ml of ammonium citrate
3.	Add 2 ml of potassium cyanide and 2 ml of hydroxylamine hydrochloride	Add 2 ml of potassium cyanide and 2 ml of hydroxylamine hydrochloride
4.	Make solution alkaline by adding ammonia solution.	Make solution alkaline by adding ammonia solution.
5.	Extract with 5 ml of dithizone until it becomes green	Extract with 5 ml of dithizone until it becomes green
6.	Combine dithizone extracts are shaken for 30 mins with 30 ml of nitric acid and the chloroform layer is discarded	Combine dithizone extracts are shaken for 30 mins with 30 ml of nitric acid and the chloroform layer is discarded
7.	To the acid solution add 5 ml of standard dithizone solution	To the acid solution add 5 ml of standard dithizone solution
8.	To the acid solution add 5 ml of standard dithizone solution	To the acid solution add 5 ml of standard dithizone solution
9.	Add 4 ml of ammonium cyanide	Add 4 ml of ammonium cyanide
10.	Shake for 30 mins	Shake for 30 mins
11.	Observe the color	Observe the color

Multiple Choice Questions (Objective)

1. What is the main principle behind the limit test for chloride?
   A) Formation of a colored solution
   B) Precipitation of chloride ions
   C) Evaporation of chloride ions
   D) Dissolution of silver nitrate
2. Which compound is used to precipitate chloride ions in the limit test for chloride?
   A) Silver sulfate
   B) Silver nitrate
   C) Potassium nitrate
   D) Sodium chloride
3. What is the chemical formula for the precipitate formed in the limit test for chloride? A) $AgNO_3$
   B) NaCl
   C) AgCl
   D) Cl_2
4. In which form does silver chloride appear when precipitated in the reaction?
   A) Blue and soluble
   B) Red and volatile
   C) White and insoluble
   D) Green and soluble
5. What is the purpose of controlling pH during the limit test for chloride?
   A) To speed up the reaction
   B) To stabilize and complete the precipitation
   C) To change the color of the precipitate
   D) To increase the solubility of the precipitate
6. How is the silver chloride precipitate collected in the limit test for chloride?
   A) By decantation

B) By centrifugation

C) By filtration

D) By evaporation

7. What step is performed after collecting the precipitate and before weighing it?

A) Recrystallization

B) Washing and drying

C) Dissolution in water

D) Heating to high temperatures

8. What type of analysis is used to quantify the chloride ions based on the precipitate formed?

A) Titrimetric analysis

B) Colorimetric analysis

C) Gravimetric analysis

D) Spectrophotometric analysis

9. Which standard is used for comparison to determine if the chloride content is within acceptable limits?

A) FDA

B) USP

C) IUPAC

D) WHO

10. What is the primary purpose of the limit test for chloride in pharmaceuticals?

A) To determine the solubility

B) To ensure safety and compliance with regulatory standards

C) To determine the pH value

D) To color the solution

11. Which item is NOT involved in the limit test for chloride?

A) Silver nitrate

B) Silver chloride

C) Sodium bicarbonate

D) Filter paper

12. Why is the precipitate washed with distilled water in the limit test for chloride?

A) To dissolve the precipitate

B) To remove soluble impurities

C) To change the precipitate color

D) To increase the reaction time

13. What happens to the washed precipitate before weighing?

A) It is dissolved in ethanol

B) It is dried to constant weight

C) It is re-filtered

D) It is melted

14. What type of reaction occurs when silver nitrate and chloride ions meet in the limit test?

A) Redox reaction

B) Double displacement reaction

C) Decomposition reaction

D) Precipitation reaction

15. What is an essential quality control measure provided by the limit test for chloride? A) Determining the viscosity of solutions

B) Ensuring the product meets safety standards for chloride content

C) Testing the flavor of the pharmaceutical

D) Measuring the boiling point of the substance

16. Which tool is essential for the final step of the limit test for chloride?

A) pH meter

B) Volumetric flask

C) Sensitive balance

D) Bunsen burner

17. What characteristic of the precipitate is crucial for its collection method?

A) Volatility

B) Insolubility

C) Flammability

D) Elasticity

18. What type of substance is primarily tested in the limit test for chloride?

A) Gases

B) Pharmaceuticals

C) Metals

D) Plastics

19. What analytical technique is involved in the limit test for chloride?

A) Electrolysis

B) Filtration

C) Crystallization

D) Sublimation

20. What is the outcome of the limit test for chloride if the standards are exceeded?

A) The sample passes the quality control.

B) The sample is approved without further testing.

C) The sample fails to meet the regulatory standards.

D) The sample requires no further analysis.

Short Answer Type Questions (Subjective)

1. What is the primary purpose of conducting limit tests in pharmaceutical analysis?
2. Define threshold limit in the context of limit tests.
3. List two analytical techniques commonly used in limit tests.
4. What is the importance of method validation in limit tests?
5. How is the sample prepared for a limit test?

6. Describe the process involved in comparing the test results with pharmacopeial standards.
7. What is the significance of detecting heavy metals in pharmaceuticals?
8. Explain why pH control is crucial in performing limit tests.
9. What are residual solvents, and why is their limit test important?
10. How does the limit test for chloride work?
11. What type of precipitate is formed in the limit test for sulfate?
12. Describe the filtration and collection step in the limit test for chloride.
13. What is gravimetric analysis in the context of limit tests?
14. Why are reference standards used in limit tests?
15. What regulatory agencies require compliance with limit tests?
16. How does the limit test for iron detect iron ions?
17. Describe the role of thioglycolic acid in the limit test for iron.
18. What reaction occurs during the limit test for arsenic?
19. How is the limit test for heavy metals typically conducted?
20. Explain the procedure for generating hydrogen sulfide in the limit test for arsenic.

Long Answer Type Questions (Subjective)

1. Discuss the principles and procedures involved in the limit test for chloride, including the chemical reactions and methods for quantification.
2. Explain the importance of quality control in pharmaceutical manufacturing and how limit tests contribute to this process.
3. Describe the analytical techniques used in limit tests and the criteria for selecting a particular method.
4. Provide a detailed explanation of the steps involved in the limit test for sulfate, from sample preparation to comparison with standards.
5. Discuss the implications of failing a limit test in the pharmaceutical industry and the potential corrective actions that could be taken.

6. Explain how the limit test for heavy metals is performed, including the specific reactions for detecting lead, arsenic, cadmium, and mercury.
7. Describe the reasoning behind the use of thioglycolic acid in the limit test for iron and how it enhances the test's effectiveness.
8. Provide an in-depth discussion on the regulatory framework for limit tests, including key agencies and their roles in ensuring pharmaceutical safety.
9. Discuss the role of pH control in limit tests and its impact on the accuracy and reliability of the test results.
10. Describe the procedure and significance of generating hydrogen sulfide gas in the limit test for arsenic, including the precautions and safety measures required during the process.

Answer Key for the 20 MCQs

1. (B) Precipitation of chloride ions
2. (B) Silver nitrate
3. (C) AgCl
4. (C) White and insoluble
5. (B) To stabilize and complete the precipitation
6. (C) By filtration
7. (B) Washing and drying
8. (C) Gravimetric analysis
9. (B) USP
10. (B) To ensure safety and compliance with regulatory standards
11. (C) Sodium bicarbonate
12. (B) To remove soluble impurities
13. (B) It is dried to constant weight
14. (D) Precipitation reaction
15. (B) Ensuring the product meets safety standards for chloride content
16. (C) Sensitive balance

17.(B) Insolubility

18.(B) Pharmaceuticals

19.(B) Filtration

20.(C) The sample fails to meet the regulatory standards.

CHAPTER – 6

ACID BASE TITRATION

INTRODUCTION:

Acid-base titration is a quantitative analytical method used to determine the concentration of an acid or base in a solution. It involves the gradual addition of a titrant (a solution of known concentration) to a solution of the analyte (the substance being analyzed) until the reaction reaches a completion point known as the equivalence point. Here's a detailed introduction to the concept:

Basic Principles of Acid-Base Titration

1. **Acid-Base Reaction:**
    a. **Acids** are substances that donate protons (H^+ ions) in a solution.
    b. **Bases** are substances that accept protons.
    c. The reaction between an acid and a base is called neutralization and produces water and a salt.
2. **Titrant and Analyte:**
    a. **Titrant:** A solution of known concentration, typically a strong acid or base, which is added to the analyte.
    b. **Analyte:** The solution of unknown concentration being analyzed.
3. **Equivalence Point:**
    a. The point at which the amount of titrant added is stoichiometrically equivalent to the amount of analyte in the solution.
    b. At the equivalence point, the number of moles of H^+ ions equals the number of moles of OH^- ions.
4. **End Point:**
    a. The point at which an indicator changes color, signaling that the equivalence point has been reached or is very close.

b. Ideally, the end point should coincide with the equivalence point.

Steps in Performing an Acid-Base Titration

1. **Preparation:**
    a. Prepare the analyte solution and place it in a flask.
    b. Choose a suitable indicator that will change color at the desired pH.
2. **Titration:**
    a. Fill a burette with the titrant solution.
    b. Slowly add the titrant to the analyte solution while continuously stirring.
    c. Monitor the pH change or the indicator color change.
3. **Detection of Equivalence Point:**
    a. Use an appropriate method to detect the equivalence point:
        i. **pH Indicators:** Substances that change color at a specific pH range. Common indicators include phenolphthalein (colorless in acid, pink in base) and methyl orange (red in acid, yellow in base).
        ii. **pH Meter:** An electronic device that measures the pH of the solution, providing a precise equivalence point.
4. **Calculation:**
    a. Record the volume of titrant added to reach the equivalence point.
    b. Use the titration formula to calculate the concentration of the analyte:

$$C_1V_1 = C_2V_2$$

Where C1 and V1 are the concentration and volume of the analyte, and C2 and V2 are the concentration and volume of the titrant.

Types of Acid-Base Titrations

1. **Strong Acid with Strong Base:**
    a. Example: HCl titrated with NaOH.
    b. The equivalence point is typically at pH 7.

2. **Weak Acid with Strong Base:**
    a. Example: Acetic acid (CH_3COOH) titrated with NaOH.
    b. The equivalence point is above pH 7 due to the production of a weak conjugate base.
3. **Strong Acid with Weak Base:**
    a. Example: HCl titrated with ammonia (NH_3).
    b. The equivalence point is below pH 7 due to the production of a weak conjugate acid.
4. **Weak Acid with Weak Base:**
    a. Example: Acetic acid titrated with ammonia.
    b. The equivalence point is not at a fixed pH and is typically determined using a pH meter.

Applications of Acid-Base Titration

1. **Pharmaceuticals:**
    a. Determining the concentration of active ingredients in drugs.
2. **Food Industry:**
    a. Measuring the acidity or alkalinity of food products.
3. **Environmental Science:**
    a. Analyzing the pH and acidity of water samples.
4. **Chemical Manufacturing:**
    a. Ensuring the correct concentrations of acidic and basic components in products.

Key Considerations

1. **Choice of Indicator:**
    a. The indicator must change color close to the equivalence point of the titration.
2. **Accuracy:**
    a. Proper calibration of titration equipment and careful addition of titrant to avoid overshooting the end point.

3. **Interference:**

   a. Substances in the analyte solution that might interfere with the titration reaction or indicator must be considered and accounted for.

THEORIES OF ACID BASE INDICATORS

Acid-base indicators are substances that change color in response to changes in pH, making them useful in determining the end point of acid-base titrations. There are several theories that explain how these indicators work. The most prominent ones are the Ostwald theory, the Quinonoid theory, and the modern understanding based on the Bronsted-Lowry theory. Here is a detailed overview of these theories:

1. Ostwald Theory

The Ostwald theory is based on the concept of ionization of weak acids and bases.

a. **Basic Premise:**

   i. Acid-base indicators are weak acids or weak bases that partially dissociate in solution.

   ii. The color change is due to the shift in the equilibrium between the undissociated (molecular) form and the dissociated (ionized) form.

b. **For an Indicator (HIn) that is a Weak Acid:**

$$\mathrm{HIn} \rightleftharpoons \mathrm{H^+} + \mathrm{In^-}$$

   i. HIn (undissociated form) has one color, while In^- (dissociated form) has a different color.

c. **Effect of pH:**

   i. In acidic solutions, the equilibrium shifts towards the left (favoring HIn), resulting in the color of HIn.

   ii. In basic solutions, the equilibrium shifts towards the right (favoring In^-), resulting in the color of In^-.

d. **Example:**

i. Phenolphthalein: Colorless in acidic solutions (HIn form) and pink in basic solutions (In^- form).

2. Quinonoid Theory

The Quinonoid theory focuses on the structural changes in the indicator molecule.

a. **Basic Premise:**

  i. Acid-base indicators exist in two tautomeric forms: one in acidic medium and the other in basic medium.

  ii. These forms are structurally different, often involving a quinonoid structure in one of the forms.

b. **For an Indicator:**

  i. The transition between the two forms involves a shift in the position of double bonds and protons, leading to a change in color.

c. **Example:**

  i. Phenolphthalein: Exists in a lactone form in acidic medium (colorless) and converts to a quinonoid form in basic medium (pink).

3. Bronsted-Lowry Theory

The Bronsted-Lowry theory extends the understanding of acid-base indicators by focusing on proton transfer.

a. **Basic Premise:**

  i. Indicators are considered as weak acids or bases that undergo proton transfer reactions.

  ii. The color change is due to the protonation or deprotonation of the indicator molecule.

b. **For an Indicator (HIn):**

  i. In acidic conditions, the indicator remains protonated (HIn), exhibiting one color.

  ii. In basic conditions, the indicator loses a proton (In^-), exhibiting another color.

c. **Example:**

    i. Methyl orange: Red in acidic conditions (protonated form) and yellow in basic conditions (deprotonated form).

Practical Considerations for Choosing an Indicator

1. **pH Range of Color Change:**
    a. Each indicator has a specific pH range over which it changes color. This range should match the expected equivalence point of the titration.
2. **Clear and Distinct Color Change:**
    a. The color change should be sharp and distinct to accurately determine the end point.
3. **Type of Titration:**
    a. The choice of indicator depends on the type of titration (strong acid-strong base, weak acid-strong base, etc.).

Examples of Common Indicators and Their pH Ranges

1. **Methyl Orange:**
    a. pH range: 3.1 (red) to 4.4 (yellow)
    b. Used in strong acid-weak base titrations.
2. **Phenolphthalein:**
    a. pH range: 8.3 (colorless) to 10.0 (pink)
    b. Used in strong acid-strong base and weak acid-strong base titrations.
3. **Bromothymol Blue:**
    a. pH range: 6.0 (yellow) to 7.6 (blue)
    b. Used in titrations involving weak acids and weak bases.
4. **Litmus:**
    a. pH range: 4.5 (red) to 8.3 (blue)
    b. General-purpose indicator.

CLASSIFICATION OF ACID BASE TITRATIONS

Acid-base titrations can be classified based on the strength of the acids and bases involved, as well as the nature of the titration process. Here's a detailed classification:

1. Based on the Strength of Acid and Base

a. Strong Acid-Strong Base Titration

i. **Description:** Involves a strong acid (completely dissociates in water) and a strong base (completely dissociates in water).

ii. **Equivalence Point:** The pH at the equivalence point is neutral (pH 7) because the salt formed does not hydrolyze.

iii. **Example:** Hydrochloric acid (HCl) titrated with sodium hydroxide (NaOH).

iv. **Indicators:** Phenolphthalein, Bromothymol blue.

v. **Titration Curve:** Shows a sharp, steep rise in pH around the equivalence point.

b. Weak Acid-Strong Base Titration

i. **Description:** Involves a weak acid (partially dissociates in water) and a strong base.

ii. **Equivalence Point:** The pH at the equivalence point is greater than 7 because the conjugate base of the weak acid hydrolyzes to produce OH^- ions.

iii. **Example:** Acetic acid (CH_3COOH) titrated with sodium hydroxide (NaOH).

iv. **Indicators:** Phenolphthalein.

v. **Titration Curve:** The curve shows a more gradual rise in pH and levels off after the equivalence point.

c. Strong Acid-Weak Base Titration

i. **Description:** Involves a strong acid and a weak base (partially dissociates in water).

ii. **Equivalence Point:** The pH at the equivalence point is less than 7 because the conjugate acid of the weak base hydrolyzes to produce H^+ ions.

iii. **Example:** Hydrochloric acid (HCl) titrated with ammonia (NH_3).

iv. **Indicators:** Methyl orange, Bromocresol green.

v. **Titration Curve:** The curve shows a more gradual decrease in pH and levels off after the equivalence point.

d. Weak Acid-Weak Base Titration

i. **Description:** Involves a weak acid and a weak base.

ii. **Equivalence Point:** The pH at the equivalence point is around 7, but the curve is not as steep as strong acid-strong base titrations.

iii. **Example:** Acetic acid (CH_3COOH) titrated with ammonia (NH_3).

iv. **Indicators:** Not as reliable due to the shallow titration curve; pH meter is often used.

v. **Titration Curve:** Shows a very gradual slope and lacks a clear, sharp equivalence point.

2. Based on the Nature of the Titration Process

a. Direct Titration

i. **Description:** The titrant is added directly to the analyte solution until the equivalence point is reached.

ii. **Procedure:** Simple and straightforward, widely used in laboratories.

iii. **Example:** Titrating hydrochloric acid with sodium hydroxide.

b. Back Titration

i. **Description:** Used when the analyte is not soluble or reacts too slowly with the titrant.

ii. **Procedure:** A known excess of a standard reagent (titrant) is added to the analyte, and the excess reagent is then titrated with another reagent.

iii. **Example:** Determining the amount of calcium carbonate by adding excess HCl and titrating the remaining HCl with NaOH.

c. Complexometric Titration

i. **Description:** Involves the formation of a complex between the analyte and the titrant.

ii. **Procedure:** Often used for determining metal ions with chelating agents like EDTA.

iii. **Example:** Determination of calcium ions using EDTA.

3. Based on the Indicator Used

a. pH Indicators

i. **Description:** Substances that change color at specific pH ranges.

ii. **Example:** Phenolphthalein, Methyl orange, Bromothymol blue.

iii. **Use:** The choice of indicator depends on the expected pH at the equivalence point.

b. pH Meter

i. **Description:** An electronic device that measures the pH of the solution continuously.

ii. **Use:** Provides precise detection of the equivalence point, especially useful in weak acid-weak base titrations.

THEORY INVOLVED IN TITRATIONS OF STRONG, WEAK, AND VERY WEAK ACIDS AND BASES

The theory involved in titrations of strong, weak, and very weak acids and bases focuses on the dissociation behavior of these acids and bases in water and their reactions with each other. The strength of an acid or base determines the shape of the titration curve, the pH at the equivalence point, and the choice of suitable indicators. Let's explore these theories in detail:

1. Strong Acid-Strong Base Titration

Theory:

a. **Strong Acids and Bases:** Strong acids (e.g., HCl, HNO_3) and strong bases (e.g., $NaOH$, KOH) completely dissociate in water.

b. Reaction: The titration involves a neutralization reaction where H^+ ions from the acid react with OH^- ions from the base to form water.

$$HCl + NaOH \rightarrow NaCl + H_2O$$

Titration Curve:

a. **Initial pH:** Very low for strong acids.

b. **Shape:** The pH rises gradually at first, then sharply near the equivalence point, and levels off after the equivalence point.

c. **Equivalence Point:** pH 7 because the salt formed (e.g., NaCl) does not hydrolyze and the solution is neutral.

Indicators:

a. **Phenolphthalein:** Changes color in the pH range 8.3-10.0.

b. **Bromothymol Blue:** Changes color in the pH range 6.0-7.6.

2. Weak Acid-Strong Base Titration

Theory:

a. **Weak Acids:** Weak acids (e.g., CH_3COOH) partially dissociate in water. The degree of dissociation is characterized by the acid dissociation constant (Ka).

b. **Reaction:** The weak acid reacts with the strong base to form water and a salt. The conjugate base of the weak acid hydrolyzes in water.

$$CH_3COOH + NaOH \rightarrow CH_3COONa + H_2O$$

c. **Buffer Region:** Before the equivalence point, the solution acts as a buffer, resisting changes in pH.

Titration Curve:

a. **Initial pH:** Higher than that of a strong acid.

b. **Shape:** The pH rises gradually, then more steeply near the equivalence point.

c. **Equivalence Point:** pH > 7 due to the hydrolysis of the conjugate base (e.g., CH_3COO^- forms OH^-).

Indicators:

a. **Phenolphthalein:** Suitable due to its color change range (pH 8.3-10.0).

3. Strong Acid-Weak Base Titration

Theory:

a. **Weak Bases:** Weak bases (e.g., NH_3) partially dissociate in water. The degree of dissociation is characterized by the base dissociation constant (Kb).

b. **Reaction:** The strong acid reacts with the weak base to form water and a salt. The conjugate acid of the weak base hydrolyzes in water.

$$HCl + NH_3 \rightarrow NH_4Cl$$

c. **Buffer Region:** Before the equivalence point, the solution acts as a buffer.

Titration Curve:

a. **Initial pH:** Lower than that of a strong base.

b. **Shape:** The pH decreases gradually, then more steeply near the equivalence point.

c. **Equivalence Point:** pH < 7 due to the hydrolysis of the conjugate acid (e.g., NH_4^+ forms H^+).

Indicators:

a. **Methyl Orange:** Suitable due to its color change range (pH 3.1-4.4).

4. Weak Acid-Weak Base Titration

Theory:

a. **Weak Acids and Bases:** Both partially dissociate in water.

b. **Reaction:** The weak acid reacts with the weak base to form water and a salt. Both the conjugate acid and conjugate base hydrolyze in water.

$$CH_3COOH + NH_3 \rightarrow CH_3COONH_4$$

Titration Curve:

a. **Initial pH:** Higher than that of a strong acid, lower than that of a strong base.

b. **Shape:** The curve is relatively shallow, with a gradual change in pH.

c. **Equivalence Point:** Around pH 7, but the exact pH depends on the relative strengths (Ka and Kb) of the weak acid and weak base.

Indicators:

a. **pH Meter:** Preferred due to the lack of a sharp change in pH, making color indicators less reliable.

Key Points in Acid-Base Titrations

1. **Equivalence Point vs. End Point:**
    a. **Equivalence Point:** The point at which stoichiometric amounts of acid and base have reacted.
    b. **End Point:** The point at which the indicator changes color.
2. **Choice of Indicator:**
    a. The choice depends on the expected pH at the equivalence point. For strong acid-strong base titrations, the equivalence point is neutral, while for other combinations, it can be acidic or basic.
3. **Buffer Regions:**
    a. In weak acid-strong base and weak base-strong acid titrations, there is a buffer region where the pH changes gradually. This is due to the presence of both the weak acid and its conjugate base or the weak base and its conjugate acid.

NEUTRALIZATION CURVES

Neutralization curves, also known as titration curves, depict the change in pH as a titrant is added to an analyte solution during an acid-base titration. These curves provide a visual representation of the titration process and help identify the equivalence point where the amounts of acid and base are stoichiometrically equal. Here's a detailed examination of neutralization curves for different types of acid-base titrations:

1. Strong Acid-Strong Base Titration

In a strong acid-strong base titration, both the acid and the base completely dissociate in water. This type of titration is straightforward and typically involves a sharp and well-defined equivalence point. Here's a detailed look into the neutralization curve for a strong acid-strong base titration:

The Titration Process

Initial Setup:

a. **Analyte (Strong Acid):** A solution of a strong acid, such as hydrochloric acid (HCl), is placed in a flask.

b. **Titrant (Strong Base):** A solution of a strong base, such as sodium hydroxide (NaOH), is added from a burette.

Reaction:

a. The neutralization reaction can be represented as:

$$HCl + NaOH \rightarrow NaCl + H_2O$$

b. Both HCl and NaOH fully dissociate in water:

$$HCl \rightarrow H^+ + Cl^-$$

$$NaOH \rightarrow Na^+ + OH^-$$

c. The H^+ ions from the acid react with the OH^- ions from the base to form water:

$$H^+ + OH^- \rightarrow H_2O$$

Titration Curve Details

1. Initial Region:

a. **pH:** The initial pH is very low, typically around 1, because the strong acid is fully dissociated.

b. **Adding Base:** As NaOH is added, the pH starts to increase slowly because each OH^- ion added neutralizes an H^+ ion, forming water.

2. Pre-Equivalence Region:

a. **Buffering Effect:** Before reaching the equivalence point, the pH increases more rapidly as more base is added. The solution still contains excess H^+ ions, but their concentration is decreasing.

b. **Shape:** The curve is relatively flat but begins to steepen as it approaches the equivalence point.

3. Equivalence Point:

a. **Definition:** The equivalence point is where the number of moles of H^+ from the acid equals the number of moles of OH^- from the base.

b. **pH:** For a strong acid-strong base titration, the pH at the equivalence point is exactly 7. This is because the resulting solution contains a neutral salt (NaCl) and water, neither of which affect the pH.

c. **Curve:** The titration curve shows a sharp, nearly vertical rise at this point due to the rapid change in pH.

4. Post-Equivalence Region:

a. **pH:** After the equivalence point, the pH continues to rise sharply as more NaOH is added because there are now excess OH^- ions in the solution.

b. **Shape:** The curve levels off again at a higher pH, typically above 12, indicating the solution is now strongly basic.

Example Titration Curve

A typical titration curve for a strong acid-strong base titration can be visualized as follows:

a. **X-Axis (Volume of NaOH added):** Shows the volume of titrant (NaOH) added to the analyte (HCl).

b. **Y-Axis (pH):** Displays the pH of the solution at various points during the titration.

Key Points in the Curve

1. **Initial pH:** Very low, around 1, due to the strong acid.
2. **Gradual Increase:** Slow pH rise as the base is added until close to the equivalence point.
3. **Steep Rise:** Sharp vertical section around the equivalence point indicating rapid pH change.
4. **Equivalence Point:** At pH 7, where stoichiometric neutralization occurs.
5. **Post-Equivalence:** Rapid increase in pH beyond the equivalence point, leveling off at a high pH.

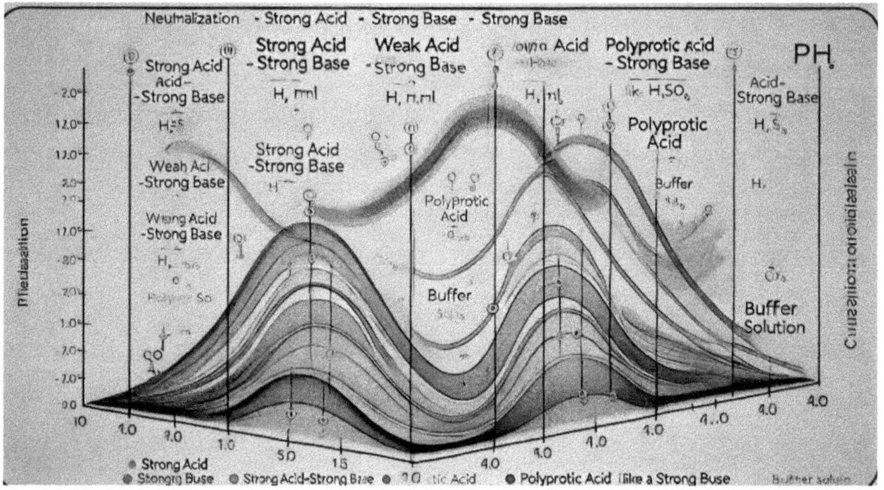

Choosing the Right Indicator

For strong acid-strong base titrations, the equivalence point is neutral (pH 7), so indicators that change color around this pH are suitable:

a. **Phenolphthalein:** Changes color from colorless to pink in the pH range of 8.3-10.0. Suitable for detecting the end point slightly beyond pH 7.

b. **Bromothymol Blue:** Changes color from yellow to blue in the pH range of 6.0-7.6. Ideal for detecting the equivalence point near pH 7.

Practical Considerations

1. **Accuracy:** Using a pH meter or a suitable indicator helps accurately determine the equivalence point.
2. **Indicator Selection:** Choose an indicator whose color change range falls within the steep part of the titration curve near the equivalence point.
3. **Volume of Titrant:** Careful measurement of the titrant volume added is crucial for precise determination of the equivalence point.

2. Weak Acid-Strong Base Titration

In a weak acid-strong base titration, the weak acid partially dissociates in water, and the strong base completely dissociates. This type of titration involves more gradual pH changes and a buffer region before the equivalence point. Here's a detailed look into the neutralization curve for a weak acid-strong base titration:

The Titration Process

Initial Setup:

a. **Analyte (Weak Acid):** A solution of a weak acid, such as acetic acid (CH_3COOH), is placed in a flask.
b. **Titrant (Strong Base):** A solution of a strong base, such as sodium hydroxide (NaOH), is added from a burette.

Reaction:

a. The neutralization reaction can be represented as:

$$CH_3COOH + NaOH \rightarrow CH_3COONa + H_2O$$

b. Acetic acid partially dissociates in water:

$$CH_3COOH \rightleftharpoons CH_3COO^- + H^+$$

c. Sodium hydroxide fully dissociates:

$$NaOH \rightarrow Na^+ + OH^-$$

d. The OH^- ions from the base react with the H^+ ions from the acid to form water:

$$H^+ + OH^- \rightarrow H_2O$$

Titration Curve Details

1. Initial Region:

a. **pH:** The initial pH is higher than that of a strong acid, typically around 3-4, due to the partial dissociation of the weak acid.

b. **Adding Base:** As NaOH is added, the pH starts to increase gradually.

2. Buffer Region:

a. **Buffering Effect:** Before reaching the equivalence point, the solution acts as a buffer, resisting drastic changes in pH. This is due to the presence of both the weak acid (CH_3COOH) and its conjugate base (CH_3COO^-).

b. **Shape:** The pH increases gradually in this region.

3. Equivalence Point:

a. **Definition:** The equivalence point is where the moles of H^+ from the weak acid equal the moles of OH^- from the strong base.

b. **pH:** For a weak acid-strong base titration, the pH at the equivalence point is greater than 7. This is because the conjugate base (CH_3COO^-) hydrolyzes, producing OH^- ions:

$$CH_3COO^- + H_2O \rightarrow CH_3COOH + OH^-$$

c. **Curve:** The titration curve shows a less steep rise compared to strong acid-strong base titrations.

4. Post-Equivalence Region:

a. **pH:** After the equivalence point, the pH rises sharply due to the excess OH^- ions from the added NaOH.

b. **Shape:** The curve levels off again at a higher pH, typically above 12, indicating the solution is now strongly basic.

Example Titration Curve

A typical titration curve for a weak acid-strong base titration can be visualized as follows:

a. **X-Axis (Volume of NaOH added):** Shows the volume of titrant (NaOH) added to the analyte (CH_3COOH).

b. **Y-Axis (pH):** Displays the pH of the solution at various points during the titration.

Key Points in the Curve

1. **Initial pH:** Higher than that of a strong acid, around 3-4, due to partial dissociation.
2. **Buffer Region:** A gradual increase in pH before the equivalence point, indicating the buffer capacity.
3. **Steep Rise:** Less steep than in strong acid-strong base titrations, reflecting the weaker acid.
4. **Equivalence Point:** At pH > 7, where stoichiometric neutralization occurs.
5. **Post-Equivalence:** Rapid increase in pH beyond the equivalence point, leveling off at a high pH.

Choosing the Right Indicator

For weak acid-strong base titrations, the equivalence point is basic (pH > 7), so indicators that change color in the basic pH range are suitable:

a. **Phenolphthalein:** Changes color from colorless to pink in the pH range of 8.3-10.0. It is suitable because it changes color after the equivalence point is reached.

Practical Considerations

1. **Accuracy:** Using a pH meter or a suitable indicator helps accurately determine the equivalence point.
2. **Indicator Selection:** Choose an indicator whose color change range falls within the steep part of the titration curve near the equivalence point.

3. **Buffer Region Analysis:** The buffer region provides valuable information about the weak acid's dissociation and buffering capacity.

3. Strong Acid-Weak Base Titration

Characteristics:

a. **Initial pH:** Starts low (around 1-2) because of the strong acid.

b. **Buffer Region:** A gradual decrease in pH before the equivalence point due to the formation of a buffer solution (mixture of weak base and its conjugate acid).

c. **Equivalence Point:** Occurs at pH < 7, where the conjugate acid of the weak base hydrolyzes, producing H^+ ions.

d. **After Equivalence Point:** The pH decreases more gradually, reflecting the excess strong acid.

Example:

a. Titrating hydrochloric acid (HCl) with ammonia (NH_3).

Titration Curve:

a. **Shape:** Sigmoidal with a less steep decrease near the equivalence point compared to strong acid-strong base titrations.

4. Weak Acid-Weak Base Titration

Characteristics:

a. **Initial pH:** Higher than that of a strong acid (around 3-4) because of the weak acid.

b. **Buffer Region:** A gradual change in pH due to the buffer action of the weak acid and its conjugate base.

c. **Equivalence Point:** Approximately around pH 7, but the exact pH depends on the relative strengths (Ka and Kb) of the weak acid and weak base.

d. **After Equivalence Point:** The pH changes slowly and less predictably compared to strong acid or strong base titrations.

Example:

a. Titrating acetic acid (CH_3COOH) with ammonia (NH_3).

Titration Curve:

a. **Shape:** Much more gradual and lacks a sharp inflection point.

Key Points and Interpretation

Understanding the key points in a neutralization curve is crucial for interpreting the results of an acid-base titration. Here are the main features and their significance for various types of titrations:

1. Initial pH

a. **Strong Acid-Strong Base:** The initial pH is very low (around 1-2) due to the complete dissociation of the strong acid.

b. **Weak Acid-Strong Base:** The initial pH is moderately low (around 3-4) because the weak acid only partially dissociates.

c. **Strong Acid-Weak Base:** The initial pH is very low (around 1-2) due to the strong acid.

d. **Weak Acid-Weak Base:** The initial pH is slightly acidic (around 4-5), reflecting partial dissociation.

Interpretation: The initial pH provides insight into the strength of the acid in the solution.

2. Buffer Region

a. **Weak Acid-Strong Base:** Before the equivalence point, the solution acts as a buffer, resisting significant pH changes.

b. **Strong Acid-Weak Base:** There is also a buffering region where the pH changes gradually.

Interpretation: The buffer region indicates the presence of both the weak acid and its conjugate base (or weak base and its conjugate acid), maintaining a relatively stable pH.

3. Equivalence Point

a. **Strong Acid-Strong Base:** The pH at the equivalence point is neutral (around 7) because the salt formed does not affect the pH.

b. **Weak Acid-Strong Base:** The pH at the equivalence point is greater than 7 due to the basic nature of the conjugate base of the weak acid.
c. **Strong Acid-Weak Base:** The pH at the equivalence point is less than 7 due to the acidic nature of the conjugate acid of the weak base.
d. **Weak Acid-Weak Base:** The pH at the equivalence point depends on the relative strengths of the weak acid and weak base and can be slightly acidic, neutral, or slightly basic.

Interpretation: The pH at the equivalence point reflects the nature of the salt formed during the titration and whether it hydrolyzes to produce an acidic or basic solution.

4. Post-Equivalence Region

a. **Strong Acid-Strong Base:** The pH rises steeply and then levels off at a high pH after the equivalence point.
b. **Weak Acid-Strong Base:** The pH increases more gradually after the equivalence point, reflecting the addition of excess strong base.
c. **Strong Acid-Weak Base:** The pH increases gradually after the equivalence point due to the excess weak base.
d. **Weak Acid-Weak Base:** The pH change after the equivalence point is more complex and depends on the weak acid and base.

Interpretation: The post-equivalence region shows how the pH changes with the addition of excess titrant, indicating the strength of the excess acid or base.

Example Neutralization Curves and Key Points

Strong Acid-Strong Base Titration

a. **Initial pH:** Very low, around 1-2.
b. **Equivalence Point:** pH 7, sharp rise at equivalence.
c. **Post-Equivalence:** Sharp rise, leveling off at high pH.

Weak Acid-Strong Base Titration

a. **Initial pH:** Moderately low, around 3-4.
b. **Buffer Region:** Gradual pH change before equivalence.

c. **Equivalence Point:** pH > 7, less steep rise.
d. **Post-Equivalence:** Gradual rise, leveling off at high pH.

Strong Acid-Weak Base Titration

a. **Initial pH:** Very low, around 1-2.
b. **Buffer Region:** Gradual pH change before equivalence.
c. **Equivalence Point:** pH < 7, less steep rise.
d. **Post-Equivalence:** Gradual rise, leveling off at moderately high pH.

Weak Acid-Weak Base Titration

a. **Initial pH:** Slightly acidic, around 4-5.
b. **Buffer Region:** Complex buffering before equivalence.
c. **Equivalence Point:** Variable pH, dependent on relative strengths.
d. **Post-Equivalence:** Complex changes, reflecting weak acid and base behavior.

Multiple Choice Questions (MCQs)

1. What is the primary purpose of acid-base titration?
   A. To identify the type of acid or base
   B. To determine the concentration of an acid or base in a solution
   C. To measure the pH of a solution
   D. To determine the temperature change in a reaction
2. What is the equivalence point in an acid-base titration?
   A. The point where the indicator changes color
   B. The point where the titrant is completely consumed
   C. The point where the moles of H^+ ions equal the moles of OH^- ions
   D. The point where the solution becomes neutral
3. Which of the following indicators is commonly used in a strong acid-strong base titration?
   A. Methyl orange

B. Phenolphthalein

C. Bromothymol blue

D. Litmus

4. What is the typical pH at the equivalence point for a weak acid-strong base titration?

A. Less than 7

B. Equal to 7

C. Greater than 7

D. Neutral

5. In the Ostwald theory of acid-base indicators, what causes the color change?

A. Structural changes in the molecule

B. Ionization of the indicator

C. Proton transfer reactions

D. Change in temperature

6. What is the pH range for phenolphthalein to change color?

A. 3.1 - 4.4

B. 4.5 - 8.3

C. 6.0 - 7.6

D. 8.3 - 10.0

7. Which titration method is suitable when the analyte reacts slowly with the titrant?

A. Direct titration

B. Back titration

C. Complexometric titration

D. Potentiometric titration

8. In a strong acid-strong base titration, what is the initial pH of the solution?

A. Around 1-2

B. Around 3-4

C. Around 5-6

D. Around 7-8

9. What happens in the buffer region of a weak acid-strong base titration?

   A. The pH remains constant

   B. The pH increases rapidly

   C. The pH changes gradually

   D. The pH decreases rapidly

10. What type of solution is formed at the equivalence point of a strong acid-weak base titration?

    A. Neutral

    B. Slightly acidic

    C. Slightly basic

    D. Strongly basic

11. What is the reaction involved in the titration of HCl with NaOH?

    A. $HCl + NaOH \rightarrow NaCl + H_2O$

    B. $HCl + NH_3 \rightarrow NH_4Cl$

    C. $CH_3COOH + NaOH \rightarrow CH_3COONa + H_2O$

    D. $CH_3COOH + NH_3 \rightarrow CH_3COONH_4$

12. Which theory of acid-base indicators focuses on the structural changes in the molecule?

    A. Ostwald theory

    B. Quinonoid theory

    C. Bronsted-Lowry theory

    D. Lewis theory

13. What is the shape of the titration curve for a weak acid-weak base titration?

    A. Sharp rise at equivalence point

    B. Gradual slope with no clear inflection point

    C. Sharp decrease at equivalence point

    D. Linear throughout

14. What is the role of a pH meter in titration?

A. To add titrant to the solution

B. To measure the pH of the solution continuously

C. To indicate the end point by changing color

D. To maintain a constant temperature

15. What is the initial pH of a solution of a weak acid like acetic acid (CH_3COOH)?

A. Around 1-2

B. Around 3-4

C. Around 5-6

D. Around 7-8

16. Which of the following is a common application of acid-base titration in the pharmaceutical industry?

A. Determining the boiling point of a substance

B. Measuring the acidity of food products

C. Analyzing the pH of water samples

D. Determining the concentration of active ingredients in drugs

17. What is the basic premise of the Bronsted-Lowry theory of acid-base indicators?

A. Indicators are weak acids or bases that undergo structural changes

B. Indicators are weak acids or bases that partially dissociate

C. Indicators undergo proton transfer reactions

D. Indicators are strong acids or bases that fully dissociate

18. During which part of the titration process is the analyte solution prepared and placed in a flask?

A. Preparation

B. Titration

C. Detection of equivalence point

D. Calculation

19. What is the typical pH at the equivalence point for a strong acid-weak base titration?

    A. Less than 7
    B. Equal to 7
    C. Greater than 7
    D. Neutral

20. What kind of titration curve is expected for a strong acid-strong base titration?

    A. Sharp, steep rise around the equivalence point
    B. Gradual rise throughout the titration
    C. Gradual slope with no clear inflection point
    D. Sharp decrease at the equivalence point

Short Answer Type Questions

1. What is acid-base titration used for?
2. Define the equivalence point in an acid-base titration.
3. What is the role of a titrant in an acid-base titration?
4. Name two common indicators used in acid-base titrations.
5. Explain the difference between the equivalence point and the end point in a titration.
6. Why is phenolphthalein used as an indicator in strong acid-strong base titrations?
7. Describe the initial pH in a weak acid-strong base titration.
8. What is a buffer region in a titration curve?
9. How does a pH meter help in detecting the equivalence point?
10. Why is the pH at the equivalence point of a weak acid-strong base titration greater than 7?
11. What is the Ostwald theory of acid-base indicators based on?
12. How does the Quinonoid theory explain the color change of indicators?

13. Define the Bronsted-Lowry theory in the context of acid-base indicators.
14. What pH range does methyl orange cover as an indicator?
15. What are the typical applications of acid-base titrations in the pharmaceutical industry?
16. Describe a direct titration process.
17. What is the key characteristic of a strong acid-weak base titration curve?
18. What happens at the equivalence point in a strong acid-strong base titration?
19. Explain the significance of the post-equivalence region in a titration curve.
20. What factors should be considered when choosing an indicator for a titration?

Long Answer Type Questions

1. Explain the basic principles of acid-base titration, including the roles of titrant and analyte.
2. Describe the steps involved in performing an acid-base titration, from preparation to calculation.
3. Compare and contrast the four types of acid-base titrations based on the strength of the acids and bases involved.
4. Discuss the applications of acid-base titration in various industries, providing specific examples.
5. Explain the Ostwald, Quinonoid, and Bronsted-Lowry theories of acid-base indicators, highlighting their differences.
6. Describe the characteristics and interpretation of a neutralization curve for a strong acid-strong base titration.
7. Explain the theory and process of a weak acid-strong base titration, including the significance of the buffer region.
8. Compare the titration curves and equivalence points of strong acid-weak base and weak acid-weak base titrations.

9. Discuss the key considerations and challenges in accurately determining the equivalence point in an acid-base titration.
10. Analyze the factors affecting the choice of indicators in different types of acid-base titrations and how they impact the results.

Answer Key

1. B. To determine the concentration of an acid or base in a solution
2. C. The point where the moles of H^+ ions equal the moles of OH^- ions
3. B. Phenolphthalein
4. C. Greater than 7
5. B. Ionization of the indicator
6. D. 8.3 - 10.0
7. B. Back titration
8. A. Around 1-2
9. C. The pH changes gradually
10. B. Slightly acidic
11. A. $HCl + NaOH \rightarrow NaCl + H_2O$
12. B. Quinonoid theory
13. B. Gradual slope with no clear inflection point
14. B. To measure the pH of the solution continuously
15. B. Around 3-4
16. D. Determining the concentration of active ingredients in drugs
17. C. Indicators undergo proton transfer reactions
18. A. Preparation
19. A. Less than 7
20. A. Sharp, steep rise around the equivalence point

CHAPTER – 7

NON AQUEOUS TITRATION

INTRODUCTION:

Non-aqueous titration is a type of titration in which the solvent used is not water. This method is employed when the substance to be analyzed is either insoluble in water or reacts incompletely with water, rendering aqueous titration methods unsuitable. Non-aqueous titration is particularly valuable in the analysis of weak acids and bases, which do not dissociate well in water but do so more readily in non-aqueous solvents.

Reasons for Using Non-Aqueous Titration

1. **Solubility**: Some substances are not soluble in water but are soluble in non-aqueous solvents.
2. **Reactivity**: Certain reactions or substances may be unstable or react slowly in water.
3. **Completeness of Reaction**: Weak acids and bases may not fully react in aqueous solutions but can be titrated more effectively in non-aqueous solvents.
4. **Accuracy**: Non-aqueous solvents can provide more precise endpoints for certain titrations.

Principles of Non-Aqueous Titration

1. **Solvent Choice**: The choice of solvent is critical in non-aqueous titration. Common solvents include acetic acid, chloroform, and dimethyl sulfoxide (DMSO). The solvent should dissolve the analyte and allow the titration reaction to proceed efficiently.
2. **Types of Non-Aqueous Titrations**:

a. **Acid-Base Titrations**: These involve the titration of weak acids or bases in non-aqueous solvents using strong bases (e.g., sodium methoxide) or acids (e.g., perchloric acid) as titrants.
b. **Complexometric Titrations**: These are used for the determination of metal ions in non-aqueous solutions.
c. **Redox Titrations**: These involve the titration of oxidizing or reducing agents in non-aqueous media.

3. **Indicators**: The choice of indicator is crucial and depends on the type of titration. Common indicators for non-aqueous titration include crystal violet, thymol blue, and methyl red.
4. **Equivalence Point Detection**: The equivalence point in non-aqueous titration can be detected using potentiometric, conductometric, or visual methods, depending on the nature of the reaction and the chosen indicator.

Procedure for Non-Aqueous Titration

1. **Preparation of the Solution**: Dissolve the analyte in the chosen non-aqueous solvent. Ensure complete dissolution.
2. **Selection of Indicator**: Add an appropriate indicator to the solution if a visual endpoint is to be determined.
3. **Titration**: Add the titrant slowly from a burette to the analyte solution while stirring. Monitor the change in color or potential, depending on the chosen method of endpoint detection.
4. **Endpoint Determination**: Identify the endpoint either by a distinct color change, a sharp change in potential (potentiometric titration), or a change in conductivity (conductometric titration).
5. **Calculation**: Calculate the concentration of the analyte based on the volume of titrant used at the equivalence point.

Applications of Non-Aqueous Titration

1. **Pharmaceutical Analysis**: Determination of the purity and concentration of pharmaceutical compounds that are weakly acidic or basic.

2. **Organic Chemistry**: Analysis of compounds that are insoluble or unstable in water.
3. **Industrial Applications**: Quality control of products such as polymers, resins, and oils.

Advantages of Non-Aqueous Titration

1. **Wider Range of Solvents**: Allows the analysis of substances that are insoluble or poorly soluble in water.
2. **Increased Sensitivity**: Provides more accurate results for weak acids and bases.
3. **Flexibility**: Can be adapted to various types of titrations, including acid-base, redox, and complexometric.

Disadvantages of Non-Aqueous Titration

1. **Solvent Handling**: Some non-aqueous solvents are toxic, flammable, or expensive.
2. **Indicator Selection**: Requires careful selection of suitable indicators for accurate endpoint detection.
3. **Equipment**: May require specialized equipment for certain types of endpoint detection, such as potentiometric titrators.

Non-aqueous titration is a valuable technique in analytical chemistry, providing accurate and reliable results for substances that are difficult to analyze using aqueous methods. Understanding the principles, procedures, and applications of non-aqueous titration is essential for effective utilization in various fields of chemical analysis.

SOLVENTS

The choice of solvent in non-aqueous titration is crucial because it influences the solubility of the analyte, the nature of the titration reaction, and the detection of the endpoint. Different solvents can stabilize the analyte, the titrant, and the reaction intermediates, leading to more precise and accurate titrations. Below are detailed descriptions of commonly used solvents in non-aqueous titration:

1. Acetic Acid

a. **Properties**: Acetic acid is a weak acid and a polar protic solvent.
b. **Uses**: It is often used in the titration of weak bases. Its acidic nature helps to suppress the ionization of weak acids, making it easier to detect the endpoint.
c. **Advantages**: Acetic acid can solubilize a wide range of organic compounds and provides a clear color change with indicators.
d. **Disadvantages**: Acetic acid's high acidity can sometimes interfere with the titration of very weak bases.

2. Glacial Acetic Acid

a. **Properties**: Glacial acetic acid is the anhydrous form of acetic acid and is a strong polar solvent.
b. **Uses**: It is suitable for titrating weak bases and for reactions that require a completely anhydrous environment.
c. **Advantages**: Its high polarity makes it effective for dissolving a variety of analytes.
d. **Disadvantages**: It is corrosive and must be handled with care. It can also absorb moisture from the air, which can affect titration results.

3. Formic Acid

a. **Properties**: Formic acid is a stronger acid than acetic acid and a polar protic solvent.
b. **Uses**: Used for titrating weak bases and as a solvent for acid-base titrations.
c. **Advantages**: It provides a high degree of ionization for weak bases and can enhance the accuracy of titration.
d. **Disadvantages**: Formic acid is more corrosive and has a stronger odor compared to acetic acid.

4. Methanol

a. **Properties**: Methanol is a polar protic solvent and a weak acid.

b. **Uses**: Commonly used in the titration of weak acids and bases. It can also be used in redox titrations.

c. **Advantages**: It has good solvating power and is relatively inexpensive.

d. **Disadvantages**: Methanol is flammable and toxic if ingested or inhaled.

5. Ethanol

a. **Properties**: Ethanol is a polar protic solvent and a weak acid.

b. **Uses**: Used in the titration of weak acids and bases and in redox titrations.

c. **Advantages**: Ethanol is less toxic than methanol and is readily available.

d. **Disadvantages**: Like methanol, ethanol is flammable.

6. Dimethyl Sulfoxide (DMSO)

a. **Properties**: DMSO is a polar aprotic solvent with a high boiling point.

b. **Uses**: Effective for the titration of very weak acids and bases.

c. **Advantages**: DMSO has a high solvating power for both polar and non-polar compounds and can stabilize ionic intermediates.

d. **Disadvantages**: It is hygroscopic and can absorb water, which may interfere with titrations. DMSO can also be toxic and requires careful handling.

7. Chloroform

a. **Properties**: Chloroform is a non-polar solvent with low reactivity.

b. **Uses**: Suitable for titrations involving non-polar compounds and in complexometric titrations.

c. **Advantages**: It can dissolve many organic compounds that are insoluble in water.

d. **Disadvantages**: Chloroform is volatile, toxic, and poses environmental hazards.

8. Tetrahydrofuran (THF)

a. **Properties**: THF is a polar aprotic solvent with a moderate boiling point.

b. **Uses**: Used in the titration of both acids and bases, particularly in polymer chemistry.

c. **Advantages**: THF can dissolve a wide range of organic and inorganic compounds.

d. **Disadvantages**: THF is highly flammable and can form explosive peroxides upon prolonged exposure to air.

9. Pyridine

a. **Properties**: Pyridine is a polar aprotic solvent with basic properties.

b. **Uses**: It is used as a solvent for the titration of weak acids.

c. **Advantages**: Pyridine can increase the ionization of weak acids, making titration endpoints more distinct.

d. **Disadvantages**: Pyridine has a very strong odor and is toxic, requiring proper ventilation and handling.

ACIDIMETRIC AND ALKALIMETRY TITRATION

Non-aqueous titration is particularly useful for acidimetric and alkalimetric titrations when the analytes or titrants are weak acids or bases that do not completely ionize in water. In these titrations, non-aqueous solvents help to achieve better solubility and more distinct endpoints.

Acidimetric Titration

Acidimetric titration involves the titration of a base with a strong acid in a non-aqueous solvent. This method is often used for the determination of organic bases, such as amines and alkaloids.

Principles of Acidimetric Titration

1. **Choice of Solvent**: A suitable non-aqueous solvent, such as glacial acetic acid, methanol, or acetic acid, is selected based on the solubility of the base and the stability of the titrant.
2. **Titrant**: The titrant is typically a strong acid, such as perchloric acid in glacial acetic acid.

3. **Indicator**: Indicators such as crystal violet, thymol blue, or methyl red are chosen based on their color change range and solubility in the solvent.
4. **Reaction**: The base reacts with the acid to form a salt. The endpoint is detected by a color change of the indicator or by potentiometric methods.

Procedure for Acidimetric Titration

1. **Preparation of Solution**: Dissolve the sample (a weak base) in the chosen non-aqueous solvent.
2. **Addition of Indicator**: Add an appropriate indicator if using a visual endpoint detection method.
3. **Titration**: Slowly add the titrant (strong acid) from a burette to the analyte solution while stirring.
4. **Endpoint Detection**: Detect the endpoint by observing a color change or using a potentiometer to measure a change in potential.
5. **Calculation**: Calculate the concentration of the base based on the volume of titrant used at the equivalence point.

Example

1. **Titration of Pyridine**:
    a. **Solvent**: Glacial acetic acid.
    b. **Titrant**: Perchloric acid in glacial acetic acid.
    c. **Indicator**: Crystal violet.
    d. **Reaction**:

$$C_5H_5N + HClO_4 \rightarrow C_5H_5NH^+ClO_4^-$$

    e. The endpoint is detected by a color change from violet to green.

Alkalimetric Titration

Alkalimetric titration involves the titration of an acid with a strong base in a non-aqueous solvent. This method is useful for determining weak acids, such as phenols and carboxylic acids.

Principles of Alkalimetric Titration

1. **Choice of Solvent**: A non-aqueous solvent, such as methanol, ethanol, or dimethyl sulfoxide (DMSO), is selected based on the solubility of the acid and the stability of the titrant.
2. **Titrant**: The titrant is typically a strong base, such as sodium methoxide or tetrabutylammonium hydroxide.
3. **Indicator**: Indicators such as thymol blue, phenolphthalein, or bromothymol blue are chosen based on their color change range and solubility in the solvent.
4. **Reaction**: The acid reacts with the base to form a salt. The endpoint is detected by a color change of the indicator or by potentiometric methods.

Procedure for Alkalimetric Titration

1. **Preparation of Solution**: Dissolve the sample (a weak acid) in the chosen non-aqueous solvent.
2. **Addition of Indicator**: Add an appropriate indicator if using a visual endpoint detection method.
3. **Titration**: Slowly add the titrant (strong base) from a burette to the analyte solution while stirring.
4. **Endpoint Detection**: Detect the endpoint by observing a color change or using a potentiometer to measure a change in potential.
5. **Calculation**: Calculate the concentration of the acid based on the volume of titrant used at the equivalence point.

Example

1. **Titration of Benzoic Acid**:
    a. **Solvent**: Methanol.
    b. **Titrant**: Sodium methoxide in methanol.
    c. **Indicator**: Phenolphthalein.
    d. **Reaction**:

$$C_6H_5COOH + CH_3ONa \rightarrow C_6H_5COONa + CH_3OH$$

e. The endpoint is detected by a color change from colorless to pink.

Advantages of Non-Aqueous Titration in Acidimetric and Alkalimetric Titrations

1. **Enhanced Solubility**: Non-aqueous solvents can dissolve analytes that are insoluble in water, leading to more accurate titrations.
2. **Improved Endpoint Detection**: Non-aqueous solvents can provide sharper and more distinct endpoints.
3. **Wider Range of Analytes**: Suitable for titrating weak acids and bases that do not fully ionize in aqueous solutions.
4. **Reduced Side Reactions**: Minimizes interference from water and other substances that may react with the analyte or titrant.

Disadvantages

1. **Toxicity and Handling**: Many non-aqueous solvents are toxic, flammable, and require careful handling and proper ventilation.
2. **Cost**: Some non-aqueous solvents can be expensive.
3. **Special Equipment**: May require specialized equipment, such as potentiometric titrators, for endpoint detection.

PRINCIPLE AND ESTIMATION OF SODIUM BENZOATE

Principle

The principle of non-aqueous titration for sodium benzoate involves the titration of benzoic acid, which is derived from sodium benzoate. Sodium benzoate, a weak base in an aqueous environment, can be titrated more effectively in a non-aqueous medium where it behaves as a strong acid or base depending on the chosen solvent and titrant. The titration in a non-aqueous solvent improves the ionization and allows for a more accurate determination of the endpoint.

Estimation of Sodium Benzoate

The estimation of sodium benzoate typically involves the following steps:

1. **Dissolution**: Dissolving the sodium benzoate in a suitable non-aqueous solvent.
2. **Titration**: Titrating the dissolved sample with a suitable titrant in the non-aqueous medium.
3. **Endpoint Detection**: Using an appropriate indicator or potentiometric method to detect the endpoint.
4. **Calculation**: Calculating the concentration of sodium benzoate based on the volume of titrant used.

Detailed Procedure

Materials and Reagents

1. **Solvent**: Glacial acetic acid or acetic anhydride.
2. **Titrant**: Perchloric acid in glacial acetic acid.
3. **Indicator**: Crystal violet, thymol blue, or potentiometric method for endpoint detection.
4. **Sample**: Sodium benzoate.

Equipment

1. Burette
2. Conical flask
3. Magnetic stirrer
4. Potentiometer (if using potentiometric detection)
5. Pipettes

Procedure

1. **Preparation of Sample Solution**:
    a. Accurately weigh a known quantity of sodium benzoate (e.g., 0.5 g).
    b. Dissolve the weighed sodium benzoate in about 50 ml of glacial acetic acid in a conical flask. Ensure complete dissolution.
2. **Preparation of Titrant**:
    a. Prepare a standard solution of perchloric acid in glacial acetic acid (usually 0.1 N). This involves accurately measuring and diluting

concentrated perchloric acid in glacial acetic acid to achieve the desired normality.

3. **Titration**:
   a. Add a few drops of the chosen indicator (e.g., crystal violet) to the sample solution if a visual endpoint is to be detected.
   b. If using a potentiometer, set it up and calibrate it as per the manufacturer's instructions.
   c. Fill the burette with the standard perchloric acid solution.
   d. Slowly titrate the sample solution with the perchloric acid solution while continuously stirring with a magnetic stirrer.
   e. If using an indicator, watch for the color change. If using a potentiometer, monitor the change in potential.
4. **Endpoint Detection**:
   a. For visual detection, the endpoint is usually identified by a distinct color change of the indicator. For example, crystal violet changes from violet to green at the endpoint.
   b. For potentiometric detection, the endpoint is indicated by a sharp change in the potential.
5. **Calculation**:
   a. Record the volume of perchloric acid used to reach the endpoint.
   b. Calculate the concentration of sodium benzoate using the following formula:
   Concentration of Sodium Benzoate (mol/L)=Weight of Sample (g)/Mol ecular Weight of Sodium Benzoate (g/mol)Volume of Titrant (L)×Nor mality of Titrant (N)
   c. Molecular weight of sodium benzoate (C7H5NaO2) is approximately 144.11 g/mol.

Example Calculation

1. Suppose 25.0 ml of 0.1 N perchloric acid is used to titrate 0.5 g of sodium benzoate.
2. The molecular weight of sodium benzoate is 144.11 g/mol.

$$\text{Moles of Titrant} = \text{Volume (L)} \times \text{Normality (N)} = 0.025 \times 0.1 = 0.0025 \text{ mol}$$

$$\text{Weight of Sodium Benzoate (mol)} = \frac{0.5 \text{ g}}{144.11 \text{ g/mol}} = 0.00347 \text{ mol}$$

Since 1 mole of sodium benzoate reacts with 1 mole of perchloric acid, the moles of sodium benzoate should equal the moles of perchloric acid at the endpoint.

$$\text{Concentration of Sodium Benzoate (mol/L)} = \frac{0.0025 \text{ mol}}{0.5 \text{ g}/144.11 \text{ g/mol}} = 0.00347 \text{ mol/L}$$

This shows the concentration of sodium benzoate in the solution.

Summary

1. **Principle**: Sodium benzoate is titrated in a non-aqueous medium to improve ionization and endpoint detection.
2. **Solvent**: Glacial acetic acid is typically used.
3. **Titrant**: Perchloric acid in glacial acetic acid.
4. **Indicator**: Crystal violet or a potentiometer.
5. **Procedure**: Dissolve, titrate, detect endpoint, and calculate concentration.

ESTIMATION OF EPHEDRINE HCL

Ephedrine hydrochloride (Ephedrine HCl) is a weak base that can be effectively titrated in a non-aqueous medium to achieve accurate results. The titration typically involves using a strong acid in a non-aqueous solvent.

Principle

Ephedrine HCl, a weak base, is titrated with a strong acid in a non-aqueous medium to ensure complete ionization and clear endpoint detection. Non-aqueous solvents such as glacial acetic acid or acetic anhydride are used to dissolve the sample, and perchloric acid in glacial acetic acid is commonly used as the titrant.

Materials and Reagents

1. **Solvent**: Glacial acetic acid or acetic anhydride.
2. **Titrant**: Perchloric acid in glacial acetic acid (0.1 N).
3. **Indicator**: Crystal violet, thymol blue, or potentiometric method for endpoint detection.
4. **Sample**: Ephedrine hydrochloride.

Equipment

1. Burette
2. Conical flask
3. Magnetic stirrer
4. Potentiometer (if using potentiometric detection)
5. Pipettes

Procedure

1. **Preparation of Sample Solution**:
    a. Accurately weigh a known quantity of ephedrine hydrochloride (e.g., 0.5 g).
    b. Dissolve the weighed ephedrine hydrochloride in about 50 ml of glacial acetic acid in a conical flask. Ensure complete dissolution.
2. **Preparation of Titrant**:
    a. Prepare a standard solution of perchloric acid in glacial acetic acid (usually 0.1 N). This involves accurately measuring and diluting concentrated perchloric acid in glacial acetic acid to achieve the desired normality.
3. **Titration**:
    a. Add a few drops of the chosen indicator (e.g., crystal violet) to the sample solution if a visual endpoint is to be detected.

b. If using a potentiometer, set it up and calibrate it as per the manufacturer's instructions.
c. Fill the burette with the standard perchloric acid solution.
d. Slowly titrate the sample solution with the perchloric acid solution while continuously stirring with a magnetic stirrer.
e. If using an indicator, watch for the color change. If using a potentiometer, monitor the change in potential.

4. **Endpoint Detection**:
   a. For visual detection, the endpoint is usually identified by a distinct color change of the indicator. For example, crystal violet changes from violet to green.
   b. For potentiometric detection, the endpoint is indicated by a sharp change in the potential.
5. **Calculation**:
   a. Record the volume of perchloric acid used to reach the endpoint.
   b. Calculate the concentration of ephedrine hydrochloride using the following formula:

$$\text{Moles of Titrant} = \text{Volume (L)} \times \text{Normality (N)} = 0.025 \times 0.1 = 0.0025 \text{ mol}$$

$$\text{Weight of Ephedrine HCl (mol)} = \frac{0.5 \text{ g}}{201.69 \text{ g/mol}} = 0.00248 \text{ mol}$$

   c. The molecular weight of ephedrine hydrochloride (C10H15NO.HCl) is approximately 201.69 g/mol.

Example Calculation

1. Suppose 25.0 ml of 0.1 N perchloric acid is used to titrate 0.5 g of ephedrine hydrochloride.
2. The molecular weight of ephedrine hydrochloride is 201.69 g/mol.

$$\text{Moles of Titrant} = \text{Volume (L)} \times \text{Normality (N)} = 0.025 \times 0.1 = 0.0025 \text{ mol}$$

$$\text{Weight of Ephedrine HCl (mol)} = \frac{0.5 \text{ g}}{201.69 \text{ g/mol}} = 0.00248 \text{ mol}$$

Since 1 mole of ephedrine hydrochloride reacts with 1 mole of perchloric acid, the moles of ephedrine hydrochloride should equal the moles of perchloric acid at the endpoint.

$$\text{Concentration of Ephedrine HCl (mol/L)} = \frac{0.0025 \text{ mol}}{0.5 \text{ g}/201.69 \text{ g/mol}} = 0.00248 \text{ mol/L}$$

This shows the concentration of ephedrine hydrochloride in the solution.

Summary

1. **Principle**: Ephedrine hydrochloride is titrated in a non-aqueous medium to improve ionization and endpoint detection.
2. **Solvent**: Glacial acetic acid is typically used.
3. **Titrant**: Perchloric acid in glacial acetic acid.
4. **Indicator**: Crystal violet or a potentiometer.
5. **Procedure**: Dissolve, titrate, detect endpoint, and calculate concentration.

Multiple Choice Questions (MCQs)

1. What is non-aqueous titration primarily used for?
   A. Analyzing strong acids and bases
   B. Analyzing substances insoluble or unstable in water
   C. Measuring the temperature change in a reaction
   D. Determining the boiling point of a substance
2. Which of the following is a common solvent used in non-aqueous titration?
   A. Water
   B. Acetic acid
   C. Benzene
   D. Glycerol

3. Why is non-aqueous titration preferred for weak acids and bases?
    A. They react incompletely in water
    B. They have high boiling points
    C. They are very soluble in water
    D. They do not dissociate in non-aqueous solvents
4. What type of titration involves the determination of metal ions in non-aqueous solutions?
    A. Acid-Base Titration
    B. Complexometric Titration
    C. Redox Titration
    D. Precipitation Titration
5. Which of the following indicators is commonly used in non-aqueous titration?
    A. Litmus
    B. Phenolphthalein
    C. Crystal violet
    D. Methyl orange
6. What is a primary advantage of using non-aqueous titration?
    A. Lower cost of solvents
    B. Higher sensitivity for weak acids and bases
    C. Faster reaction times
    D. Less toxic solvents
7. In non-aqueous titration, how is the equivalence point typically detected?
    A. Temperature change
    B. Visual observation of color change
    C. Weight change
    D. Volume change
8. What solvent is commonly used for the titration of weak bases in non-aqueous titration?

A. Methanol

B. Glacial acetic acid

C. Water

D. Ethanol

9. What is the role of a potentiometer in non-aqueous titration?

A. To add titrant to the solution

B. To measure the pH of the solution continuously

C. To detect the endpoint by measuring potential changes

D. To indicate the temperature change

10. Which non-aqueous solvent is known for its high solvating power for both polar and non-polar compounds?

A. Water

B. Dimethyl sulfoxide (DMSO)

C. Chloroform

D. Tetrahydrofuran (THF)

11. What is a key disadvantage of using non-aqueous titration?

A. Higher cost of solvents

B. Less accurate results

C. Slower reaction times

D. Limited types of titrations

12. For the estimation of sodium benzoate, which solvent is typically used?

A. Methanol

B. Water

C. Glacial acetic acid

D. Ethanol

13. In the estimation of ephedrine HCl, what is the titrant used?

A. Sodium methoxide

B. Perchloric acid

C. Hydrochloric acid

D. Sodium hydroxide

14. Why is glacial acetic acid used in non-aqueous titration?

A. It is non-polar

B. It is a weak acid and a polar protic solvent

C. It is a strong base

D. It has a high boiling point

15. Which indicator changes from violet to green at the endpoint in non-aqueous titration?

A. Phenolphthalein

B. Methyl orange

C. Crystal violet

D. Thymol blue

16. What type of titration is used for determining weak acids like benzoic acid in non-aqueous solvents?

A. Acidimetric Titration

B. Redox Titration

C. Complexometric Titration

D. Precipitation Titration

17. What is the molecular weight of sodium benzoate (C7H5NaO2)?

A. 144.11 g/mol

B. 120.12 g/mol

C. 150.13 g/mol

D. 200.20 g/mol

18. Which solvent is known to be highly flammable and can form explosive peroxides upon prolonged exposure to air?

A. Methanol

B. Dimethyl sulfoxide (DMSO)

C. Chloroform

D. Tetrahydrofuran (THF)

19. What is the purpose of adding an indicator in non-aqueous titration?

A. To increase the solubility of the analyte

B. To visually detect the endpoint

C. To speed up the reaction

D. To stabilize the titrant

20. Why is it important to handle non-aqueous solvents with care?

A. They are very cheap

B. They are all non-toxic

C. Many are toxic, flammable, or expensive

D. They always react quickly

Short Answer Type Questions (Subjective)

1. What is non-aqueous titration and why is it used?
2. Name two reasons why non-aqueous titration might be preferred over aqueous titration.
3. What types of compounds are typically analyzed using non-aqueous titration?
4. Explain the principle behind non-aqueous titration.
5. List three common solvents used in non-aqueous titration.
6. How does the choice of solvent affect non-aqueous titration?
7. What is the role of an indicator in non-aqueous titration?
8. How is the equivalence point detected in non-aqueous titration?
9. Describe the procedure for performing a non-aqueous titration.
10. What are the advantages of using non-aqueous titration?
11. What are some disadvantages associated with non-aqueous titration?
12. Why is glacial acetic acid commonly used as a solvent in non-aqueous titration?
13. What properties make dimethyl sulfoxide (DMSO) a useful solvent in non-aqueous titration?

14. What type of titration is typically performed using perchloric acid in glacial acetic acid as the titrant?
15. Explain the principle and procedure for the estimation of sodium benzoate using non-aqueous titration.
16. What is the molecular weight of sodium benzoate?
17. Describe the procedure for the estimation of ephedrine HCl using non-aqueous titration.
18. What is the role of a potentiometer in non-aqueous titration?
19. How does the titration of a weak base differ from that of a weak acid in non-aqueous titration?
20. Explain the significance of endpoint detection in non-aqueous titration.

Long Answer Type Questions (Subjective)

1. Discuss the principles and applications of non-aqueous titration in detail.
2. Compare and contrast aqueous and non-aqueous titration, highlighting their advantages and disadvantages.
3. Explain the types of non-aqueous titrations, providing examples of each.
4. Describe in detail the procedure and calculations involved in the estimation of sodium benzoate using non-aqueous titration.
5. Discuss the properties, uses, advantages, and disadvantages of five different solvents used in non-aqueous titration.
6. Explain the principles and procedures for performing acidimetric and alkalimetric titrations in non-aqueous media.
7. Describe the estimation of ephedrine HCl using non-aqueous titration, including the role of solvents, titrants, and indicators.
8. How is endpoint detection achieved in non-aqueous titration? Compare the use of visual indicators and potentiometric methods.
9. Discuss the challenges and safety considerations associated with non-aqueous titration.

10. Explain the significance of solvent choice in non-aqueous titration and how it influences the accuracy and reliability of the results. Provide examples of suitable solvents for different types of analytes.

Answer Key

1. B. Analyzing substances insoluble or unstable in water
2. B. Acetic acid
3. A. They react incompletely in water
4. B. Complexometric Titration
5. C. Crystal violet
6. B. Higher sensitivity for weak acids and bases
7. B. Visual observation of color change
8. B. Glacial acetic acid
9. C. To detect the endpoint by measuring potential changes
10. B. Dimethyl sulfoxide (DMSO)
11. A. Higher cost of solvents
12. C. Glacial acetic acid
13. B. Perchloric acid
14. B. It is a weak acid and a polar protic solvent
15. C. Crystal violet
16. A. Acidimetric Titration
17. A. 144.11 g/mol
18. D. Tetrahydrofuran (THF)
19. B. To visually detect the endpoint
20. C. Many are toxic, flammable, or expensive

CHAPTER – 8

PRECIPITATION TITRATIONS

INTRODUCTION:

Precipitation titrations are a type of volumetric analysis in which the titrant reacts with the analyte to form an insoluble precipitate. These titrations are used to determine the concentration of a particular ion in a solution by adding a reagent that forms an insoluble compound with that ion. The endpoint of the titration is reached when no more precipitate forms, indicating that the reaction is complete. Here's a detailed introduction to precipitation titrations:

Principles of Precipitation Titrations

1. **Precipitation Reaction:**
   a. The fundamental principle of a precipitation titration is the formation of an insoluble precipitate.
   b. For instance, when titrating chloride ions (Cl^-) with a solution of silver nitrate ($AgNO_3$), the reaction forms an insoluble precipitate of silver chloride

$$Ag^+(aq) + Cl^-(aq) \rightarrow AgCl(s)$$

2. **Stoichiometry**:
   a. The stoichiometry of the reaction is crucial as it defines the equivalence point. In the above reaction, one mole of Ag^+ reacts with one mole of Cl^-.
3. **Indicator**:
   a. An indicator is often used to determine the endpoint of the titration. The indicator should react with either the titrant or the analyte to produce a visible change (color change or formation of a secondary precipitate).

Types of Precipitation Titrations

1. **Argentometric Titrations**:
    a. These involve silver nitrate as the titrant and are used to determine halides (Cl^-, Br^-, I^-) and other anions that form insoluble silver salts.
2. **Mohr's Method**:
    a. In Mohr's method, chromate ions (CrO42−) are used as an indicator. When all chloride ions have reacted with silver ions, any further addition of silver nitrate will react with chromate to form a red precipitate of silver chromate (Ag2CrO4):

    $$2Ag^{+}(aq) + CrO_4^{2-}(aq) \rightarrow Ag_2CrO_4(s)$$

3. **Volhard's Method**:
    a. This method uses thiocyanate (SCN−) as a titrant. After precipitating chloride with an excess of silver nitrate, the remaining silver ions are titrated with potassium thiocyanate (KSCN) using iron(III) ions (Fe3+) as an indicator. A red complex of iron(III) thiocyanate indicates the endpoint:

    $$Fe^{3+}(aq) + SCN^{-}(aq) \rightarrow [Fe(SCN)]^{2+}(aq)$$

4. **Fajans Method**:
    a. This method uses adsorption indicators like fluorescein. The indicator adsorbs onto the surface of the precipitate particles and changes color when the charge on the particles changes at the endpoint.

Procedures for Precipitation Titrations

1. **Preparation of the Sample**:
    a. The sample solution is prepared and placed in a titration flask.
2. **Addition of Indicator**:

a. An appropriate indicator is added to the solution. The choice of indicator depends on the specific type of precipitation titration being conducted.

3. **Titration Process**:
    a. The titrant is added from a burette to the analyte solution slowly and with constant stirring to ensure even mixing.
4. **Endpoint Detection**:
    a. The endpoint is detected by a visible change, such as the appearance of a precipitate, color change of an indicator, or formation of a secondary precipitate.
5. **Calculation of Concentration**:
    a. The volume of titrant used to reach the endpoint is recorded. Using the stoichiometry of the reaction, the concentration of the analyte can be calculated.

Advantages and Limitations

Advantages:

1. High precision and accuracy for suitable analytes.
2. Can be used to determine a variety of ions in solution.

Limitations:

1. Requires a clear and distinct endpoint, which may not always be easy to detect.
2. Not suitable for very low concentrations of analyte due to solubility limits.

Applications

1. Determination of halides (Cl^-, Br^-, I^-).
2. Analysis of sulfate, phosphate, and other anions that form insoluble precipitates.
3. Water analysis for hardness (calcium and magnesium ions).
4. Determination of metals like silver and mercury.

Precipitation titrations are a powerful analytical technique in chemistry, providing a reliable means of quantifying specific ions in a solution through the formation of insoluble precipitates.

MOHR'S METHODOF PRECIPITATION TITRATION

Mohr's method is a classical technique used in precipitation titrations, specifically designed for the determination of chloride, bromide, and cyanide ions. This method uses a silver nitrate solution as the titrant and potassium chromate as the indicator. Here's a detailed exploration of Mohr's method:

Principles of Mohr's Method

1. **Reaction Involved**:
    a. The primary reaction in Mohr's method is between the chloride ions (Cl−) in the sample and the silver ions (Ag+) from the silver nitrate solution to form an insoluble precipitate of silver chloride (AgCl):

    $$Ag^{+}(aq) + Cl^{-}(aq) \rightarrow AgCl(s)$$

2. **Indicator**:
    a. Potassium chromate (K2CrO4) is used as the indicator. Once all the chloride ions have precipitated as silver chloride, the first excess of silver ions will react with chromate ions to form a red-brown precipitate of silver chromate (Ag2CrO4), indicating the endpoint:

    $$2Ag^{+}(aq) + CrO_4^{2-}(aq) \rightarrow Ag_2CrO_4(s)$$

Procedure for Mohr's Method

1. **Preparation**:
    a. Prepare the sample solution containing chloride ions.
    b. Standardize the silver nitrate solution using a standard chloride solution.
2. **Titration**:

a. Add a few drops of potassium chromate indicator to the sample solution.
b. Titrate the sample with the standardized silver nitrate solution. The titrant is added slowly with constant stirring to ensure complete mixing and uniform precipitation.

3. **Detection of Endpoint**:
   a. The endpoint is reached when a distinct color change occurs from yellow (chromate) to a red-brown precipitate of silver chromate.
   b. The appearance of the red-brown color indicates the presence of excess silver ions, signifying that all chloride ions have reacted.

Calculations

To calculate the concentration of chloride ions in the sample, use the following steps:

1. Record the volume of silver nitrate solution used at the endpoint.
2. Use the molarity (M) of the silver nitrate solution and the volume (V) used in the titration to calculate the moles of silver ions:

$$\text{Moles of } Ag^{+} = M_{AgNO_3} \times V_{AgNO_3}$$

3. Since the stoichiometry of the reaction between Ag+ and Cl− is 1:1, the moles of chloride ions in the sample will be equal to the moles of silver ions.
4. Calculate the concentration of chloride ions in the sample by dividing the moles of chloride by the volume of the sample.

Example Calculation

Suppose 25.00 mL of a chloride-containing sample requires 12.50 mL of 0.100 M silver nitrate solution to reach the endpoint.

1. Calculate the moles of silver nitrate used:

$$\text{Moles of } AgNO_3 = 0.100\,\text{M} \times 0.01250\,\text{L} = 0.00125\,\text{moles}$$

2. Moles of Cl− are equal to the moles of Ag+:

$$\text{Moles of } Cl^{-} = 0.00125 \text{ moles}$$

3. Calculate the concentration of chloride ions in the sample:

$$\text{Concentration of } Cl^{-} = \frac{0.00125 \text{ moles}}{0.02500 \text{ L}} = 0.0500 \text{ M}$$

Advantages and Limitations of Mohr's Method

Advantages:

1. Simple and straightforward with easily recognizable endpoints.
2. Applicable to a variety of halide determinations.

Limitations:

1. The pH of the solution must be controlled, typically between 6.5 and 10, to prevent the formation of interfering precipitates.
2. Not suitable for solutions with interfering ions that form precipitates with silver or chromate ions.
3. The method is less effective at very low concentrations due to the solubility of silver chromate and silver chloride.

Applications

Mohr's method is widely used in various fields, including:

1. Water analysis for chloride content.
2. Analysis of food products for salt content.
3. Environmental monitoring for halide pollutants.

VOLHARD'S METHOD OF PRECIPITATION TITRATION

Volhard's method is another classical technique used in precipitation titrations, particularly suited for the determination of halides such as chloride, bromide, and iodide ions. This method involves a back-titration process, utilizing silver nitrate to precipitate the halides and then titrating the excess silver nitrate with thiocyanate using iron(III) ions as an indicator. Here's a detailed overview of Volhard's method:

Principles of Volhard's Method

1. **Precipitation Reaction**:
    a. The analyte (typically a halide) reacts with an excess of a standard solution of silver nitrate to form an insoluble silver halide precipitate:

    $$Ag^{+}(aq) + X^{-}(aq) \rightarrow AgX(s)$$

    b. Here, X− represents the halide ion (e.g., Cl−, Br−, or I−).
2. **Back-Titration**:
    a. The excess silver nitrate is then titrated with a standard solution of potassium thiocyanate (KSCN), forming a soluble silver thiocyanate complex:

    $$Ag^{+}(aq) + SCN^{-}(aq) \rightarrow AgSCN(s)$$

3. **Indicator**:
    a. Iron(III) ions (Fe3+) are used as an indicator. When all the excess silver ions have reacted with the thiocyanate, the first addition of excess thiocyanate will form a red-colored complex with iron(III) ions, indicating the endpoint:

    $$Fe^{3+}(aq) + SCN^{-}(aq) \rightarrow [Fe(SCN)]^{2+}(aq)$$

Procedure for Volhard's Method

1. **Sample Preparation**:
    a. The sample containing the halide ions is dissolved in water, and an excess of standard silver nitrate solution is added to precipitate the halide completely.
2. **Filtration (if necessary)**:
    a. The mixture is filtered to remove the precipitate of silver halide, leaving the excess silver nitrate in the filtrate. In some cases, filtration might not be necessary if the subsequent steps are done carefully.

3. **Back-Titration**:
    a. The filtrate containing the excess silver nitrate is titrated with a standard solution of potassium thiocyanate.
    b. A few drops of ferric ammonium sulfate or iron(III) nitrate solution are added as an indicator.
4. **Detection of Endpoint**:
    a. The endpoint is detected by the appearance of a red color, indicating the formation of the iron (III) thiocyanate complex, which signifies that all the excess silver ions have reacted.

Calculations

To calculate the concentration of the halide ions in the sample:

1. **Calculate the moles of silver nitrate added initially**:
    a. Use the volume and molarity of the silver nitrate solution to find the total moles of Ag+ added:

$$\text{Moles of } AgNO_3 = M_{AgNO_3} \times V_{AgNO_3}$$

2. **Calculate the moles of thiocyanate used in the back-titration**:
    a. Use the volume and molarity of the potassium thiocyanate solution to find the moles of SCN− used:

$$\text{Moles of } KSCN = M_{KSCN} \times V_{KSCN}$$

    b. Since the reaction between Ag+ and SCN− is 1:1, the moles of SCN− used will be equal to the moles of excess Ag+ left after the precipitation reaction.
3. **Calculate the moles of Ag+ that reacted with the halide**:
    a. Subtract the moles of Ag+ that reacted with SCN− from the total moles of Ag+ added:

$$\text{Moles of } Ag^+ \text{ (reacted with halide)} = \text{Total moles of } Ag^+ - \text{Moles of } SCN^-$$

4. **Determine the concentration of the halide**:
   a. Since the stoichiometry of the reaction between Ag+ and X− is 1:1, the moles of halide ions will be equal to the moles of Ag+ that reacted with the halide.
   b. Calculate the concentration of the halide in the sample

$$\text{Concentration of halide} = \frac{\text{Moles of halide}}{\text{Volume of the sample}}$$

Example Calculation

Suppose 50.00 mL of a chloride-containing sample is titrated with 25.00 mL of 0.100 M silver nitrate solution, and the excess silver nitrate is back-titrated with 10.00 mL of 0.050 M potassium thiocyanate solution.

1. **Total moles of AgNO3 added**:

$$\text{Moles of } AgNO_3 = 0.100\,\text{M} \times 0.02500\,\text{L} = 0.00250\,\text{moles}$$

2. **Moles of KSCN used in back-titration**:

$$\text{Moles of } KSCN = 0.050\,\text{M} \times 0.01000\,\text{L} = 0.00050\,\text{moles}$$

3. **Moles of Ag+ that reacted with chloride**:

$$\text{Moles of } Ag^{+} \text{ (reacted with chloride)} = 0.00250\,\text{moles} - 0.00050\,\text{moles} = 0.00200\,\text{ı}$$

4. **Concentration of chloride in the sample**:

$$\text{Concentration of } Cl^{-} = \frac{0.00200\,\text{moles}}{0.05000\,\text{L}} = 0.0400\,\text{M}$$

Advantages and Limitations of Volhard's Method

Advantages:

1. Applicable to a wide range of halides and other anions.
2. Useful in solutions with low concentrations of analyte.
3. The endpoint is clear and easy to detect.

Limitations:

1. Requires careful control of experimental conditions, especially pH.
2. Interferences from other ions that form precipitates or complexes with silver or thiocyanate.
3. More complex and time-consuming compared to direct titration methods.

Applications

Volhard's method is used in various fields, including:

1. Determination of halides in water and wastewater.
2. Analysis of chloride content in food products.
3. Pharmaceutical analysis for halide impurities.
4. Environmental monitoring of halide pollutants.

MODIFIED VOLHARD'S METHOD OF PRECIPITATION TITRATION

The Modified Volhard's method is an adaptation of the traditional Volhard's method used in precipitation titrations. This modification is often employed to improve the accuracy and reliability of the titration, especially when dealing with complex matrices or when the direct application of the Volhard's method might be challenging. Here's a detailed overview of the Modified Volhard's method:

Principles of the Modified Volhard's Method

The Modified Volhard's method follows the same general principles as the original Volhard's method but with modifications to improve accuracy and minimize potential interferences. The primary steps include:

1. **Precipitation Reaction**:
    a. The analyte (typically a halide) is reacted with an excess of a standard silver nitrate solution to form an insoluble silver halide precipitate.
    $Ag^+(aq) + X^-(aq) \rightarrow AgX(s)$
    b. Here, $X-$ represents the halide ion (e.g., $Cl-$, $Br-$, or $I-$).

2. **Removal of Precipitate**:

a. The precipitate is removed by filtration or centrifugation to ensure that only the excess silver ions remain in the solution.

3. **Back-Titration**:
   a. The excess silver nitrate in the filtrate is titrated with a standard solution of potassium thiocyanate.
   b. $Ag^{+}(aq) + SCN^{-}(aq) \rightarrow AgSCN(s)$
4. **Indicator**:
   a. Iron(III) ions (Fe3+) are used as an indicator. When all the excess silver ions have reacted with thiocyanate, the first addition of excess thiocyanate will form a red-colored complex with iron(III) ions, indicating the endpoint:
   b. $Fe^{3+}(aq) + SCN^{-}(aq) \rightarrow [Fe(SCN)]^{2+}(aq)$

Modifications in the Procedure

1. **Acidic Medium**:
   a. The titration is often conducted in an acidic medium (usually nitric acid) to prevent the formation of other precipitates that could interfere with the detection of the endpoint.
   b. This ensures that the silver halide precipitate remains insoluble and improves the sharpness of the endpoint detection.
2. **Addition of Nitrobenzene**:
   a. Nitrobenzene or other organic solvents may be added to the solution to coat the precipitate and prevent it from re-dissolving during the titration.
   b. This helps to stabilize the precipitate and improve the accuracy of the titration.

Detailed Procedure for the Modified Volhard's Method

1. **Sample Preparation**:
   a. Dissolve the sample containing the halide ions in distilled water.

b. Add a known excess amount of standard silver nitrate solution to the sample to ensure complete precipitation of the halide.

2. **Acidification**:
   a. Acidify the mixture with nitric acid to maintain an acidic medium.
3. **Addition of Nitrobenzene** (if applicable):
   a. Add a small amount of nitrobenzene to the solution to coat the precipitate and prevent its re-dissolution.
4. **Filtration**:
   a. Filter the mixture to remove the precipitate of silver halide, ensuring that only the excess silver ions remain in the filtrate.
5. **Back-Titration**:
   a. Add a few drops of ferric ammonium sulfate or iron(III) nitrate solution as an indicator to the filtrate.
   b. Titrate the excess silver nitrate with a standard solution of potassium thiocyanate until the first permanent red color appears, indicating the endpoint.

Calculations

1. **Total moles of silver nitrate added**:
   a. Calculate the total moles of silver nitrate added to the sample:

$$\text{Moles of } AgNO_3 = M_{AgNO_3} \times V_{AgNO_3}$$

2. **Moles of thiocyanate used in back-titration**:
   a. Calculate the moles of potassium thiocyanate used in the back-titration:

$$\text{Moles of } KSCN = M_{KSCN} \times V_{KSCN}$$

3. **Moles of excess silver ions**:
   a. The moles of excess silver ions are equal to the moles of thiocyanate used:

$$\text{Moles of excess } Ag^+ = \text{Moles of } KSCN$$

4. **Moles of halide ions in the sample**:
   a. Subtract the moles of excess silver ions from the total moles of silver nitrate added to find the moles of halide ions:

$$\text{Moles of halide} = \text{Total moles of } AgNO_3 - \text{Moles of excess } Ag^+$$

5. **Concentration of halide ions**:
   a. Calculate the concentration of halide ions in the sample:

$$\text{Concentration of halide} = \frac{\text{Moles of halide}}{\text{Volume of the sample}}$$

Example Calculation

Suppose 50.00 mL of a chloride-containing sample is titrated with 25.00 mL of 0.100 M silver nitrate solution, and the excess silver nitrate is back-titrated with 10.00 mL of 0.050 M potassium thiocyanate solution.

1. **Total moles of AgNO3 added**:

$$\text{Moles of } AgNO_3 = 0.100\,\text{M} \times 0.02500\,\text{L} = 0.00250\,\text{moles}$$

2. **Moles of KSCN used in back-titration**:

$$\text{Moles of } KSCN = 0.050\,\text{M} \times 0.01000\,\text{L} = 0.00050\,\text{moles}$$

3. **Moles of excess Ag+**:

$$\text{Moles of excess } Ag^+ = 0.00050\,\text{moles}$$

4. **Moles of Cl− in the sample**:

$$\text{Moles of } Cl^- = 0.00250\,\text{moles} - 0.00050\,\text{moles} = 0.00200\,\text{moles}$$

5. **Concentration of Cl− in the sample**:

$$\text{Concentration of } Cl^- = \frac{0.00200\,\text{moles}}{0.05000\,\text{L}} = 0.0400\,\text{M}$$

Advantages and Limitations of the Modified Volhard's Method

Advantages:

1. Improved accuracy and precision compared to the traditional Volhard's method.
2. Effective in complex matrices where direct titration might be problematic.
3. Clear and distinct endpoint detection.

Limitations:

1. More complex and time-consuming than direct titration methods.
2. Requires careful control of experimental conditions, such as pH and filtration.
3. Potential interferences from other ions that can form complexes or precipitates with silver or thiocyanate.

Applications

The Modified Volhard's method is used in various fields, including:

1. Determination of halides in water and wastewater.
2. Analysis of chloride content in food products.
3. Pharmaceutical analysis for halide impurities.
4. Environmental monitoring of halide pollutants.

FAJANS METHOD OF PRECIPITATION TITRATION

Fajans method is a type of precipitation titration that uses adsorption indicators to determine the endpoint. This method is particularly useful for detecting halides and other anions by utilizing the formation of a colored complex on the precipitate surface at the endpoint. Here's a detailed exploration of Fajans method:

Principles of Fajans Method

1. **Precipitation Reaction**:
    a. The analyte (typically a halide) reacts with a standard solution of a titrant (such as silver nitrate) to form an insoluble precipitate:

$$Ag^+(aq) + X^-(aq) \rightarrow AgX(s)$$

b. Here, X^- represents the halide ion (e.g., Cl^-, Br^-, or I^-).

2. **Adsorption Indicator**:
   a. An adsorption indicator is a dye that adsorbs onto the surface of the precipitate and undergoes a color change at the endpoint.
   b. Common indicators include fluorescein, eosin, and dichlorofluorescein.
   c. The indicator binds to the surface of the precipitate due to a charge reversal when the titrant is in excess, resulting in a visible color change.

Procedure for Fajans Method

1. **Sample Preparation**:
   a. Prepare the sample solution containing the halide ions.
   b. Standardize the titrant solution, typically silver nitrate.
2. **Addition of Indicator**:
   a. Add a small amount of the adsorption indicator to the sample solution.
3. **Titration**:
   a. Slowly add the standardized titrant solution (e.g., silver nitrate) to the sample with constant stirring.
   b. As the titrant is added, the halide ions precipitate out as silver halide.
4. **Detection of Endpoint**:
   a. The endpoint is detected when the color of the adsorption indicator changes, indicating that the titrant is in slight excess and has adsorbed onto the surface of the precipitate.
   b. For example, with fluorescein as the indicator, the color changes from yellow-green to pink.

Calculations

To calculate the concentration of halide ions in the sample:

1. **Record the volume of titrant used at the endpoint**.
2. **Calculate the moles of titrant used**:

$$\text{Moles of titrant} = M_{\text{titrant}} \times V_{\text{titrant}}$$

3. **Determine the moles of halide ions**:
    a. Since the stoichiometry of the reaction between Ag+ and X− is 1:1, the moles of halide ions in the sample are equal to the moles of titrant used.
4. **Calculate the concentration of halide ions**:

$$\text{Concentration of halide ions} = \frac{\text{Moles of halide}}{\text{Volume of the sample}}$$

Example Calculation

Suppose 50.00 mL of a chloride-containing sample requires 20.00 mL of 0.100 M silver nitrate solution to reach the endpoint with fluorescein as the indicator.

1. **Calculate the moles of silver nitrate used**:

$$\text{Moles of AgNO}_3 = 0.100\,\text{M} \times 0.02000\,\text{L} = 0.00200\,\text{moles}$$

2. **Moles of Cl− in the sample**:
    a. The moles of Cl− are equal to the moles of AgNO3:

$$\text{Moles of } Cl^- = 0.00200\,\text{moles}$$

3. **Concentration of Cl− in the sample**:

$$\text{Concentration of } Cl^- = \frac{0.00200\,\text{moles}}{0.05000\,\text{L}} = 0.0400\,\text{M}$$

Advantages and Limitations of Fajans Method

Advantages:

1. Clear and distinct endpoint detection with a visible color change.
2. Can be used for a variety of anions that form insoluble precipitates.
3. More sensitive than some other titration methods, allowing detection of smaller amounts of analyte.

Limitations:

1. Requires a suitable adsorption indicator that works well with the specific precipitate.
2. pH and ionic strength of the solution must be controlled to ensure accurate results.
3. Interferences from other ions that can form precipitates or complexes with the titrant or indicator.

Applications

Fajans method is widely used in various fields, including:

1. Determination of halides in water and wastewater.
2. Analysis of chloride content in food products.
3. Pharmaceutical analysis for halide impurities.
4. Environmental monitoring of halide pollutants.

ESTIMATION OF SODIUM CHLORIDE

The estimation of sodium chloride (NaCl) through precipitation titration can be effectively performed using the Mohr's method, which involves titration with silver nitrate (AgNO3) in the presence of potassium chromate (K2CrO4) as an indicator. This method is suitable for determining the chloride content in a sample, such as water, food products, or other chloride-containing solutions.

Principles of Mohr's Method

1. **Precipitation Reaction**:
   a. Sodium chloride reacts with silver nitrate to form an insoluble precipitate of silver chloride:

$$NaCl(aq) + AgNO_3(aq) \rightarrow AgCl(s) + NaNO_3(aq)$$

2. **Indicator**:
   a. Potassium chromate is used as an indicator. When all chloride ions have reacted with silver ions, the first excess of silver ions reacts with

chromate ions to form a red-brown precipitate of silver chromate, indicating the endpoint:

$$2Ag^{+}(aq) + CrO_4^{2-}(aq) \rightarrow Ag_2CrO_4(s)$$

Detailed Procedure for Estimation of Sodium Chloride

Materials and Reagents

1. Sample solution containing sodium chloride
2. Standard silver nitrate solution (e.g., 0.1 M)
3. Potassium chromate indicator solution (5% w/v)
4. Distilled water
5. Burette, pipette, and volumetric flasks
6. Erlenmeyer flask or titration beaker

Steps

1. **Preparation of Sample Solution**:
    a. Dissolve the sample containing sodium chloride in distilled water and transfer it to a volumetric flask to make up to a known volume. For example, prepare 100 mL of sample solution.
2. **Addition of Indicator**:
    a. Transfer an aliquot (e.g., 25.00 mL) of the sample solution to an Erlenmeyer flask.
    b. Add 1-2 mL of potassium chromate indicator solution to the sample solution. The solution will turn yellow.
3. **Titration**:
    a. Fill a burette with the standard silver nitrate solution.
    b. Titrate the sample solution with the silver nitrate solution, adding it slowly and with constant stirring.
    c. As silver nitrate is added, silver chloride precipitates out, and the solution remains yellow.
4. **Detection of Endpoint**:

a. Continue adding the silver nitrate solution until a red-brown color persists, indicating the formation of silver chromate. This is the endpoint of the titration.

Calculations

To calculate the concentration of sodium chloride in the sample:

1. **Record the volume of silver nitrate used**:
   a. Note the volume of silver nitrate solution required to reach the endpoint.
2. **Calculate the moles of silver nitrate used**:

$$\text{Moles of } AgNO_3 = M_{AgNO_3} \times V_{AgNO_3}$$

   a. Where MAgNO3 is the molarity of the silver nitrate solution and VAgNO3 is the volume of silver nitrate solution used in liters.
3. **Determine the moles of sodium chloride**:
   a. Since the reaction between NaCl and AgNO3 is 1:1, the moles of NaCl in the sample are equal to the moles of AgNO3 used.
4. **Calculate the concentration of sodium chloride**:

$$\text{Concentration of NaCl} = \frac{\text{Moles of NaCl}}{\text{Volume of the sample aliquot}}$$

   a. The volume of the sample aliquot is the volume of the sample solution that was titrated (e.g., 25.00 mL).
5. **Express the result**:
   a. The concentration of NaCl can be expressed in moles per liter (M) or converted to grams per liter (g/L) by multiplying by the molar mass of NaCl (58.44 g/mol).

Example Calculation

Suppose 25.00 mL of a sample solution requires 18.00 mL of 0.100 M silver nitrate solution to reach the endpoint with potassium chromate as the indicator.

1. **Calculate the moles of silver nitrate used:**

$$\text{Moles of } AgNO_3 = 0.100\,\text{M} \times 0.01800\,\text{L} = 0.00180\,\text{moles}$$

2. **Moles of NaCl in the sample:**
   a. The moles of NaCl are equal to the moles of AgNO3:

$$\text{Moles of } NaCl = 0.00180\,\text{moles}$$

3. **Concentration of NaCl in the sample aliquot:**

$$\text{Concentration of NaCl} = \frac{0.00180\,\text{moles}}{0.02500\,\text{L}} = 0.0720\,\text{M}$$

4. **Convert to grams per liter:**
   a. Multiply by the molar mass of NaCl (58.44 g/mol):

$$\text{Concentration of NaCl} = 0.0720\,\text{M} \times 58.44\,\text{g/mol} = 4.21\,\text{g/L}$$

Advantages and Limitations of Mohr's Method

Advantages:

1. Simple and straightforward procedure.
2. Clear and distinct endpoint detection with a visible color change.
3. Suitable for various chloride-containing samples.

Limitations:

1. The method is pH-sensitive and works best in neutral to slightly alkaline conditions (pH 6.5-10).
2. Interference from other ions that form precipitates with silver or chromate.
3. Not suitable for colored or turbid samples that may obscure the endpoint detection.

Applications

Mohr's method is widely used in various fields, including:

1. Water analysis for chloride content.
2. Food industry for determining the salt content in products.

3. Environmental monitoring of chloride levels in wastewater and natural waters.
4. Clinical analysis of chloride in biological fluids.

Multiple Choice Questions (MCQs)

1. What is the fundamental principle behind precipitation titrations?
   A) Formation of a color change
   B) Formation of an insoluble precipitate
   C) Formation of a gas
   D) Formation of a soluble complex
2. In the reaction $Ag^+(aq) + Cl^-(aq) \rightarrow AgCl(s)$, what is formed?
   A) A soluble complex
   B) A gas
   C) An insoluble precipitate
   D) A color change
3. What role does stoichiometry play in precipitation titrations?
   A) Determines the color change
   B) Defines the equivalence point
   C) Determines the endpoint
   D) Changes the solubility of the precipitate
4. Which of the following is used as an indicator in Mohr's method?
   A) Fluorescein
   B) Potassium chromate
   C) Iron(III) ions
   D) Methyl orange
5. What color change indicates the endpoint in Mohr's method?
   A) Yellow to red-brown
   B) Red to blue

C) Green to yellow

D) Blue to pink

6. What is the primary titrant used in argentometric titrations?

A) Potassium permanganate

B) Silver nitrate

C) Hydrochloric acid

D) Sodium hydroxide

7. In Volhard's method, what is the function of iron(III) ions?

A) Primary titrant

B) Precipitate former

C) Indicator

D) Buffer

8. Which method uses thiocyanate (SCN^-) as a titrant?

A) Mohr's method

B) Volhard's method

C) Fajans method

D) Modified Volhard's method

9. What is an adsorption indicator?

A) An indicator that adsorbs onto the surface of the precipitate

B) An indicator that forms a gas

C) An indicator that changes pH

D) An indicator that dissolves in the solution

10. Which indicator is used in Fajans method?

A) Potassium chromate

B) Iron(III) ions

C) Fluorescein

D) Methyl orange

11. What is the endpoint detected by in the Modified Volhard's method?

A) Formation of a gas

B) Formation of a red-colored complex

C) Formation of a blue-colored complex

D) Formation of a precipitate

12. What modification is often made in the Modified Volhard's method to improve accuracy?

A) Use of a gas indicator

B) Addition of nitrobenzene

C) Use of a buffer solution

D) Addition of sodium hydroxide

13. What is the primary reaction involved in Mohr's method?

A) $Ag^+(aq) + Cl^-(aq) \rightarrow AgCl(s)$

B) $Ag^+(aq) + SCN^-(aq) \rightarrow AgSCN(s)$

C) $Ag^+(aq) + Br^-(aq) \rightarrow AgBr(s)$

D) $Ag^+(aq) + I^-(aq) \rightarrow AgI(s)$

14. Which of the following is a limitation of precipitation titrations?

A) High precision for all analytes

B) Not suitable for very low concentrations of analyte

C) Suitable for detecting gases

D) High sensitivity to temperature changes

15. What is the advantage of Mohr's method?

A) Simple and straightforward with easily recognizable endpoints

B) High sensitivity to temperature changes

C) Complex procedure

D) Requires specific equipment

16. Which method is used for water analysis for chloride content?

A) Volhard's method

B) Mohr's method

C) Fajans method

D) Modified Volhard's method

17. What color change indicates the endpoint in Fajans method with fluorescein as the indicator?

A) Yellow-green to pink

B) Blue to red

C) Red to yellow

D) Green to blue

18. In the estimation of sodium chloride using Mohr's method, what is the precipitate formed?

A) Sodium chromate

B) Silver chloride

C) Sodium nitrate

D) Silver nitrate

19. Which method involves a back-titration process?

A) Mohr's method

B) Volhard's method

C) Fajans method

D) Modified Volhard's method

20. Which method uses chromate ions as an indicator?

A) Mohr's method

B) Volhard's method

C) Fajans method

D) Modified Volhard's method

Short Answer Type Questions

1. What is the fundamental principle behind precipitation titrations?
2. Describe the stoichiometry of the reaction between Ag^+ and Cl^- ions in a precipitation titration.
3. What is the role of an indicator in precipitation titrations?
4. Name the titrant used in argentometric titrations.

5. Which ions are typically determined using Mohr's method?
6. What indicator is used in Mohr's method and what color change indicates the endpoint?
7. Explain the primary reaction involved in Mohr's method.
8. In Volhard's method, what is the role of thiocyanate ions (SCN^-)?
9. What is the purpose of using iron(III) ions (Fe^{3+}) as an indicator in Volhard's method?
10. Describe the endpoint detection in Volhard's method.
11. What are adsorption indicators, and in which method are they used?
12. Name two common adsorption indicators used in Fajans method.
13. How is the endpoint detected in Fajans method using fluorescein as an indicator?
14. What modification is often made in the Modified Volhard's method to improve accuracy?
15. Why is an acidic medium used in the Modified Volhard's method?
16. Explain the reaction that occurs between NaCl and $AgNO_3$ in Mohr's method.
17. What is the endpoint color change in Mohr's method when potassium chromate is used as an indicator?
18. List two advantages of precipitation titrations.
19. What are the limitations of precipitation titrations?
20. Provide an application of Mohr's method in environmental monitoring.

Long Answer Type Questions

1. Discuss the principles and procedures of precipitation titrations, highlighting the formation of insoluble precipitates and the role of stoichiometry.

2. Describe in detail Mohr's method of precipitation titration, including the reactions involved, the indicator used, and the endpoint detection.
3. Explain Volhard's method of precipitation titration, outlining the steps involved in the back-titration process and the calculations required to determine the concentration of halides.
4. Compare and contrast Mohr's method and Volhard's method of precipitation titration, focusing on their principles, procedures, and applications.
5. Describe the Modified Volhard's method, including the modifications made to improve accuracy and the detailed procedure for conducting this titration.
6. Explain the principles and applications of Fajans method in precipitation titration, including the use of adsorption indicators and the procedure for detecting the endpoint.
7. Provide a step-by-step procedure for the estimation of sodium chloride using Mohr's method, including the preparation of the sample, titration process, and calculation of the concentration.
8. Discuss the advantages and limitations of using Mohr's method for the determination of chloride content in various samples.
9. Explain the calculations involved in determining the concentration of chloride ions using precipitation titrations, providing an example calculation for better understanding.
10. Describe the applications of precipitation titrations in different fields such as water analysis, food industry, and environmental monitoring, highlighting the importance of these techniques in analytical chemistry.

Answer Key

1. B (Formation of an insoluble precipitate)
2. C (An insoluble precipitate)

3. B (Defines the equivalence point)
4. B (Potassium chromate)
5. A (Yellow to red-brown)
6. B (Silver nitrate)
7. C (Indicator)
8. B (Volhard's method)
9. A (An indicator that adsorbs onto the surface of the precipitate)
10. C (Fluorescein)
11. B (Formation of a red-colored complex)
12. B (Addition of nitrobenzene)
13. A ($Ag^{+}(aq) + Cl^{-}(aq) \rightarrow AgCl(s)$)
14. B (Not suitable for very low concentrations of analyte)
15. A (Simple and straightforward with easily recognizable endpoints)
16. B (Mohr's method)
17. A (Yellow-green to pink)
18. B (Silver chloride)
19. B (Volhard's method)
20. A (Mohr's method)

CHAPTER – 9

COMPLEXOMETRIC TITRATION

INTRODUCTION:

Complexometric titration is a form of volumetric analysis in which the formation of a complex ion is used to indicate the endpoint of a titration. This technique is particularly useful for the determination of metal ions in solution.

Key Concepts in Complexometric Titration

1. **Complex Formation**:
    a. A complex ion consists of a central metal ion bonded to one or more molecules or ions called ligands. These ligands donate electron pairs to the metal ion to form coordinate bonds.
    b. The stability of the complex is defined by the formation constant (KfK_fKf).
2. **Chelating Agents**:
    a. A chelating agent is a ligand that can form multiple bonds with a single metal ion. The most common chelating agent used in complexometric titrations is ethylenediaminetetraacetic acid (EDTA).
    b. EDTA can form stable complexes with most metal ions, making it a versatile titrant.
3. **Indicators**:
    a. An indicator is used to signal the endpoint of the titration. The indicator itself forms a complex with the metal ion, which changes color when it is displaced by the EDTA.
    b. Common indicators include Eriochrome Black T, Calmagite, and Murexide.

Procedure of Complexometric Titration

1. **Preparation of the Sample**:
   a. The sample containing the metal ions is dissolved in a suitable solvent, usually water. The pH of the solution may need to be adjusted to ensure that the metal ions are in the appropriate form for complexation.
2. **Addition of the Indicator**:
   a. A small amount of the indicator is added to the solution. The solution changes color based on the metal-indicator complex formed.
3. **Titration**:
   a. The titrant (EDTA solution) is slowly added to the sample solution from a burette. The EDTA binds to the metal ions in the solution, forming a stable complex.
   b. As the EDTA is added, it displaces the indicator from the metal ions, causing a color change.
4. **Endpoint Detection**:
   a. The endpoint is reached when all the metal ions have formed complexes with the EDTA, and the indicator is no longer bound to the metal ions. This results in a distinct color change in the solution.
   b. The volume of EDTA used to reach the endpoint is recorded.
5. **Calculations**:
   a. The concentration of the metal ions in the sample can be calculated using the volume of EDTA used, the concentration of the EDTA solution, and the stoichiometry of the complexation reaction.

Example: Determination of Calcium and Magnesium Ions

1. **Sample Preparation**:
   a. A water sample containing calcium and magnesium ions is prepared. The pH is adjusted to around 10 using a buffer solution.
2. **Indicator Addition**:

a. Eriochrome Black T is added to the sample, turning it wine red.

3. **Titration**:
    a. EDTA solution is added from a burette. As EDTA binds to the calcium and magnesium ions, the solution color changes from wine red to pure blue.
4. **Endpoint**:
    a. The endpoint is detected when the solution turns from wine red to blue, indicating all calcium and magnesium ions have been complexed with EDTA.
5. **Calculation**:
    a. The volume of EDTA used is noted, and the concentration of calcium and magnesium ions in the water sample is calculated based on the known concentration of the EDTA solution.

Advantages of Complexometric Titration

1. **Accuracy**: High precision in determining metal ion concentrations.
2. **Versatility**: Applicable to a wide range of metal ions.
3. **Specificity**: Selective for specific metal ions when appropriate indicators and conditions are used.
4. **Simple Equipment**: Requires basic laboratory equipment such as burettes and pipettes.

Applications

1. **Water Hardness Analysis**: Determination of calcium and magnesium ion concentrations in water.
2. **Pharmaceutical Analysis**: Determination of metal impurities in pharmaceuticals.
3. **Environmental Monitoring**: Analysis of metal contaminants in soil and water.
4. **Food Industry**: Determination of metal content in food products.

Complexometric titration is a powerful analytical technique widely used in various fields for its accuracy, simplicity, and ability to analyze complex mixtures of metal ions.

CLASSIFICATION

Complexometric titration can be classified based on several criteria, including the type of titrant used, the method of endpoint detection, and the nature of the analyte. Here are the main classifications in detail:

1. Classification by Titrant

a. EDTA Titration

i. **Direct Titration**: The metal ion solution is titrated directly with a standard EDTA solution. An indicator is used to signal the endpoint.

ii. **Back Titration**: Used when the direct titration is not feasible. An excess of EDTA is added to the metal ion solution, and the excess EDTA is titrated with a standard solution of a second metal ion.

iii. **Indirect Titration**: The analyte is first reacted with a reagent to form a metal complex, which is then titrated with EDTA.

b. Other Complexing Agents

i. **Cyanide Titration**: Cyanide ions are used to form complexes with certain metal ions.

ii. **Ammonia Titration**: Ammonia can form complexes with certain transition metals.

2. Classification by Endpoint Detection

a. Visual Indicators

i. **Metal Ion Indicators**: Change color when they bind to the metal ion. The most common are Eriochrome Black T and Calmagite.

ii. **Color Change of Solution**: The color change directly observed in the solution, indicating the endpoint.

b. Instrumental Methods

i. **Potentiometric Titration**: Uses a potentiometer to detect changes in voltage corresponding to the formation of the metal-EDTA complex.

ii. **Spectrophotometric Titration**: Measures changes in absorbance of the solution as the titration progresses.

iii. **Conductometric Titration**: Monitors changes in the electrical conductivity of the solution.

iv. **Amperometric Titration**: Measures changes in current during the titration process.

3. Classification by Analyte

a. Single Metal Ion

i. **Simple Complexometric Titration**: Involves a single metal ion in the solution. The titration curve and endpoint are straightforward.

b. Mixed Metal Ions

i. **Selective Complexometric Titration**: Involves multiple metal ions. Selective complexation and masking agents may be used to titrate one metal ion in the presence of others.

ii. **Sequential Complexometric Titration**: Different metal ions are titrated in a specific order by changing the pH or using different indicators.

4. Classification by pH Conditions

a. Constant pH Titration

i. **Buffered Solutions**: The pH of the solution is kept constant using a buffer to ensure consistent complexation behavior.

b. Variable pH Titration

i. **pH Adjustment**: The pH is adjusted during the titration process to selectively titrate different metal ions at their optimal pH levels.

Detailed Examples

Direct EDTA Titration of Calcium

i. **Procedure**: A water sample containing calcium ions is titrated with EDTA using Eriochrome Black T as an indicator. The solution changes from wine red to blue at the endpoint.
ii. **Application**: Determining water hardness.

Back Titration of Nickel

i. **Procedure**: Excess EDTA is added to a nickel solution, and the remaining EDTA is titrated with a standard zinc solution. The indicator used is Xylenol Orange, which changes color at the endpoint.
ii. **Application**: Analysis of nickel content in alloys.

Spectrophotometric Titration of Iron

i. **Procedure**: An iron solution is titrated with EDTA while monitoring the absorbance at a specific wavelength. The change in absorbance indicates the endpoint.
ii. **Application**: Determination of trace iron in pharmaceuticals.

Advantages and Applications

i. **Water Hardness Testing**: Commonly used to measure the concentration of calcium and magnesium ions in water.
ii. **Pharmaceuticals**: Used to ensure metal ion content is within specified limits.
iii. **Environmental Analysis**: Detects metal pollutants in soil and water.
iv. **Food Industry**: Determines metal content in various food products.
v. **Industrial Applications**: Used in quality control processes for metals and alloys.

Complexometric titration, especially using EDTA, is a versatile and accurate method for analyzing metal ions, with widespread applications across different fields.

METAL ION INDICATORS

In complexometric titration, metal ion indicators (also known as metallochromic indicators) play a crucial role in detecting the endpoint. These indicators are compounds that change color when they bind to metal ions. This color change signifies the completion of the titration process. Below are the details of some commonly used metal ion indicators, their mechanisms, and their applications.

Common Metal Ion Indicators

1. Eriochrome Black T (EBT)

a. **Chemical Structure**: C20H12N3NaO7S

b. **Color Change**:

   i. Free Indicator: Blue

   ii. Metal-Indicator Complex: Red

   iii. Endpoint: Blue

c. **Mechanism**: Eriochrome Black T forms a wine-red complex with metal ions like calcium and magnesium at a pH of around 10. When EDTA is added, it complexes with the metal ions, releasing the EBT, which then turns blue.

d. **Applications**: Widely used in water hardness determination and for titrating calcium and magnesium ions.

2. Calmagite

a. **Chemical Structure**: C17H14N3NaO5S

b. **Color Change**:

   i. Free Indicator: Blue

   ii. Metal-Indicator Complex: Red

   iii. Endpoint: Blue

c. **Mechanism**: Similar to Eriochrome Black T, Calmagite forms a red complex with metal ions at a slightly alkaline pH. EDTA displaces the indicator, resulting in a color change to blue.

d. **Applications**: Used in the titration of calcium and magnesium ions, especially in water analysis.

3. Murexide (Ammonium Purpurate)

a. **Chemical Structure**: C8H8N6O6

b. **Color Change**:

   i. Free Indicator: Yellow

   ii. Metal-Indicator Complex: Purple

   iii. Endpoint: Yellow

c. **Mechanism**: Murexide forms a purple complex with metal ions such as calcium. Upon the addition of EDTA, the metal ions are complexed by EDTA, and the solution turns back to yellow.

d. **Applications**: Primarily used for titrating calcium ions in the presence of magnesium ions.

4. Xylenol Orange

a. **Chemical Structure**: C31H32N2Na4O13S

b. **Color Change**:

   i. Free Indicator: Yellow

   ii. Metal-Indicator Complex: Red

   iii. Endpoint: Yellow

c. **Mechanism**: Xylenol Orange forms a red complex with metal ions like iron and zinc. The addition of EDTA results in a yellow endpoint as the metal ions are sequestered by EDTA.

d. **Applications**: Used for titrating metals such as iron, zinc, and thorium.

Mechanism of Action

Metal ion indicators work based on the principle of competitive binding between the indicator and the chelating agent (such as EDTA) for the metal ions. Here's a general outline of the mechanism:

1. **Indicator Binding**: The indicator initially binds to the metal ions, forming a colored complex.
2. **Titration with EDTA**: As EDTA is added to the solution, it competes with the indicator for the metal ions.

3. **Displacement of Indicator**: EDTA, having a higher affinity for the metal ions, displaces the indicator, freeing it from the metal complex.
4. **Color Change**: The freed indicator exhibits a color change, signifying the endpoint of the titration.

Selection Criteria for Indicators

1. **Stability**: The indicator-metal complex should be less stable than the EDTA-metal complex to ensure complete displacement by EDTA.
2. **Distinct Color Change**: The color change should be clear and distinct to accurately determine the endpoint.
3. **pH Range**: The indicator should work effectively within the pH range of the titration process.

Practical Considerations

1. **Buffer Solutions**: Maintaining the correct pH is essential, as the performance of the indicator and the stability of the metal-EDTA complex depend on it.
2. **Indicator Concentration**: The amount of indicator used should be sufficient to produce a noticeable color change but not too much to obscure the endpoint.

Example Procedures

Water Hardness Determination using EBT

1. **Preparation**: A water sample is taken, and the pH is adjusted to around 10 using an ammonia buffer.
2. **Indicator Addition**: A few drops of Eriochrome Black T are added to the sample, turning it wine red.
3. **Titration**: The sample is titrated with EDTA solution. As EDTA binds the calcium and magnesium ions, the color changes to blue at the endpoint.
4. **Calculation**: The concentration of calcium and magnesium ions is calculated based on the volume of EDTA used.

Iron Determination using Xylenol Orange

1. **Preparation**: An iron solution is prepared, and the pH is adjusted to around 2-3.
2. **Indicator Addition**: A few drops of Xylenol Orange are added, turning the solution red.
3. **Titration**: EDTA is added until the solution changes from red to yellow.
4. **Calculation**: The concentration of iron is determined from the EDTA volume used.

Metal ion indicators are vital for accurately determining the endpoint in complexometric titrations, ensuring precise quantification of metal ions in various samples.

MASKING AND DEMASKING REAGENTS

In complexometric titration, masking and demasking reagents are used to selectively control the reaction between metal ions and the titrant (usually EDTA). These reagents are crucial in differentiating between various metal ions in a mixture, allowing for the accurate determination of specific ions without interference from others.

Masking Reagents

Masking reagents selectively react with certain metal ions to form stable, non-reactive complexes. These complexes do not participate in the titration with the primary titrant (EDTA), effectively "masking" the metal ions from the titration process.

Common Masking Reagents and Their Mechanisms

1. **Cyanide (CN^-)**
   a. **Mechanism**: Cyanide forms very stable complexes with many metal ions such as zinc, copper, and cadmium, rendering them inert during the titration.
   b. **Example Reaction**:

$$Cu^{2+} + 4CN^- \rightarrow [Cu(CN)_4]^{2-}$$

c. **Application**: Masking copper and zinc ions in the presence of other metal ions.

2. **Triethanolamine (TEA)**

a. **Mechanism**: TEA forms stable complexes with iron and aluminum ions, preventing them from reacting with EDTA.

b. **Example Reaction**:

$$Fe^{3+} + 3(C_6H_{15}NO_3) \rightarrow [Fe(C_6H_{15}NO_3)_3]^{3+}$$

c. **Application**: Masking iron in the analysis of calcium and magnesium ions.

3. **Fluoride (F⁻)**

a. **Mechanism**: Fluoride forms strong complexes with aluminum, preventing its interference during the titration.

b. **Example Reaction**:

$$Al^{3+} + 6F^- \rightarrow [AlF_6]^{3-}$$

c. **Application**: Masking aluminum ions in the presence of other metal ions.

4. **Tartrate and Citrate Ions**

a. **Mechanism**: These ions form stable complexes with calcium and magnesium, preventing their reaction with EDTA.

b. **Example Reaction**:

$$Ca^{2+} + 2C_4H_4O_6^{2-} \rightarrow [Ca(C_4H_4O_6)_2]^{2-}$$

c. **Application**: Masking calcium and magnesium in the presence of other metal ions like zinc.

Demasking Reagents

Demasking reagents are used to release metal ions from their masked complexes, making them available for reaction with the titrant (EDTA). This process is necessary when you need to titrate a metal ion that was previously masked to avoid interference.

Common Demasking Reagents and Their Mechanisms

1. **Mercaptoacetic Acid (Thioglycolic Acid)**
   a. **Mechanism**: Breaks the stable cyanide complexes of metals like copper, zinc, and cadmium, freeing the metal ions for titration.
   b. **Example Reaction**:

   $$[Cu(CN)_4]^{2-} + 2HSCH_2COOH \rightarrow Cu^{2+} + 4CN^- + 2HSCH_2COO^-$$

   c. **Application**: Demasking of copper and zinc after their initial titration.
2. **Hydrochloric Acid (HCl)**
   a. **Mechanism**: Breaks down complexes like those formed by fluoride or cyanide, releasing the metal ions.
   b. **Example Reaction**:

   $$[AlF_6]^{3-} + 6H^+ \rightarrow Al^{3+} + 6HF$$

   c. **Application**: Demasking aluminum ions after masking with fluoride.
3. **Formaldehyde**
   a. **Mechanism**: Breaks down the complexes formed by triethanolamine, releasing metal ions such as iron.
   b. **Example Reaction**:

   $$[Fe(C_6H_{15}NO_3)_3]^{3+} + 3HCHO \rightarrow Fe^{3+} + 3(C_6H_{15}NO_3HCHO)$$

   c. **Application**: Demasking iron ions after initial masking.

Practical Example: Sequential Titration

Determination of Calcium and Magnesium in Water

1. **Masking Magnesium**:
   a. Add a masking agent like triethanolamine to the water sample to form a complex with magnesium ions.

b. Titrate the solution with EDTA to determine the calcium content, using Eriochrome Black T as the indicator.

2. **Demasking Magnesium**:

    a. Add a demasking agent (such as formaldehyde) to release magnesium ions from the complex.

    b. Continue titration with EDTA to determine the magnesium content.

Importance in Analytical Chemistry

1. **Selectivity**: Masking and demasking reagents allow for the selective titration of specific metal ions in the presence of others, enhancing the precision and accuracy of the analysis.
2. **Versatility**: These reagents expand the range of complexometric titrations to include mixtures of metal ions that would otherwise interfere with each other.
3. **Efficiency**: By selectively masking and demasking ions, complexometric titration can be performed more efficiently, reducing the need for multiple separate analyses.

Masking and demasking reagents are essential tools in complexometric titration, enabling the accurate and selective determination of metal ions in complex mixtures.

ESTIMATION OF MAGNESIUM SULPHATE

Estimating magnesium sulfate ($MgSO_4$) in complexometric titration typically involves titrating the magnesium ions with a standardized EDTA solution in the presence of a suitable metal ion indicator. Here's a detailed procedure for the estimation of magnesium sulfate using complexometric titration:

Procedure for Estimating Magnesium Sulfate

1. Preparation of Sample

a. **Weighing and Dissolving**: Weigh an accurately measured amount of magnesium sulfate ($MgSO_4$) into a volumetric flask.

b. **Dissolve**: Dissolve the $MgSO_4$ in distilled water to make a known volume of solution. This ensures a precise concentration for titration.

2. Preparation of Buffer Solution

a. **pH Adjustment**: Adjust the pH of the magnesium sulfate solution to around 10 using a suitable buffer solution. This pH is optimal for the formation of stable complexes between magnesium ions and EDTA.

3. Adding Metal Ion Indicator

a. **Selection of Indicator**: Choose a metal ion indicator that forms a stable complex with magnesium ions. Eriochrome Black T is commonly used, which forms a wine-red complex with magnesium ions at pH 10.

b. **Indicator Addition**: Add a few drops of Eriochrome Black T indicator solution to the magnesium sulfate solution. The solution should turn wine-red due to the formation of the magnesium-indicator complex.

4. Titration Process

a. **Standardization of EDTA**: Before titration, standardize the EDTA solution using a primary standard such as calcium carbonate ($CaCO_3$) to determine its exact concentration.

b. **Titration Setup**: Fill a burette with the standardized EDTA solution. Use a pipette to transfer a measured volume of the magnesium sulfate solution into a conical flask.

c. **Titration Procedure**: Titrate the magnesium sulfate solution with the EDTA solution, while swirling the flask to ensure thorough mixing.

d. **Endpoint Detection**: The endpoint is reached when the wine-red color of the magnesium-indicator complex changes to a pure blue color. This change occurs when all magnesium ions have reacted with EDTA, leaving the indicator free in its blue form.

5. Calculation of Magnesium Sulfate Concentration

a. **Calculation**: Calculate the concentration of magnesium sulfate in the original solution using the following formula:

$$\text{Moles of MgSO}_4 = \text{Moles of EDTA used} \times \frac{\text{Moles of Mg}^{2+}}{\text{Moles of EDTA}}$$

Where:

i. Moles of EDTA used is determined from the titration.

ii. Moles of Mg^{2+} is 1:1 with moles of EDTA used, assuming complete complexation.

b. **Convert to Mass**: Convert moles of $MgSO_4$ to mass if the initial mass of $MgSO_4$ used is known.

Considerations

1. **Precision**: Ensure accurate measurements of volumes and concentrations to achieve precise results.
2. **Indicator Choice**: The choice of indicator and pH control are critical for accurate endpoint detection.
3. **Standardization**: Properly standardize the EDTA solution to ensure reliable titration results.

Application

Estimating magnesium sulfate concentration is crucial in various industries, including agriculture (as a fertilizer), pharmaceuticals, and food processing. Complexometric titration provides a robust method for determining magnesium ions precisely, allowing for quality control and regulatory compliance in these sectors.

ESTIMATION OF CALCIUM GLUCONATE

Estimating calcium gluconate in complexometric titration involves titrating the calcium ions with a standardized EDTA solution in the presence of a suitable metal ion indicator. Here's a detailed procedure for the estimation of calcium gluconate using complexometric titration:

Procedure for Estimating Calcium Gluconate

1. Preparation of Sample

a. **Preparation**: Dissolve an accurately weighed amount of calcium gluconate in distilled water to make a known volume of solution. This ensures a precise concentration for titration.

2. **Preparation of Buffer Solution**

   a. **pH Adjustment**: Adjust the pH of the calcium gluconate solution to around 10 using an ammonia-ammonium chloride buffer solution. This pH is optimal for the formation of stable complexes between calcium ions and EDTA.

3. **Adding Metal Ion Indicator**

   a. **Selection of Indicator**: Choose a metal ion indicator that forms a stable complex with calcium ions. Eriochrome Black T is commonly used, which forms a wine-red complex with calcium ions at pH 10.

   b. **Indicator Addition**: Add a few drops of Eriochrome Black T indicator solution to the calcium gluconate solution. The solution should turn wine-red due to the formation of the calcium-indicator complex.

4. **Titration Process**

   a. **Standardization of EDTA**: Before titration, standardize the EDTA solution using a primary standard such as calcium carbonate ($CaCO_3$) to determine its exact concentration.

   b. **Titration Setup**: Fill a burette with the standardized EDTA solution. Use a pipette to transfer a measured volume of the calcium gluconate solution into a conical flask.

   c. **Titration Procedure**: Titrate the calcium gluconate solution with the EDTA solution, while swirling the flask to ensure thorough mixing.

   d. **Endpoint Detection**: The endpoint is reached when the wine-red color of the calcium-indicator complex changes to a pure blue color. This change occurs when all calcium ions have reacted with EDTA, leaving the indicator free in its blue form.

5. Calculation of Calcium Gluconate Concentration

a. **Calculation**: Calculate the concentration of calcium gluconate in the original solution using the following formula:

$$\text{Moles of CaGluconate} = \text{Moles of EDTA used} \times \frac{\text{Moles of Ca}^{2+}}{\text{Moles of EDTA}}$$

Where:

i. Moles of EDTA used is determined from the titration.

ii. Moles of Ca^{2+} is 1:1 with moles of EDTA used, assuming complete complexation.

b. **Convert to Mass**: Convert moles of calcium gluconate to mass if the initial mass of calcium gluconate used is known.

Considerations

1. **Precision**: Ensure accurate measurements of volumes and concentrations to achieve precise results.
2. **Indicator Choice**: The choice of indicator and pH control are critical for accurate endpoint detection.
3. **Standardization**: Properly standardize the EDTA solution to ensure reliable titration results.

Application

Estimating calcium gluconate concentration is important in pharmaceutical formulations and medical applications, where accurate dosage and formulation control are essential. Complexometric titration provides a robust method for determining calcium ions precisely, allowing for quality control and regulatory compliance in these sectors.

Multiple Choice Questions

1. What is the primary use of complexometric titration?
   a) Determining acidity levels
   b) Determining metal ion concentrations

c) Measuring pH
d) Determining sugar content

2. What is the most common chelating agent used in complexometric titrations?
   a) Cyanide
   b) Ammonia
   c) EDTA
   d) Hydrochloric acid
3. What role does the indicator play in complexometric titration?
   a) It reacts with the titrant to form a precipitate
   b) It signals the endpoint of the titration
   c) It dissolves the analyte
   d) It stabilizes the complex ion
4. Which indicator is commonly used in the determination of calcium and magnesium ions?
   a) Phenolphthalein
   b) Eriochrome Black T
   c) Methyl orange
   d) Bromothymol blue
5. At what pH is Eriochrome Black T effective in forming a complex with metal ions?
   a) pH 2
   b) pH 4
   c) pH 7
   d) pH 10
6. What is the endpoint detection in complexometric titration typically indicated by?
   a) Formation of a precipitate
   b) Temperature change
   c) Color change

d) pH change

7. What is the color change observed when using Eriochrome Black T as an indicator in a titration involving calcium and magnesium ions?
   a) Red to blue
   b) Blue to red
   c) Yellow to green
   d) Green to yellow
8. Which method involves adding an excess of EDTA to the metal ion solution and then titrating the excess with a second metal ion solution?
   a) Direct titration
   b) Back titration
   c) Indirect titration
   d) Potentiometric titration
9. What is the role of a buffer solution in complexometric titration?
   a) To dissolve the sample
   b) To maintain a constant pH
   c) To act as an indicator
   d) To form a precipitate
10. Which of the following is NOT a common metal ion indicator?
    a) Calmagite
    b) Murexide
    c) Phenolphthalein
    d) Xylenol Orange
11. What is the purpose of using masking reagents in complexometric titration?
    a) To enhance the color change of the indicator
    b) To selectively react with and mask certain metal ions
    c) To dissolve the analyte
    d) To maintain the pH
12. Which of the following is an example of a masking reagent?

a) Eriochrome Black T
b) Xylenol Orange
c) Triethanolamine (TEA)
d) Hydrochloric acid

13. What does the demasking reagent do in complexometric titration?
a) Forms a complex with the indicator
b) Releases metal ions from their masked complexes
c) Changes the pH of the solution
d) Forms a precipitate with the analyte

14. Which of the following is a demasking reagent?
a) Cyanide
b) Triethanolamine (TEA)
c) Mercaptoacetic acid (Thioglycolic acid)
d) Ammonia

15. In the estimation of magnesium sulfate, which indicator is commonly used?
a) Phenolphthalein
b) Calmagite
c) Eriochrome Black T
d) Murexide

16. What color change indicates the endpoint in the titration of magnesium sulfate with EDTA using Eriochrome Black T?
a) Yellow to blue
b) Blue to red
c) Wine red to blue
d) Green to yellow

17. In the estimation of calcium gluconate, what buffer solution is typically used?
a) Acetate buffer
b) Phosphate buffer

c) Ammonia-ammonium chloride buffer

d) Borate buffer

18. What pH is maintained during the titration of calcium gluconate with EDTA?

a) pH 2

b) pH 4

c) pH 7

d) pH 10

19. Which metal ion indicator turns yellow when the endpoint is reached in the titration of iron with EDTA?

a) Eriochrome Black T

b) Murexide

c) Xylenol Orange

d) Calmagite

20. What is the common application of complexometric titration in the food industry?

a) Measuring acidity

b) Determining sugar content

c) Determining metal content

d) Measuring pH

Short Answer Type Questions (Subjective)

1. Define complexometric titration and its primary use.
2. What is a complex ion and how is it formed?
3. Explain the role of a chelating agent in complexometric titration.
4. Why is EDTA commonly used as a titrant in complexometric titrations?
5. Describe the function of an indicator in complexometric titration.
6. How is the endpoint of a complexometric titration detected?
7. Why is the pH of the solution adjusted during a complexometric titration?

8. What is the significance of the formation constant (Kf) in complexometric titration?
9. Give an example of a common metal ion indicator used in complexometric titration.
10. Explain the procedure of a direct EDTA titration of calcium.
11. What is back titration and when is it used in complexometric titration?
12. How does a metal ion indicator work in detecting the endpoint of a titration?
13. What are masking reagents and why are they used in complexometric titrations?
14. Provide an example of a common masking reagent and its application.
15. What is the role of demasking reagents in complexometric titration?
16. Describe the procedure for estimating magnesium sulfate using complexometric titration.
17. How do you calculate the concentration of metal ions from the volume of EDTA used?
18. Why is it important to standardize the EDTA solution before titration?
19. Explain the significance of buffering the solution during a complexometric titration.
20. What are the applications of complexometric titration in environmental analysis?

Long Answer Type Questions (Subjective)

1. Discuss the principles and procedure of complexometric titration, highlighting the role of EDTA and indicators.
2. Explain the classification of complexometric titrations based on the type of titrant used, providing examples for each type.
3. Describe the different methods of endpoint detection in complexometric titration and discuss their advantages and disadvantages.

4. Explain the concept of masking and demasking in complexometric titration with suitable examples.
5. Discuss the procedure for estimating calcium and magnesium ions in water using complexometric titration.
6. Explain the classification of complexometric titrations based on the nature of the analyte and provide detailed examples.
7. Describe the importance of pH control in complexometric titration and the role of buffer solutions.
8. Discuss the mechanism of action of metal ion indicators in complexometric titration, providing examples of common indicators used.
9. Explain the procedure and calculations involved in estimating calcium gluconate using complexometric titration.
10. Discuss the applications of complexometric titration in pharmaceutical analysis, providing examples of specific metal impurities that can be determined using this technique.

Answer Key

1. b) Determining metal ion concentrations
2. c) EDTA
3. b) It signals the endpoint of the titration
4. b) Eriochrome Black
5. d) pH 10
6. c) Color change
7. a) Red to blue
8. b) Back titration
9. b) To maintain a constant pH
10. c) Phenolphthalein -
11. b) To selectively react with and mask certain metal ions
12. c) Triethanolamine (TEA)

13.b) Releases metal ions from their masked

14.c) Mercaptoacetic acid (Thioglycolic acid)

15.c) Eriochrome Black T

16.c) Wine red to blue

17.c) Ammonia-ammonium chloride buffer

18.d) pH 10

19.c) Xylenol Orange

20.c) Determining metal content

CHAPTER – 10

GRAVIMETRY

INTRODUCTION:

Gravimetry is a type of quantitative chemical analysis that measures the mass of a substance to determine its concentration or quantity in a sample. This method is based on the principle that certain compounds can be precipitated out of a solution, and the mass of these precipitates can be measured with high accuracy. Here's a detailed introduction to gravimetry:

Principles of Gravimetry

1. **Quantitative Precipitation**: The substance to be measured is converted into a compound that can be precipitated out of the solution. The precipitation reaction must be complete, meaning all of the analyte must be converted into the precipitate.
2. **Filtration and Washing**: The precipitate is filtered from the solution using filter paper or a sintered glass filter. It is then washed to remove any impurities or adhering ions that could affect the mass.
3. **Drying or Ignition**: The precipitate is dried to a constant mass or ignited to decompose the precipitate to a known stable form. This ensures that the mass measured is only due to the desired compound.
4. **Weighing**: The dried or ignited precipitate is weighed using an analytical balance with high precision.
5. **Calculations**: The mass of the precipitate is used to calculate the amount or concentration of the analyte in the original sample using stoichiometric relationships.

Types of Gravimetric Analysis

1. **Precipitation Gravimetry**: The analyte is converted to a sparingly soluble precipitate. For example, chloride ions can be precipitated as silver chloride ($AgCl$) using silver nitrate ($AgNO_3$).
2. **Volatilization Gravimetry**: The analyte is volatilized (converted to gas) and collected or removed. The remaining mass of the sample is measured to determine the amount of the volatilized analyte. For example, the determination of water content in a hydrate by heating it to drive off the water.

Steps in a Gravimetric Analysis

1. **Sample Preparation**: The sample is dissolved in a suitable solvent if it is not already in solution. The solution should be clear, and the analyte should be present in a known and suitable form for precipitation.
2. **Precipitation**: The precipitating reagent is added to the solution containing the analyte. The addition is usually done slowly with constant stirring to promote the formation of large, easily filterable particles. Conditions such as pH, temperature, and concentration must be controlled to ensure complete and selective precipitation.
3. **Digestion**: The precipitate is often allowed to "digest" by keeping it in the hot solution for some time. This helps in forming larger, purer crystals by re-dissolution and re-precipitation of smaller particles.
4. **Filtration and Washing**: The precipitate is separated from the solution using filtration. The filter cake is washed with a suitable solvent to remove impurities.
5. **Drying or Ignition**: The filtered precipitate is dried in an oven at a specific temperature or ignited in a furnace if the precipitate needs to be converted to a more stable form.
6. **Weighing**: The dried or ignited precipitate is weighed accurately using an analytical balance.

7. **Calculations**: The mass of the precipitate is used to calculate the quantity of the analyte in the original sample based on the stoichiometry of the precipitation reaction.

Advantages of Gravimetry

1. **High Accuracy and Precision**: Gravimetric methods are among the most accurate and precise analytical techniques.
2. **Simplicity and Low Cost**: The equipment required is simple and inexpensive.
3. **Absolute Method**: Gravimetry is often considered an absolute method because it directly measures the mass of the analyte without the need for calibration against a standard.

Disadvantages of Gravimetry

1. **Time-Consuming**: The process of precipitation, filtration, drying, or ignition and weighing can be time-consuming.
2. **Requires Skill**: Accurate results require careful execution of each step and attention to detail.
3. **Interference**: Other substances in the sample can interfere with the precipitation or cause co-precipitation, leading to errors.

Applications of Gravimetry

1. **Environmental Analysis**: Determination of pollutants in air and water.
2. **Pharmaceuticals**: Analysis of active ingredients in drugs.
3. **Materials Science**: Determination of composition and purity of materials.
4. **Geochemistry**: Analysis of minerals and ores.

Gravimetry remains a fundamental technique in analytical chemistry due to its robustness and reliability, despite the availability of more modern and faster methods.

PRINCIPLE OF GRAVIMETRIC ANALYSIS

Gravimetric analysis is based on the principle of measuring the mass of a substance to determine its quantity or concentration. In gravimetry, this involves converting the analyte into a pure, stable, and known compound that can be isolated and weighed accurately. Here is a detailed explanation of the principles involved in gravimetric analysis:

Fundamental Principles of Gravimetric Analysis

1. **Quantitative Conversion**:
    a. **Precipitation**: The analyte is converted into an insoluble precipitate by adding a suitable precipitating agent. This reaction should go to completion, ensuring that all the analyte is precipitated out of the solution.
    b. **Volatilization**: In some cases, the analyte is converted into a gaseous form, which can be collected or removed, and the residue or the gas is weighed.
2. **Pure and Stable Product**:
    a. The precipitate or the volatile product must be pure and stable under the conditions of the experiment. Any impurities or decomposition can lead to errors in the final mass measurement.
3. **Known Composition**:
    a. The chemical composition of the precipitate or volatile product must be known accurately. This is crucial for calculating the amount of the original analyte from the mass of the product.
4. **Complete Separation**:
    a. The precipitate must be completely separated from the solution through filtration. Any loss of the precipitate or incomplete precipitation can lead to inaccuracies.
5. **Accurate Weighing**:
    a. The final product is dried to a constant mass or ignited to a stable form and then weighed using a precise analytical balance. This step is critical as the mass measurement directly affects the accuracy of the analysis.

Detailed Steps and Principles

1. **Sample Preparation**:
   a. Dissolve the sample in an appropriate solvent to ensure the analyte is in a suitable form for the subsequent reactions.
   b. The solution should be clear, and the analyte should be fully dissolved to avoid incomplete precipitation.
2. **Precipitation**:
   a. Add a precipitating agent to the solution containing the analyte. This reagent reacts with the analyte to form an insoluble compound.
   b. The conditions such as pH, temperature, and concentration should be optimized to ensure complete and selective precipitation.
   c. Stir the solution to promote the formation of larger, purer precipitate particles, which are easier to filter.
3. **Digestion**:
   a. Allow the precipitate to "digest" by keeping it in the hot solution for some time. This step helps in recrystallizing smaller particles into larger ones, reducing impurities and improving the purity of the precipitate.
4. **Filtration and Washing**:
   a. Filter the precipitate using appropriate filtration methods (e.g., filter paper or sintered glass filters).
   b. Wash the precipitate thoroughly with a suitable solvent (often water or dilute acid) to remove any impurities or adhering ions that might affect the mass.
5. **Drying or Ignition**:
   a. Dry the precipitate to a constant mass in an oven or desiccator to remove any residual moisture.

b. Alternatively, ignite the precipitate in a furnace to convert it into a more stable form. This step is especially important for precipitates that might contain water of hydration or other volatile components.

6. **Weighing**:
    a. Weigh the dried or ignited precipitate accurately using an analytical balance.
    b. Ensure that the balance is calibrated, and the environment is controlled to avoid errors due to air currents, temperature changes, or static electricity.
7. **Calculations**:
    a. Use the mass of the precipitate to calculate the amount or concentration of the analyte in the original sample.
    b. Apply stoichiometric relationships based on the known chemical composition of the precipitate to determine the quantity of the analyte.

Example Calculation

To illustrate, let's consider the determination of chloride ions (Cl^-) in a sample using silver nitrate ($AgNO_3$) as the precipitating agent:

1. Dissolve the sample containing Cl^- in water.
2. Add an excess of $AgNO_3$ solution to the sample solution to precipitate AgCl:

$$Ag^+ + Cl^- \rightarrow AgCl(s)$$

3. Filter and wash the AgCl precipitate.
4. Dry the precipitate to a constant mass.
5. Weigh the dried AgCl.
6. Calculate the amount of Cl^- in the sample using the molar mass of AgCl and the stoichiometry of the reaction.

For example, if the mass of AgCl obtained is mmm grams:

$$\text{Amount of Cl}^- = \frac{m \times \text{Molar mass of Cl}}{\text{Molar mass of AgCl}}$$

Factors Affecting Gravimetric Analysis

1. **Solubility of the Precipitate**: The precipitate should have low solubility to ensure complete precipitation.
2. **Purity of the Precipitate**: Impurities can be co-precipitated, leading to errors.
3. **Particle Size**: Larger particles are easier to filter and wash, reducing contamination.
4. **Complete Reaction**: Ensure the reaction between the analyte and precipitating agent goes to completion.

Applications

Gravimetric analysis is used in various fields, including:

1. **Environmental Analysis**: Measuring pollutants in water and air.
2. **Pharmaceuticals**: Determining the active ingredients in drugs.
3. **Materials Science**: Assessing the purity and composition of materials.
4. **Geochemistry**: Analyzing minerals and ores for metal content.

STEPS INVOLVED IN GRAVIMETRIC ANALYSIS

Gravimetric analysis involves a series of systematic steps to determine the quantity of an analyte based on its mass. Here's a detailed explanation of the steps involved in gravimetric analysis:

Steps in Gravimetric Analysis

1. **Sample Preparation**:
    a. **Weighing**: Weigh an appropriate amount of the sample that contains the analyte you want to quantify. This weight should be accurately recorded to ensure precise calculations later.

b. **Dissolution**: Dissolve the sample in a suitable solvent to bring the analyte into solution. Ensure complete dissolution to avoid incomplete precipitation later.

2. **Precipitation**:
   a. **Choice of Precipitating Agent**: Select a precipitating agent that reacts specifically with the analyte to form a compound that is insoluble in the solvent used. The choice of precipitant depends on the nature of the analyte and its chemical properties.
   b. **Precipitation Reaction**: Add the precipitating agent to the sample solution. The reaction should be such that the precipitate formed is pure, easily filterable, and quantitative (i.e., all analyte must precipitate out).
   c. **Conditions Control**: Control factors such as pH, temperature, and concentration to ensure complete and selective precipitation. Stir the solution gently to promote the formation of larger, easily filterable particles.
3. **Digestion (Optional)**:
   a. **Digestion Time**: Allow the precipitate to "digest" in the hot solution for a specific period. This step helps in the growth of larger crystals and reduces the presence of impurities through re-precipitation.
   b. **Stirring**: Stir the solution during digestion to maintain homogeneity and promote crystal growth.
4. **Filtration**:
   a. **Filtering**: Filter the precipitate using a suitable filter paper or a sintered glass crucible to separate it from the solution.
   b. **Washing**: Wash the precipitate thoroughly with a small amount of solvent to remove any soluble impurities or excess reagent that may adhere to the precipitate.
5. **Drying or Ignition**:

a. **Drying**: Transfer the wet precipitate to an oven and dry it to a constant mass. This step removes any remaining solvent and ensures the precipitate's mass is accurately determined.
b. **Ignition**: In some cases, especially for inorganic compounds or compounds containing volatile components, ignite the precipitate in a furnace to convert it into a stable form (e.g., oxides).

6. **Weighing**:
   a. **Accurate Weighing**: Weigh the dried or ignited precipitate using an analytical balance with high precision. Record the mass accurately to four decimal places or better, depending on the sensitivity of the balance.
7. **Calculations**:
   a. **Stoichiometric Calculation**: Use the mass of the precipitate and its known chemical composition to calculate the amount of the analyte present in the original sample.
   b. **Molar Relationships**: Apply stoichiometric relationships based on the balanced chemical equation of the precipitation reaction to determine the quantity of analyte.
8. **Verification**:
   a. **Quality Control**: Perform quality control checks to ensure the accuracy and reliability of the results obtained.
   b. **Repeatability**: If necessary, repeat the analysis to ensure reproducibility and validate the findings.

Example Scenario

To illustrate, consider the determination of sulfate ions (SO_4^{2-}) in a sample using barium chloride ($BaCl_2$) as the precipitating agent:

1. **Sample Preparation**: Weigh a sample containing sulfate ions and dissolve it in water.
2. **Precipitation**: Add excess $BaCl_2$ solution to precipitate $BaSO_4$:

$$Ba^{2+} + SO_4^{2-} \rightarrow BaSO_4(s)$$

3. **Filtration and Washing**: Filter the $BaSO_4$ precipitate and wash it with water to remove any soluble impurities.
4. **Drying**: Dry the $BaSO_4$ precipitate in an oven to remove water.
5. **Weighing**: Weigh the dried $BaSO_4$ precipitate using an analytical balance.
6. **Calculations**: Calculate the amount of sulfate ions in the sample based on the mass of $BaSO_4$ precipitate and the stoichiometry of the reaction.

Advantages and Limitations

1. **Advantages**:
    a. High precision and accuracy.
    b. Applicable across various industries and fields.
    c. Provides quantitative data on the analyte's concentration.
2. **Limitations**:
    a. Time-consuming compared to some modern analytical techniques.
    b. Requires careful control of experimental conditions.
    c. Susceptible to errors from impurities and incomplete reactions.

PURITY OF THE PRECIPITATE

In gravimetric analysis, the purity of the precipitate is crucial because it directly impacts the accuracy and reliability of the final analytical results. Here's a detailed explanation of what purity of the precipitate entails and how it is ensured:

Importance of Purity in Gravimetric Analysis

1. **Accuracy of Results**:
    a. The mass of the precipitate is used to calculate the amount of the analyte in the original sample. Any impurities in the precipitate will lead to overestimation or underestimation of the analyte concentration.
2. **Precision**:

a. Impurities can affect the consistency and reproducibility of the analysis. A pure precipitate ensures that each measurement reflects the true amount of analyte present.

3. **Interferences**:

   a. Impurities can co-precipitate with the analyte, leading to errors in quantification. They can also affect the physical properties of the precipitate, such as solubility and stability.

Ensuring Purity of the Precipitate

1. **Selective Precipitation**:

   a. Choose a precipitating agent that forms a specific and insoluble compound with the analyte. This helps in selective precipitation and minimizes the inclusion of impurities.

2. **Digestion and Aging**:

   a. Allow the precipitate to "digest" or age in the solution for a specific period. This process promotes the growth of larger, purer crystals by re-dissolving and re-precipitating smaller particles. It helps in improving the purity of the precipitate.

3. **Filtration and Washing**:

   a. Use appropriate filtration techniques to separate the precipitate from the solution. Filter paper or sintered glass filters are commonly used.

   b. Wash the precipitate thoroughly with a suitable solvent (e.g., water or dilute acid) to remove soluble impurities, excess reagents, or ions that might adhere to the surface of the precipitate.

4. **Drying or Ignition**:

   a. Dry the precipitate to a constant mass in an oven or desiccator. This step removes residual solvent and ensures that the mass measured is only due to the precipitate itself, not any trapped water.

b. In cases where the precipitate is to be converted into a more stable form, ignite it in a furnace to drive off volatile components and convert it into a stable oxide or other form.

5. **Quality Control Checks**:
   a. Perform quality control checks throughout the process to monitor the purity of the precipitate.
   b. Use analytical techniques such as gravimetry itself, spectroscopy, or chromatography to verify the absence of impurities and the purity of the final product.

Factors Affecting Purity

1. **Solubility of the Precipitate**:
   a. Choose a precipitate with low solubility in the solvent used. This ensures that the precipitate remains intact and does not dissolve back into the solution during washing or drying.
2. **Reaction Conditions**:
   a. Optimize reaction conditions such as pH, temperature, and concentration to maximize the yield and purity of the precipitate.
3. **Handling and Storage**:
   a. Minimize contamination during handling and storage of the precipitate. Use clean equipment and containers to avoid introducing impurities.

Example Application

For instance, in the determination of chloride ions (Cl^-) using silver nitrate ($AgNO_3$) as the precipitating agent:

1. Silver chloride (AgCl) is formed as a white precipitate:

$$Ag^+ + Cl^- \rightarrow AgCl(s)$$

2. Ensure that the AgCl precipitate is thoroughly washed to remove any soluble silver ions or other contaminants that could affect its purity.

Conclusion

The purity of the precipitate in gravimetric analysis is maintained through careful selection of precipitating agents, thorough washing, proper drying or ignition, and meticulous quality control checks. These steps are essential to ensure accurate and reliable quantitative results in analytical chemistry.

CO-PRECIPITATION AND POST PRECIPITATION

In gravimetric analysis, co-precipitation and post-precipitation are phenomena that can significantly impact the accuracy and reliability of the analytical results. Understanding these concepts is crucial for ensuring the purity of the precipitate and thus the accuracy of the final quantification of the analyte. Let's delve into each of these in detail:

Co-Precipitation

Co-precipitation refers to the undesired inclusion of impurities or contaminants in the precipitate along with the analyte of interest. This occurs when substances other than the intended analyte are incorporated into the precipitate due to physical or chemical interactions during the precipitation process. Co-precipitation can lead to overestimation or underestimation of the analyte concentration if not properly controlled.

Mechanisms of Co-Precipitation

1. **Adsorption**: Impurities may adsorb onto the surface of the precipitate particles, especially if they have similar properties (e.g., surface charge or hydrophobicity).
2. **Inclusion**: Small particles of impurities may become trapped within the crystal lattice or structure of the precipitate during its formation.
3. **Occlusion**: Impurities may be physically enclosed or embedded within the precipitate particles as they form, making them difficult to remove by washing.

Ways to Minimize Co-Precipitation

1. **Selective Precipitation**: Choose a precipitating agent that forms a precipitate selectively with the analyte and not with other substances present in the solution.
2. **Digestion or Aging**: Allow the precipitate to age or "digest" in the solution for a period. This can promote the growth of larger, purer crystals and reduce the inclusion of impurities.
3. **Optimize Reaction Conditions**: Control parameters such as pH, temperature, and concentration to ensure complete and selective precipitation of the analyte.
4. **Thorough Washing**: Wash the precipitate thoroughly with a suitable solvent to remove any loosely bound impurities or contaminants that may have adhered to the surface of the precipitate.
5. **Use of Masking Agents**: Sometimes, masking agents are used to complex with interfering ions in solution, preventing their co-precipitation with the analyte.

Post-Precipitation

Post-precipitation refers to the phenomenon where additional precipitation occurs after the main precipitation reaction is completed. This can happen due to changes in the solution conditions or the introduction of new reagents after the initial precipitation step.

Causes of Post-Precipitation

1. **Changes in Solubility**: Solubility of the precipitate can change with temperature, pH, or the addition of complexing agents, leading to re-precipitation.
2. **Secondary Reactions**: Secondary reactions may occur that lead to the formation of new precipitates or the redissolution and re-precipitation of the initial precipitate.

Control of Post-Precipitation

1. **Stabilize Solution Conditions**: Maintain stable and appropriate solution conditions (pH, temperature) throughout the analysis to minimize changes that could induce post-precipitation.
2. **Avoid Introduction of New Reagents**: Once the main precipitation is complete, avoid introducing new reagents that could alter the chemical equilibrium and induce further precipitation reactions.

Importance in Gravimetric Analysis

Both co-precipitation and post-precipitation can introduce systematic errors into gravimetric analysis results by affecting the purity of the precipitate. These errors can lead to inaccurate quantification of the analyte and undermine the reliability of the analytical data. Therefore, careful control of these phenomena through proper experimental design, technique, and attention to detail is essential to ensure accurate and precise results in gravimetric analysis.

Example Application

For instance, in the determination of chloride ions (Cl^-) using silver nitrate ($AgNO_3$) as the precipitating agent:

1. Co-precipitation may occur if other ions in the sample, such as bromide (Br^-), also precipitate as silver bromide (AgBr) due to their similar reactivity with Ag^+ ions.
2. Post-precipitation could occur if the pH of the solution changes after initial precipitation, leading to additional precipitation of silver ions as hydroxides or carbonates.

ESTIMATION OF BARIUM SULPHATE

Estimating barium sulfate ($BaSO_4$) in gravimetric analysis involves determining the amount of $BaSO_4$ precipitate formed from a sample containing barium ions (Ba^{2+}) and sulfate ions (SO_4^{2-}). Here's a detailed step-by-step process for the gravimetric estimation of barium sulfate:

Steps for Estimating Barium Sulfate in Gravimetry

1. **Sample Preparation**:
   a. Weigh an appropriate amount of the sample containing barium ions (Ba^{2+}) and sulfate ions (SO_4^{2-}). Record the mass accurately.
2. **Precipitation of Barium Sulfate**:
   a. Transfer the sample into a suitable beaker or flask and dissolve it in distilled water or a suitable solvent if necessary.
   b. Add an excess of a precipitating agent to the sample solution. Commonly used precipitating agents for $BaSO_4$ include sodium sulfate (Na_2SO_4) or sodium carbonate (Na_2CO_3) solutions.
   c. The reaction can be represented as:

$$Ba^{2+} + SO_4^{2-} \rightarrow BaSO_4(s)$$

   d. Stir the solution to ensure thorough mixing and to facilitate the precipitation of $BaSO_4$. The precipitation should be complete and selective, with all Ba^{2+} ions reacting to form $BaSO_4$.
3. **Digestion (Optional)**:
   a. Allow the precipitate to age or "digest" in the solution for a specific period. This helps in the formation of larger and purer $BaSO_4$ crystals by re-dissolving and re-precipitating smaller particles.
4. **Filtration and Washing**:
   a. Filter the $BaSO_4$ precipitate using a suitable filter paper or a sintered glass crucible. Wash the precipitate thoroughly with distilled water or a dilute acid (e.g., dilute hydrochloric acid) to remove any soluble impurities or excess reagent.
5. **Drying**:
   a. Transfer the washed $BaSO_4$ precipitate onto a weighed filter paper or into a pre-weighed crucible.

b. Dry the precipitate to a constant mass in an oven at a specified temperature (usually around 110-120°C). Ensure that all moisture is removed to obtain a stable and reproducible mass.

6. **Ignition (Optional)**:
   a. If necessary, ignite the dried $BaSO_4$ precipitate in a furnace at a high temperature (usually around 800-900°C). This step converts $BaSO_4$ into barium oxide (BaO), which may be desired for certain applications or to remove any organic impurities.
7. **Weighing**:
   a. After drying or ignition, cool the crucible or filter paper with the $BaSO_4$ precipitate to room temperature in a desiccator.
   b. Weigh the crucible or filter paper containing the $BaSO_4$ precipitate using an analytical balance with high precision. Record the mass accurately.
8. **Calculations**:
   a. Calculate the amount of $BaSO_4$ precipitate formed based on its mass. Use the stoichiometry of the precipitation reaction to determine the amount of barium ions (Ba^{2+}) in the original sample.
9. For example, if mBaSO4 is the mass of $BaSO_4$ obtained:

$$\text{Amount of Ba}^{2+} = \frac{m_{\text{BaSO}_4} \times \text{Molar mass of BaSO}_4}{\text{Molar mass of Ba}^{2+}}$$

Ensure to consider the stoichiometry of the reaction and the molar masses of $BaSO_4$ and Ba^{2+} accurately.

Quality Control and Verification

1. Perform quality control checks throughout the analysis to ensure the accuracy and reliability of the results.
2. Repeat the analysis if necessary to confirm the reproducibility of the gravimetric determination.

3. Use calibration standards or reference materials to validate the analytical procedure and results.

Applications

Gravimetric estimation of barium sulfate is widely used in various industries and fields, including environmental analysis, pharmaceuticals, and materials science. It provides accurate and precise quantification of barium ions in samples, ensuring compliance with regulatory standards and quality control requirements.

Multiple Choice Questions (MCQs)

1. What is the primary principle of gravimetric analysis?

   a) Measuring volume

   b) Measuring mass

   c) Measuring temperature

   d) Measuring pH

2. In gravimetric analysis, what is the purpose of drying the precipitate to a constant mass? a) To remove impurities

   b) To ensure accurate mass measurement

   c) To change the chemical composition

   d) To increase the precipitate size

3. Which step involves adding a precipitating agent to the solution containing the analyte?

   a) Digestion

   b) Filtration

   c) Precipitation

   d) Weighing

4. What is a common method to ensure the purity of the precipitate in gravimetric analysis? a) Increasing the temperature

   b) Washing with a suitable solvent

c) Adding more sample

d) Decreasing the pH

5. Which of the following is NOT a type of gravimetric analysis?

a) Precipitation gravimetry

b) Volatilization gravimetry

c) Chromatography

d) Filtration gravimetry

6. What is the role of digestion in gravimetric analysis?

a) To dissolve the precipitate

b) To promote the formation of larger, purer crystals

c) To filter the solution

d) To weigh the precipitate

7. In the estimation of barium sulfate, what is the reaction that occurs when barium ions react with sulfate ions?

a) Ba2++SO42−→BaSO4(s)

b) Ba2++Cl−→BaCl2(s)

c) Ba2++NO3−→Ba(NO3)2(s)

d) Ba2++OH−→Ba(OH)2(s)

8. What is the purpose of using an analytical balance in gravimetric analysis?

a) To dissolve the sample

b) To accurately measure the mass of the precipitate

c) To filter the precipitate

d) To dry the precipitate

9. Which of the following factors does NOT affect the purity of the precipitate in gravimetric analysis?

a) Temperature control

b) Solubility of the precipitate

c) Color of the precipitate

d) Washing of the precipitate

10. What is co-precipitation in the context of gravimetric analysis?

a) Precipitation of only the desired analyte

b) Inclusion of impurities in the precipitate

c) Loss of precipitate during filtration

d) Measurement of the precipitate's mass

11. Which of the following methods can minimize co-precipitation?

a) Increasing the reaction temperature

b) Using a masking agent

c) Reducing the sample size

d) Adding more precipitating agent

12. What is post-precipitation in gravimetric analysis?

a) Precipitation that occurs after the main precipitation reaction

b) Loss of precipitate during washing

c) Dissolution of the precipitate

d) Measurement of the precipitate's mass

13. Why is thorough washing of the precipitate important in gravimetric analysis?

a) To increase the precipitate's size

b) To remove impurities and excess reagents

c) To dry the precipitate

d) To dissolve the sample

14. Which of the following is a disadvantage of gravimetric analysis?

a) High precision and accuracy

b) Time-consuming process

c) Low cost

d) Simplicity

15. What is the final step in gravimetric analysis before calculations are performed?

a) Drying

b) Filtration

c) Weighing

d) Digestion

16. In gravimetric analysis, which property of the precipitate is crucial for accurate results?

    a) Color

    b) Mass

    c) Solubility

    d) Shape

17. How is the mass of the analyte calculated in gravimetric analysis?

    a) By measuring the volume of the solution

    b) By using the mass of the precipitate and stoichiometry

    c) By measuring the temperature

    d) By using a pH meter

18. What is the purpose of using a sintered glass filter in gravimetric analysis?

    a) To dissolve the sample

    b) To filter the precipitate

    c) To dry the precipitate

    d) To weigh the precipitate

19. In the estimation of barium sulfate, what is the formula for calculating the amount of barium ions?

    a) mBaSO4×Molar mass of Ba2+/Molar mass of BaSO4

    b) mBaSO4×Molar mass of SO42−/Molar mass of BaSO4

    c) mBaSO4×Molar mass of BaSO4/Molar mass of Ba2+

    d) mBaSO4×Molar mass of Ba2+/Molar mass of SO42−

20. What is the importance of controlling the pH during the precipitation step in gravimetric analysis?

    a) To increase the sample size

    b) To ensure selective and complete precipitation

c) To change the color of the precipitate

d) To increase the temperature of the solution

Short Answer Type Questions

1. What is gravimetry?
2. What are the basic principles of gravimetric analysis?
3. How is the analyte typically precipitated in gravimetric analysis?
4. What is the purpose of drying or igniting the precipitate in gravimetric analysis?
5. Name two types of gravimetric analysis.
6. What is the importance of washing the precipitate in gravimetric analysis?
7. What does the term 'quantitative precipitation' mean in the context of gravimetric analysis?
8. Why is it important to control the pH during the precipitation step?
9. What are some common applications of gravimetric analysis?
10. Explain co-precipitation in gravimetric analysis.
11. What is post-precipitation, and why can it be problematic in gravimetric analysis?
12. How is the mass of the precipitate typically measured in gravimetric analysis?
13. Why is selective precipitation important for the purity of the precipitate?
14. Describe the digestion step in gravimetric analysis.
15. What role does an analytical balance play in gravimetric analysis?
16. Why is stoichiometry important in gravimetric calculations?
17. What factors can affect the solubility of the precipitate?
18. Explain the term 'complete separation' in the context of gravimetric analysis.
19. Why might a precipitate be ignited in a furnace during gravimetric analysis?
20. How can the purity of a precipitate be verified in gravimetric analysis?

Long Answer Type Questions

1. Describe the detailed steps involved in a typical gravimetric analysis, from sample preparation to calculation of the analyte quantity.
2. Explain the principles of gravimetric analysis and how they ensure accurate and reliable quantitative measurements.
3. Discuss the factors that can affect the purity of the precipitate in gravimetric analysis and how to control these factors.
4. Compare and contrast co-precipitation and post-precipitation, including their causes and how they can be minimized.
5. Outline the process for estimating barium sulfate ($BaSO_4$) in a sample using gravimetric analysis.
6. What are the advantages and disadvantages of gravimetric analysis compared to other analytical techniques?
7. Explain how the mass of the analyte is calculated using stoichiometry in gravimetric analysis, providing an example calculation.
8. Discuss the importance of accurate weighing in gravimetric analysis and the measures taken to ensure precise measurements.
9. Describe the applications of gravimetric analysis in environmental science, pharmaceuticals, and materials science.
10. Explain the role of filtration and washing in gravimetric analysis and how they contribute to the accuracy and reliability of the results.

Answer Key

1. b) Measuring mass
2. b) To ensure accurate mass measurement
3. c) Precipitation
4. b) Washing with a suitable solvent
5. c) Chromatography
6. b) To promote the formation of larger, purer crystals

7. a) $Ba^{2+} + SO_4^{2-} \rightarrow BaSO_4(s)$
8. b) To accurately measure the mass of the precipitate
9. c) Color of the precipitate
10. b) Inclusion of impurities in the precipitate
11. b) Using a masking agent
12. a) Precipitation that occurs after the main precipitation reaction
13. b) To remove impurities and excess reagents
14. b) Time-consuming process
15. c) Weighing
16. b) Mass
17. b) By using the mass of the precipitate and stoichiometry
18. b) To filter the precipitate
19. a) $m_{BaSO_4} \times \text{Molar mass of } Ba^{2+} / \text{Molar mass of } BaSO_4$
20. b) To ensure selective and complete precipitation

CHAPTER – 11

DIAZOTIZATION

INTRODUCTION:

Diazotization is a chemical reaction in which a primary aromatic amine (aniline or its derivatives) reacts with nitrous acid (generated in situ from sodium nitrite and a mineral acid such as hydrochloric acid) to form a diazonium salt. This reaction is significant in organic synthesis, especially in the preparation of azo dyes and other aromatic compounds. Here's a detailed introduction to the diazotization process:

Mechanism of Diazotization

1. **Formation of Nitrous Acid (HNO_2):**
    a. Nitrous acid is not typically available in a pure form but is generated in situ by reacting sodium nitrite ($NaNO_2$) with a strong acid like hydrochloric acid (HCl).
    b. The reaction is:
        i. $$NaNO_2 + HCl \rightarrow HNO_2 + NaCl$$
2. **Reaction of the Amine with Nitrous Acid:**
    a. The primary aromatic amine ($ArNH_2$) reacts with nitrous acid to form the diazonium ion (ArN_2^+).
    b. This process involves several steps:
        i. **Protonation of Nitrous Acid:** \
        $$HNO_2 + H^+ \rightarrow H_2NO_2^+$$
        ii. **Formation of Nitrosyl Cation:**
        $$H_2NO_2^+ \rightarrow NO^+ + H_2O$$
        iii. **Reaction with the Amine:**

$$ArNH_2 + NO^+ \rightarrow ArNH\text{-}NO^+$$

iv. **Formation of the Diazonium Ion:**

$$ArNH\text{-}NO^+ \rightarrow ArN_2^+ + H_2O$$

Conditions and Procedure

1. **Temperature Control:**
   a. The diazotization reaction is typically carried out at low temperatures (0-5°C) to stabilize the diazonium ion and prevent decomposition.
2. **Preparation:**
   a. Dissolve the aromatic amine in a dilute acid solution (usually HCl or H_2SO_4).
   b. Cool the solution in an ice bath to maintain a low temperature.
   c. Slowly add a cold solution of sodium nitrite, ensuring continuous stirring and temperature control.

Applications of Diazotization

1. **Azo Coupling:**
   a. Diazotization is often followed by coupling with phenols or aromatic amines to form azo compounds (ArN=NAr'), which are widely used as dyes and pigments.
   b. Example:

$$ArN_2^+ + Ar'OH \rightarrow ArN{=}NAr' + H^+$$

2. **Sandmeyer Reaction:**
   a. The diazonium group can be replaced by various substituents using copper salts (CuX) in the Sandmeyer reaction to form halides, cyanides, or other derivatives.
   b. Example:

$$ArN_2^+ + CuCl \rightarrow ArCl + N_2 + Cu^+$$

3. **Replacement Reactions:**
    a. The diazonium group can be replaced by hydrogen (reduction), fluorine (via the Schiemann reaction), or hydroxyl (via hydrolysis) to synthesize various substituted aromatic compounds.

Safety and Precautions

1. **Stability of Diazonium Salts:**
    a. Diazonium salts are generally unstable and can decompose explosively, especially at higher temperatures.
    b. Proper temperature control and handling precautions are essential.
2. **Handling Nitrous Acid:**
    a. Nitrous acid is a potent oxidizer and should be handled with care.
    b. Proper ventilation and protective equipment (gloves, goggles) are necessary.

Example of Diazotization Reaction

Preparation of Benzene Diazonium Chloride:

1. Dissolve aniline ($C_6H_5NH_2$) in dilute hydrochloric acid.
2. Cool the solution to 0-5°C.
3. Add a cold solution of sodium nitrite ($NaNO_2$) dropwise while maintaining the temperature.
4. The resulting benzene diazonium chloride ($C_6H_5N_2Cl$) can be used for further reactions.

BASIC PRINCIPLES OF DIAZOTIZATION

Diazotization is a critical reaction in organic chemistry involving the conversion of primary aromatic amines into diazonium salts. Understanding the basic principles underlying this process is essential for its application in synthesis. Here are the fundamental principles of diazotization:

Basic Principles of Diazotization

1. **Primary Aromatic Amines:**

a. Diazotization is specific to primary aromatic amines ($ArNH_2$), where "Ar" denotes an aromatic ring such as benzene.

2. **Generation of Nitrous Acid:**
   a. Nitrous acid (HNO_2) is not stable and is generated in situ by reacting a nitrite salt (typically sodium nitrite, $NaNO_2$) with a mineral acid (such as hydrochloric acid, HCl).
   b. The reaction is:

$$NaNO_2 + HCl \rightarrow HNO_2 + NaCl$$

3. **Formation of Diazonium Salts:**
   a. The primary aromatic amine reacts with nitrous acid to form a diazonium salt ($ArN_2^+X^-$), where X^- is usually a halide like Cl^- or Br^-.
   b. The general reaction is:

$$ArNH_2 + HNO_2 + HX \rightarrow ArN_2^+X^- + 2H_2O$$

4. **Mechanism:**
   a. **Protonation of Nitrous Acid:**

$$HNO_2 + H^+ \rightarrow H_2NO_2^+$$

   b. **Formation of Nitrosyl Cation:**

$$H_2NO_2^+ \rightarrow NO^+ + H_2O$$

   c. **Reaction with Amine:**

$$ArNH_2 + NO^+ \rightarrow ArNH\text{-}NO^+$$

   d. **Formation of Diazonium Ion:**

$$ArNH\text{-}NO^+ \rightarrow ArN_2^+ + H_2O$$

Conditions for Diazotization

1. **Temperature Control:**

a. Diazotization reactions are generally performed at low temperatures (0-5°C) to stabilize the diazonium salts and prevent their decomposition.

2. **Acidic Medium:**

a. A strong acid (like HCl or H_2SO_4) is necessary to protonate nitrous acid and facilitate the formation of the nitrosyl cation (NO^+).

3. **Stoichiometry:**

a. Precise stoichiometric amounts of the primary amine, sodium nitrite, and acid are crucial for a successful diazotization reaction.

Applications of Diazotization

1. **Azo Coupling Reactions:**

a. Diazotized aromatic amines can couple with phenols or aromatic amines to form azo compounds (ArN=NAr'), which are widely used as dyes.

b. Example:

$$ArN_2^+ + Ar'OH \rightarrow ArN{=}NAr' + H^+$$

2. **Sandmeyer Reaction:**

a. Diazotization followed by the Sandmeyer reaction allows the introduction of various substituents into the aromatic ring.

b. Example:

$$ArN_2^+ + CuCl \rightarrow ArCl + N_2 + Cu^+$$

3. **Replacement Reactions:**

a. The diazonium group can be replaced by other groups, such as hydroxyl (ArOH) via hydrolysis or fluorine (ArF) via the Schiemann reaction.

Safety and Handling

1. **Stability of Diazonium Salts:**

a. Diazonium salts are generally unstable and can decompose explosively, especially at higher temperatures.
b. Proper temperature control and safe handling practices are essential.

2. **Handling Nitrous Acid:**
   a. Nitrous acid is a strong oxidizer and should be handled with appropriate safety measures, including the use of personal protective equipment (gloves, goggles) and good ventilation.

Example of Diazotization Procedure

Preparation of Benzene Diazonium Chloride:

1. **Dissolve Aniline:**
   a. Dissolve aniline ($C_6H_5NH_2$) in dilute hydrochloric acid.
2. **Cooling:**
   a. Cool the solution in an ice bath to maintain a temperature of 0-5°C.
3. **Add Sodium Nitrite:**
   a. Slowly add a cold solution of sodium nitrite ($NaNO_2$) while stirring continuously and maintaining the temperature.
4. **Formation of Diazonium Salt:**
   a. Benzene diazonium chloride ($C_6H_5N_2Cl$) forms in the solution and can be used for further reactions or isolated if required.

METHODS OF DIAZOTIZATION

Diazotization can be performed through several methods depending on the specific requirements and nature of the aromatic amine being used. Here, we'll discuss the detailed methods of diazotization, including their procedures, advantages, and potential applications.

Methods of Diazotization

1. **Classical Method**
2. **Alkaline Method**
3. **Continuous Flow Method**
4. **Microwave-Assisted Diazotization**

5. **Photochemical Diazotization**

1. Classical Method

Procedure:

1. **Preparation of the Aromatic Amine Solution:**
    a. Dissolve the primary aromatic amine in dilute hydrochloric acid (or another suitable mineral acid).
2. **Cooling:**
    a. Place the solution in an ice bath to maintain a temperature of 0-5°C.
3. **Generation of Nitrous Acid:**
    a. Prepare a separate cold solution of sodium nitrite ($NaNO_2$).
4. **Addition of Sodium Nitrite:**
    a. Slowly add the sodium nitrite solution to the aromatic amine solution while stirring continuously. The temperature must be kept low to stabilize the diazonium salt.
5. **Formation of Diazonium Salt:**
    a. The diazonium salt forms in the solution and can be used immediately for further reactions or precipitated if needed.

Advantages:

1. Simple and widely used.
2. Suitable for a variety of aromatic amines.

Applications:

1. Synthesis of azo dyes.
2. Intermediate in Sandmeyer reactions.

2. Alkaline Method

Procedure:

1. **Preparation of the Aromatic Amine Solution:**
    a. Dissolve the primary aromatic amine in water.
2. **Addition of Sodium Nitrite:**
    a. Add a solution of sodium nitrite to the aromatic amine solution.

3. **Alkaline Environment:**
    a. Maintain the solution at a slightly alkaline pH by adding a small amount of sodium hydroxide.
4. **Acidification:**
    a. Gradually add a mineral acid (such as hydrochloric acid) to the solution, ensuring the temperature remains low (0-5°C).
5. **Formation of Diazonium Salt:**
    a. The diazonium salt forms under these conditions.

Advantages:

1. Useful for amines that are unstable in acidic conditions.
2. Can be performed with less stringent temperature control.

Applications:

1. Preparation of diazonium salts from sensitive aromatic amines.

3. Continuous Flow Method

Procedure:

1. **Setup:**
    a. Use a continuous flow reactor system where solutions of the aromatic amine, sodium nitrite, and acid are continuously pumped into the reactor.
2. **Reaction:**
    a. The diazotization reaction occurs within the flow reactor, typically equipped with a cooling system to maintain the desired temperature.
3. **Collection:**
    a. The diazonium salt solution is collected at the outlet of the reactor.

Advantages:

1. Suitable for large-scale industrial synthesis.
2. Improved safety and control over reaction conditions.
3. Enhanced mixing and heat transfer.

Applications:

1. Large-scale production of diazonium salts for dyes and pharmaceuticals.

4. Microwave-Assisted Diazotization

Procedure:

1. **Preparation of the Aromatic Amine Solution:**
    a. Dissolve the primary aromatic amine in a suitable solvent with acid and sodium nitrite.
2. **Microwave Irradiation:**
    a. Place the solution in a microwave reactor and apply microwave irradiation for a short period (usually a few minutes).
3. **Formation of Diazonium Salt:**
    a. The reaction rapidly forms the diazonium salt due to the efficient heating and mixing provided by microwaves.

Advantages:

1. Significantly reduced reaction time.
2. Enhanced yields and purity.
3. Energy-efficient.

Applications:

1. Rapid synthesis of diazonium salts for research and development purposes.

5. Photochemical Diazotization

Procedure:

1. **Preparation of the Aromatic Amine Solution:**
    a. Dissolve the primary aromatic amine in a solvent with a source of nitrite.
2. **Irradiation:**
    a. Expose the solution to UV light or another suitable light source.
3. **Formation of Diazonium Salt:**
    a. The photochemical energy promotes the formation of nitrosyl cation (NO^+) and subsequently the diazonium ion (ArN_2^+).

Advantages:

1. Mild reaction conditions.
2. Potential for selective activation.

Applications:

1. Synthesis of diazonium salts for photochemistry and material science applications.

APPLICATION OF DIAZOTIZATION

Diazotization is a highly versatile reaction in organic chemistry with numerous applications across various fields. The formation of diazonium salts from aromatic amines opens up a range of subsequent reactions and applications, particularly in the synthesis of dyes, pharmaceuticals, and advanced materials. Here are detailed applications of diazotization:

Applications of Diazotization

1. Azo Dye Synthesis
2. Sandmeyer Reaction
3. Replacement Reactions
4. Synthesis of Aryl Halides
5. Synthesis of Aryl Nitriles
6. Preparation of Phenols
7. Synthesis of Fluorobenzenes
8. Organic Synthesis Intermediates
9. Pharmaceutical Applications

1. Azo Dye Synthesis

Description:

a. Azo dyes are synthesized by coupling diazonium salts with phenols or aromatic amines. The resulting azo compounds (ArN=NAr') are widely used as dyes due to their vivid colors.

Procedure:

1. Prepare the diazonium salt from a primary aromatic amine via diazotization.

2. Couple the diazonium salt with a phenol or an aromatic amine in a basic medium.

Example:

$$ArN_2^+ + Ar'OH \rightarrow ArN{=}NAr' + H^+$$

Applications:

a. Textile dyes
b. Food colorants
c. Pigments in inks and paints

2. Sandmeyer Reaction

Description:

a. The Sandmeyer reaction involves the substitution of the diazonium group with various nucleophiles using copper(I) salts as catalysts.

Procedure:

1. Prepare the diazonium salt from a primary aromatic amine.
2. React the diazonium salt with a copper(I) salt (e.g., CuCl, CuBr) to introduce the desired substituent.

Example:

$$ArN_2^+ + CuCl \rightarrow ArCl + N_2 + Cu^+$$

Applications:

a. Synthesis of aryl halides
b. Introduction of functional groups like cyanides (ArCN) and thiols (ArSH)

3. Replacement Reactions

Description:

a. Diazotization can be followed by replacement reactions to substitute the diazonium group with various other groups, expanding the versatility of the method.

Applications:

Hydrolysis to Phenols:

$$ArN_2^+ + H_2O \rightarrow ArOH + N_2 + H^+$$

Reduction to Aryl Hydrogens:

$$ArN_2^+ + H_3PO_2 \rightarrow ArH + N_2 + H_3PO_3$$

Application Example:

a. Preparation of phenols from anilines

4. Synthesis of Aryl Halides

Description:

a. Aryl halides can be synthesized by replacing the diazonium group with halides using appropriate halide salts or acids.

Procedure:

1. Prepare the diazonium salt from a primary aromatic amine.
2. React the diazonium salt with halide ions (Cl^-, Br^-, I^-).

Example:

$$ArN_2^+ + HCl \rightarrow ArCl + N_2 + H^+$$

Applications:

a. Synthesis of chloro-, bromo-, and iodo-benzenes
b. Intermediates for further chemical transformations

5. Synthesis of Aryl Nitriles

Description:

a. Aryl nitriles are synthesized by reacting diazonium salts with cuprous cyanide (CuCN).

Procedure:

1. Prepare the diazonium salt from a primary aromatic amine.
2. React the diazonium salt with CuCN to form the aryl nitrile.

Example:

$$ArN_2^+ + CuCN \rightarrow ArCN + N_2 + Cu^+$$

Applications:

a. Synthesis of benzonitriles, which are valuable intermediates in organic synthesis and pharmaceuticals.

6. Preparation of Phenols

Description:

a. Phenols can be prepared from diazonium salts through hydrolysis.

Procedure:

1. Prepare the diazonium salt from a primary aromatic amine.
2. Heat the diazonium salt in an aqueous solution to form the phenol.

Example:

$$ArN_2^+ + H_2O \rightarrow ArOH + N_2 + H^+$$

Applications:

a. Synthesis of phenolic compounds used in resins, plastics, and pharmaceuticals.

7. Synthesis of Fluorobenzenes

Description:

a. Fluorobenzenes are synthesized using the Schiemann reaction, where the diazonium salt reacts with tetrafluoroborate.

Procedure:

1. Prepare the diazonium salt from a primary aromatic amine.
2. React the diazonium salt with fluoroboric acid (HBF_4) to form the fluorobenzene.

Example:

$$ArN_2^+ + HBF_4 \rightarrow ArF + N_2 + BF_3 + H^+$$

Applications:

a. Synthesis of fluorinated aromatic compounds for pharmaceuticals and agrochemicals.

8. Organic Synthesis Intermediates

Description:

a. Diazonium salts serve as versatile intermediates in organic synthesis, allowing the introduction of various functional groups into the aromatic ring.

Applications:

a. Building blocks for complex organic molecules
b. Synthesis of heterocycles and other aromatic compounds

9. Pharmaceutical Applications

Description:

a. Diazotization and subsequent reactions are used in the synthesis of various pharmaceuticals, particularly in the introduction of functional groups and the construction of aromatic systems.

Applications:

a. Synthesis of active pharmaceutical ingredients (APIs)
b. Intermediate steps in the production of drugs like sulfa drugs, antihistamines, and more.

Multiple Choice Questions (MCQs)

1. What is diazotization?
    a) A reaction involving alkyl halides
    b) A reaction involving primary aromatic amines and nitrous acid
    c) A reduction reaction of aldehydes
    d) A polymerization reaction
2. What compound is typically used to generate nitrous acid in situ for diazotization?

a) Sodium chloride
b) Sodium nitrite
c) Sodium sulfate
d) Sodium hydroxide

3. What is the main product formed when a primary aromatic amine reacts with nitrous acid?
   a) Azo compound
   b) Diazonium salt
   c) Phenol
   d) Aniline
4. Which of the following acids is commonly used in the diazotization reaction?
   a) Acetic acid
   b) Sulfuric acid
   c) Hydrochloric acid
   d) Nitric acid
5. At what temperature range is the diazotization reaction typically carried out to stabilize the diazonium ion?
   a) 25-30°C
   b) 0-5°C
   c) 50-60°C
   d) -10-0°C
6. What is the first step in the mechanism of diazotization?
   a) Formation of nitrosyl cation
   b) Reaction with the amine
   c) Protonation of nitrous acid
   d) Formation of diazonium ion
7. Which of the following is an application of diazotization?
   a) Formation of alcohols

b) Synthesis of azo dyes

c) Polymerization of ethylene

d) Hydrogenation of alkenes

8. What is the Sandmeyer reaction used for?

a) Synthesis of azo dyes

b) Introduction of various substituents into the aromatic ring

c) Formation of ethers

d) Hydrolysis of esters

9. Which ion is involved in the Schiemann reaction for the synthesis of fluorobenzenes?

a) Cl^-

b) NO_3^-

c) BF_4^-

d) SO_4^{2-}

10. What is the major safety concern when handling diazonium salts?

a) They are highly toxic

b) They can decompose explosively

c) They emit harmful gases

d) They cause corrosion

11. Which method of diazotization is suitable for large-scale industrial synthesis?

a) Classical method

b) Alkaline method

c) Continuous flow method

d) Photochemical diazotization

12. What is an advantage of microwave-assisted diazotization?

a) Longer reaction time

b) Reduced reaction time

c) Less energy-efficient

d) Higher temperatures required

13. What type of medium is required for the classical method of diazotization?

a) Basic medium

b) Neutral medium

c) Acidic medium

d) Alkaline medium

14. What is the product when a diazonium salt reacts with a phenol?

a) Aniline

b) Azo compound

c) Halobenzene

d) Phenol

15. What is formed in the reaction between benzene diazonium chloride and copper chloride (CuCl)?

a) Benzene diazonium nitrate

b) Benzene

c) Chlorobenzene

d) Bromobenzene

16. What is the key intermediate in the synthesis of aryl nitriles using diazonium salts?

a) CuCl

b) CuCN

c) NaOH

d) H_2SO_4

17. Which reaction involves the hydrolysis of diazonium salts to form phenols?

a) Sandmeyer reaction

b) Schiemann reaction

c) Hydrolysis reaction

d) Reduction reaction

18. What is the outcome of the reduction of diazonium salts with hypophosphorous acid (H_3PO_2)?
    a) Phenol formation
    b) Azo dye formation
    c) Aryl halide formation
    d) Aryl hydrogen formation
19. Which reaction involves the coupling of diazonium salts with aromatic amines?
    a) Sandmeyer reaction
    b) Azo coupling reaction
    c) Schiemann reaction
    d) Reduction reaction
20. What is a common application of diazonium salts in the pharmaceutical industry?
    a) Synthesis of polymers
    b) Intermediate steps in drug production
    c) Preparation of alkyl halides
    d) Production of sulfuric acid

Short Answer Type Questions (Subjective)

1. What is diazotization?
2. Describe the process of generating nitrous acid in situ for diazotization.
3. What is the role of temperature control in the diazotization reaction?
4. Write the general reaction for the formation of diazonium salts.
5. Explain the protonation step in the mechanism of diazotization.
6. What is the significance of azo coupling in diazotization?
7. Describe the Sandmeyer reaction and its importance.
8. What are the safety precautions required while handling diazonium salts?
9. How is benzene diazonium chloride prepared from aniline?

10. Why are primary aromatic amines specifically used in diazotization reactions?
11. What is the importance of using a strong acid in diazotization?
12. Explain the alkaline method of diazotization.
13. What are the advantages of microwave-assisted diazotization?
14. Describe the photochemical diazotization method.
15. How are azo dyes synthesized using diazonium salts?
16. What is the role of copper salts in the Sandmeyer reaction?
17. How are aryl halides synthesized using diazonium salts?
18. Explain the Schiemann reaction for the synthesis of fluorobenzenes.
19. Describe the replacement reactions involving diazonium salts.
20. What are the applications of diazonium salts in pharmaceutical synthesis?

Long Answer Type Questions (Subjective)

1. Describe in detail the mechanism of diazotization, including all the intermediate steps and the final formation of the diazonium ion.
2. Discuss the conditions required for a successful diazotization reaction and explain why each condition is important.
3. Explain the various applications of diazotization in organic synthesis, highlighting the significance of azo dye synthesis and the Sandmeyer reaction.
4. Describe the continuous flow method of diazotization. What are its advantages and applications in industrial synthesis?
5. Compare and contrast the classical method and the alkaline method of diazotization, discussing the advantages and disadvantages of each.
6. Explain the procedure and advantages of microwave-assisted diazotization. How does it improve the efficiency of the diazotization process?
7. Discuss the safety and handling precautions required when working with diazonium salts and nitrous acid. Why are these precautions necessary?

8. Describe the synthesis of aryl nitriles using diazonium salts. Include the reaction mechanism and its applications in organic synthesis.
9. Explain how phenols are prepared from diazonium salts through hydrolysis. What are the practical applications of this reaction?
10. Discuss the role of diazonium salts as intermediates in the pharmaceutical industry, providing examples of drugs synthesized using diazotization and subsequent reactions.

Answer Key

1. b) A reaction involving primary aromatic amines and nitrous acid
2. b) Sodium nitrite
3. b) Diazonium salt
4. c) Hydrochloric acid
5. b) 0-5°C
6. c) Protonation of nitrous acid
7. b) Synthesis of azo dyes
8. b) Introduction of various substituents into the aromatic ring
9. c) BF_4^-
10. b) They can decompose explosively
11. c) Continuous flow method
12. b) Reduced reaction time
13. c) Acidic medium
14. b) Azo compound
15. c) Chlorobenzene
16. b) CuCN
17. c) Hydrolysis reaction
18. d) Aryl hydrogen formation
19. b) Azo coupling reaction
20. b) Intermediate steps in drug production

CHAPTER – 12

REDOX TITRATIONS

INTRODUCTION:

Redox titrations, also known as oxidation-reduction titrations, are a type of titration based on a redox reaction between the analyte and the titrant. These titrations are used to determine the concentration of an unknown solution by reacting it with a solution of known concentration.

Principles of Redox Titrations

1. **Oxidation-Reduction Reactions**:
   a. **Oxidation**: Loss of electrons.
   b. **Reduction**: Gain of electrons.
   c. Redox reactions involve the transfer of electrons from the oxidizing agent to the reducing agent.
2. **Oxidizing and Reducing Agents**:
   a. **Oxidizing Agent**: The substance that gains electrons (is reduced).
   b. **Reducing Agent**: The substance that loses electrons (is oxidized).
3. **Redox Potential**:
   a. Each redox couple has a specific potential, and the difference in potential drives the redox reaction.
   b. The Nernst equation can be used to calculate the electrode potential of a half-cell.
4. **Equivalence Point**:
   a. The point at which the amount of titrant added is stoichiometrically equivalent to the quantity of analyte in the sample.
   b. At this point, the number of electrons lost by the reducing agent equals the number of electrons gained by the oxidizing agent.

Types of Redox Titrations

1. **Direct Redox Titration**:

a. Involves direct addition of titrant to the analyte solution.

b. Example: Titration of iron(II) with potassium permanganate.

2. **Back Titration**:

a. An excess of a standard solution of a reagent is added to the analyte. The remaining excess reagent is then titrated with another standard solution.

b. Used when the endpoint is more easily detected with a different reagent.

Common Redox Titrants

1. **Potassium Permanganate ($KMnO_4$)**:

a. A strong oxidizing agent, often used in acidic medium.

b. Indicator itself due to its deep purple color.

2. **Potassium Dichromate ($K_2Cr_2O_7$)**:

a. Another strong oxidizing agent, usually used in acidic medium.

b. Requires an external indicator like diphenylamine.

3. **Iodine (I_2)**:

a. Used as an oxidizing agent in titrations involving reducing agents.

b. Starch is often used as an indicator, forming a blue complex with iodine.

4. **Sodium Thiosulfate ($Na_2S_2O_3$)**:

a. A common reducing agent used in iodometric titrations.

b. Reacts with iodine to form iodide ions, which is colorless.

Indicators in Redox Titrations

1. **Starch**: Used in iodometric titrations. Forms a blue-black complex with iodine, which disappears at the endpoint.

2. **Diphenylamine**: Used in dichromate titrations. Changes color from green to violet at the endpoint.

3. **Redox Indicators**: These are substances that change color at a particular electrode potential.

Procedures for Redox Titrations

1. **Preparation**:
    a. Prepare the analyte solution and the titrant.
    b. Choose a suitable indicator or use a self-indicating titrant.
2. **Standardization**:
    a. Standardize the titrant solution using a primary standard.
3. **Titration**:
    a. Add the titrant to the analyte solution until the equivalence point is reached.
    b. Monitor the color change of the indicator or the solution itself.
4. **Calculation**:
    a. Calculate the concentration of the analyte using the volume of titrant added and the stoichiometry of the redox reaction.

Applications of Redox Titrations

1. **Determination of Iron Content**:
    a. Iron in ores can be analyzed by titration with potassium permanganate.
2. **Analysis of Bleaching Agents**:
    a. Sodium hypochlorite (bleach) can be titrated with sodium thiosulfate to determine its concentration.
3. **Determination of Vitamin C**:
    a. Vitamin C (ascorbic acid) can be titrated with iodine.
4. **Environmental Analysis**:
    a. Measurement of dissolved oxygen in water bodies using iodometric titration.

CONCEPTS OF OXIDATION AND REDUCTION

In the context of redox titrations, oxidation and reduction are fundamental concepts that drive the titration process. Here's a detailed explanation of these concepts as they relate to redox titrations:

Oxidation and Reduction in Redox Titrations

1. Oxidation (Oxidizing Agent):

a. **Definition**: Oxidation refers to the loss of electrons by a species during a chemical reaction.

b. **In Redox Titrations**: The substance acting as the oxidizing agent gains electrons from the analyte, causing the analyte to lose electrons.

c. **Example**: In the titration of iron(II) ions with potassium permanganate ($KMnO_4$), iron(II) ions are oxidized to iron(III) ions, while permanganate ions (MnO_4^-) are reduced to manganese(II) ions (Mn^{2+}).

2. Reduction (Reducing Agent):

a. **Definition**: Reduction refers to the gain of electrons by a species during a chemical reaction.

b. **In Redox Titrations**: The substance acting as the reducing agent loses electrons to the titrant, causing the titrant to gain electrons.

c. **Example**: In the titration of potassium dichromate ($K_2Cr_2O_7$) with ferrous ammonium sulfate ($Fe(NH_4)_2(SO_4)_2$), the dichromate ions ($Cr_2O_7^{2-}$) are reduced to chromium(III) ions (Cr^{3+}), while the iron(II) ions are oxidized to iron(III) ions.

Key Points:

a. **Redox Reaction**: Redox titrations are based on redox reactions where one species is oxidized and another is reduced.

b. **Equivalence Point**: At the equivalence point of a redox titration, the moles of electrons transferred from the reducing agent (analyte) equal the moles of electrons accepted by the oxidizing agent (titrant).

c. **Indicators**: Indicators in redox titrations often change color based on the redox state of the solution, indicating when the reaction is complete.

Practical Applications:

a. **Quantitative Analysis**: Redox titrations are widely used for quantitative analysis of substances that can undergo oxidation or reduction reactions.

b. **Standardization**: Titrants such as potassium permanganate, potassium dichromate, and iodine are often standardized against primary standards before use in titrations.

c. **Environmental Monitoring**: Redox titrations can be used in environmental monitoring to determine levels of pollutants, such as dissolved oxygen in water.

TYPES OF REDOX TITRATIONS

Redox titrations encompass several types, each tailored to different analytical needs and reactions. Here are the main types of redox titrations commonly used:

1. Direct Redox Titration

a. **Definition**: Involves the direct reaction between the analyte and the titrant.

b. **Application**: Used when the reaction between the analyte and titrant proceeds rapidly and is easily detectable.

c. **Example**: Titration of ferrous ions (Fe^{2+}) with potassium permanganate ($KMnO_4$) in acidic medium, where Fe^{2+} is oxidized to Fe^{3+} and MnO_4^- is reduced to Mn^{2+}.

2. Back Titration

a. **Definition**: Involves adding an excess of a standard titrant to the analyte and then titrating the excess titrant with another standard solution.

b. **Application**: Used when the endpoint of the direct titration is difficult to observe or when the reaction rate is slow.

c. **Example**: Determination of the concentration of hydrogen peroxide (H_2O_2) by titrating the excess potassium permanganate with ferrous ammonium sulfate.

3. Iodometric (Iodimetric) Titration

a. **Definition**: Uses iodine (I_2) as a titrant or as an indicator in a redox reaction.

b. **Application**: Commonly used to determine reducing agents such as sulfite, thiosulfate, and hydrogen peroxide.
c. **Example**: Determination of ascorbic acid (Vitamin C) content in a solution by titrating it with iodine.

4. Dichromate Titration

a. **Definition**: Involves the use of potassium dichromate ($K_2Cr_2O_7$) as a titrant.
b. **Application**: Used to determine reducing agents in acidic medium.
c. **Example**: Determination of iron (II) ions in a sample using potassium dichromate, where Fe^{2+} is oxidized to Fe^{3+} and dichromate ($Cr_2O_7^{2-}$) is reduced to chromium (III) ions.

5. Permanganate Titration

a. **Definition**: Uses potassium permanganate ($KMnO_4$) as a titrant.
b. **Application**: Commonly used for oxidizing agents or substances that can be easily oxidized in acidic medium.
c. **Example**: Titration of oxalate ions ($C_2O_4^{2-}$) with potassium permanganate, where oxalate is oxidized to carbon dioxide and permanganate ions are reduced to manganese dioxide (MnO_2).

6. Titration with Sodium Thiosulfate

a. **Definition**: Involves using sodium thiosulfate ($Na_2S_2O_3$) as a titrant.
b. **Application**: Used in iodometric titrations to determine the concentration of iodine or substances that react with iodine.
c. **Example**: Determination of chlorine content in water by titrating excess iodine with sodium thiosulfate.

PRINCIPLES OF CERIMETRY

Cerimetry is a technique used in redox titrations that involves the use of cerium(IV) sulfate ($Ce(SO_4)_2$) as a titrant. It is based on the redox reaction between cerium(IV) ions (Ce^{4+}) and the analyte, typically a reducing agent. Here are the key principles of cerimetry:

1. **Cerium(IV) Ion as a Titrant**:
   a. Cerium(IV) sulfate ($Ce(SO_4)_2$) is commonly used as the titrant in cerimetry.
   b. Cerium(IV) ions are strong oxidizing agents and can readily accept electrons from reducing agents.
2. **Redox Reaction**:
   a. The principle involves the redox reaction between cerium(IV) ions and the analyte.
   b. Cerium(IV) ions are reduced to cerium(III) ions (Ce^{3+}) during the titration process, while the analyte undergoes oxidation.
3. **Indicator Systems**:
   a. Cerimetry often employs indicator systems to detect the endpoint of the titration.
   b. Common indicators include dyes or complexes that change color when cerium(IV) ions are completely reduced to cerium(III) ions.
4. **Equivalence Point**:
   a. The equivalence point is reached when all the cerium(IV) ions have reacted with the analyte.
   b. At this point, the amount of cerium(IV) ions added is stoichiometrically equivalent to the amount of reducing agent (analyte) present.
5. **Calculation of Analyte Concentration**:
   a. The concentration of the analyte can be calculated based on the volume of cerium(IV) titrant used and the stoichiometry of the reaction.
   b. Typically, a primary standard of known concentration is used to standardize the cerium(IV) titrant before performing the titration.

Example of Cerimetry:

An example of cerimetry involves the determination of iron(II) ions (Fe^{2+}) in a sample using cerium(IV) sulfate as the titrant:

1. **Reaction**:

$$Ce^{4+} + Fe^{2+} \rightarrow Ce^{3+} + Fe^{3+}$$

2. **Procedure**:
    a. Prepare a solution of cerium(IV) sulfate.
    b. Standardize the cerium(IV) solution using a primary standard.
    c. Add the cerium(IV) solution to the analyte containing iron(II) ions until the color change indicates the endpoint.
    d. Calculate the concentration of iron(II) ions based on the volume of cerium(IV) solution used.

Advantages of Cerimetry:

1. **Selective**: Cerimetry can be selective for certain analytes based on their reducing properties.
2. **Sensitive**: It can be sensitive to low concentrations of analytes, especially when using indicator systems.
3. **Versatile**: Cerimetry can be applied to various types of samples and analytes with appropriate adjustments.

Cerimetry is a valuable technique in analytical chemistry, offering precise and reliable determination of analyte concentrations through careful control of redox reactions involving cerium(IV) ions.

APPLICATIONS OF CERIMETRY

Cerimetry, a technique utilizing cerium(IV) sulfate as a titrant in redox titrations, finds application in various analytical contexts due to its specific properties and advantages. Here are some key applications of cerimetry in redox titrations:

1. Determination of Iron in Iron Ores

a. **Application**: Cerimetry is commonly used to determine the iron content in iron ores.
b. **Principle**: Iron(II) ions (Fe^{2+}) in the ore sample are oxidized to iron(III) ions (Fe^{3+}) by cerium(IV) ions (Ce^{4+}).
c. **Procedure**:
    i. The iron ore sample is dissolved and the iron ions are complexed to prevent interference.
    ii. Cerium(IV) sulfate is titrated against the iron solution until the endpoint is reached, indicated by a color change.
d. **Advantages**: Cerimetry offers a reliable method for accurately determining iron content in ores, which is crucial for quality control in the iron and steel industry.

2. Analysis of Reducing Agents in Pharmaceutical Formulations

a. **Application**: Cerimetry is used to quantify reducing agents in pharmaceutical formulations.
b. **Principle**: Pharmaceutical formulations often contain reducing agents that can be titrated with cerium(IV) ions.
c. **Procedure**:
    i. The formulation is dissolved and prepared for titration.
    ii. Cerium(IV) sulfate is added until the endpoint, often signaled by a change in color due to an indicator.
d. **Advantages**: It provides a sensitive and selective method for assessing the concentration of reducing agents in pharmaceutical products, ensuring product quality and compliance with regulatory standards.

3. Environmental Monitoring of Redox-Active Species

a. **Application**: Cerimetry is applied in environmental chemistry to monitor redox-active species in water and soil samples.
b. **Principle**: Redox-active species such as manganese, iron, and organic compounds can be quantified using cerimetry.

c. **Procedure**:

   i. Water or soil samples are prepared and treated to release the redox-active species.

   ii. Cerium(IV) sulfate is titrated against the sample until the endpoint, indicated by a change in color or potential.

d. **Advantages**: It offers a robust method for assessing the presence and concentration of redox-active pollutants, contributing to environmental management and remediation efforts.

4. Quality Control in Food and Beverage Industry

a. **Application**: Cerimetry is utilized in the food and beverage industry to determine antioxidant concentrations.

b. **Principle**: Antioxidants, which are reducing agents, can be quantified using cerium(IV) titration.

c. **Procedure**:

   i. Food or beverage samples are prepared and treated to extract antioxidants.

   ii. Cerium(IV) sulfate solution is added until the endpoint is reached, indicated by a color change or other suitable indicator.

d. **Advantages**: It provides a reliable method for assessing antioxidant levels in food products, ensuring product stability and compliance with food safety regulations.

PRINCIPLES OF IODIMETRY

Iodimetry is a type of redox titration that involves the use of iodine (I_2) or iodide ions (I^-) as the titrant. This technique is particularly useful for determining substances that can be oxidized by iodine under acidic conditions. Here are the key principles of iodimetry:

1. Oxidation by Iodine (I_2):

a. **Iodine as Oxidizing Agent**: Iodine is a strong oxidizing agent in acidic medium, capable of oxidizing many substances.

b. **Reaction**: Iodine can oxidize substances that are easily reducible, such as sulfite ions (SO_3^{2-}), thiosulfate ions ($S_2O_3^{2-}$), and ascorbic acid (Vitamin C).

c. **Example Reaction**: The oxidation of ascorbic acid by iodine can be represented as:

$$C_6H_8O_6 + I_2 \rightarrow C_6H_6O_6 + 2I^- + 2H^+$$

2. Redox Reaction in Iodimetry:

a. **Iodine and Iodide Ions**: Iodine (I_2) in the presence of excess iodide ions (I^-) can exist in equilibrium:

$$I_2 + 2I^- \rightleftharpoons I_3^-$$

b. **Titration**: During titration, iodine or iodide ions react with the analyte. The iodine concentration is determined by a suitable indicator or by back-titration with a standard solution of sodium thiosulfate ($Na_2S_2O_3$).

3. Endpoint Detection:

a. **Starch-Iodine Complex**: A common indicator used in iodimetry is starch, which forms a deep blue complex with iodine.

b. **Color Change**: The endpoint of the titration is detected when the starch-iodine complex changes from blue to colorless, indicating that all the analyte has reacted with iodine.

4. Standardization of Iodine Solution:

a. **Primary Standard**: Before use, the iodine solution is standardized against a primary standard, such as sodium thiosulfate ($Na_2S_2O_3$), which is weighed accurately and dissolved to a known concentration.

b. **Back Titration**: Alternatively, the iodine solution can be standardized by back-titrating it with a known concentration of sodium thiosulfate after reacting it with a known amount of a standard reducing agent.

5. Applications of Iodimetry:

a. **Determination of Reducing Agents**: Iodimetry is widely used for the determination of substances that can reduce iodine, such as ascorbic acid (Vitamin C) in pharmaceuticals and food products.

b. **Analysis of Sulfur Compounds**: It is also used to quantify sulfur compounds, such as sulfites and thiosulfates, in environmental and industrial samples.

c. **Measurement of Dissolved Oxygen**: In environmental monitoring, iodimetry can be employed to determine dissolved oxygen levels in water samples.

6. Advantages:

a. **Selective**: Iodimetry is selective for substances that react specifically with iodine or iodide ions under acidic conditions.

b. **Sensitive**: It can detect low concentrations of analytes due to the highly visible endpoint with starch as an indicator.

c. **Versatile**: Iodimetry can be adapted for various types of samples and analytes, making it a versatile technique in analytical chemistry.

APPLICATIONS OF IODIMETRY

Iodimetry, a specific type of redox titration utilizing iodine (I_2) or iodide ions (I^-) as a titrant, finds diverse applications in analytical chemistry due to its selective oxidation properties and reliable endpoint detection. Here are some key applications of iodimetry in redox titrations:

1. Determination of Ascorbic Acid (Vitamin C)

a. **Application**: Iodimetry is widely used to determine the concentration of ascorbic acid (Vitamin C) in pharmaceuticals, food products, and biological samples.

b. **Principle**: Ascorbic acid is a reducing agent that can readily react with iodine under acidic conditions:

$$C_6H_8O_6 + I_2 \rightarrow C_6H_6O_6 + 2I^- + 2H^+$$

c. **Procedure**: The sample containing ascorbic acid is titrated with iodine solution until the starch-iodine complex turns from blue to colorless, indicating the endpoint.

d. **Advantages**: Provides a precise method for quantifying the antioxidant properties of Vitamin C in various products, ensuring compliance with regulatory standards.

2. Analysis of Sulfite and Thiosulfate

a. **Application**: Iodimetry is used for the determination of sulfite (SO_3^{2-}) and thiosulfate ($S_2O_3^{2-}$) ions in environmental samples, food processing, and water treatment industries.

b. **Principle**: Sulfite and thiosulfate are reducing agents that react with iodine to form sulfate ions and iodide ions:

$$SO_3^{2-} + 2I_2 + 2H^+ \rightarrow SO_4^{2-} + 2I^- + H_2O$$

c. **Procedure**: The sample is treated to release sulfite or thiosulfate ions, followed by titration with iodine until the starch-iodine complex indicates the endpoint.

d. **Advantages**: Offers a reliable method for monitoring sulfite and thiosulfate levels in industrial processes and environmental samples, ensuring compliance with safety and quality standards.

3. Determination of Dissolved Oxygen in Water

a. **Application**: Iodimetry is employed to measure dissolved oxygen levels in water samples, crucial for assessing water quality in environmental monitoring.

b. **Principle**: Dissolved oxygen oxidizes iodide ions (I^-) to iodine (I_2) under acidic conditions:

$$O_2 + 2I^- + 2H^+ \rightarrow I_2 + H_2O$$

c. **Procedure**: Water samples are treated with an acidic solution containing iodide ions, and the liberated iodine is titrated with a standard sodium thiosulfate solution.

d. **Advantages**: Provides a quantitative measure of dissolved oxygen levels, critical for assessing aquatic ecosystem health and compliance with regulatory standards.

4. Analysis of Reducing Sugars in Food Products

a. **Application**: Iodimetry is used to determine the concentration of reducing sugars (e.g., glucose, fructose) in food products, including honey, fruit juices, and syrups.

b. **Principle**: Reducing sugars react with iodine under acidic conditions, leading to the formation of iodide ions and a color change in the starch-iodine complex.

c. **Procedure**: The sample is hydrolyzed and treated with excess iodine, and the remaining iodine is titrated with sodium thiosulfate until the starch-iodine complex turns colorless.

d. **Advantages**: Offers a reliable method for quantifying reducing sugar content in food products, ensuring accurate labeling and quality control.

PRINCIPLES OF IODOMETRY

Iodometry is a type of redox titration that involves the use of iodide ions (I^-) as the titrant. It is distinct from iodimetry, where iodine (I_2) is the titrant. Here are the key principles of iodometry in redox titrations:

1. Oxidation of Iodide Ions (I^-):

a. **Iodide as Reducing Agent**: In iodometry, iodide ions act as reducing agents.

b. **Reaction**: Iodide ions can be oxidized by strong oxidizing agents, such as:

$$2I^- \rightarrow I_2 + 2e^-$$

c. **Example**: The oxidation of iodide ions by a strong oxidizing agent like potassium permanganate ($KMnO_4$) in acidic medium:

$$5I^- + 2MnO_4^- + 16H^+ \rightarrow 5I_2 + 2Mn^{2+} + 8H_2O$$

2. Redox Titration Principle:

a. **Titration Setup**: The analyte containing the oxidizing agent is titrated with iodide ions in the presence of an appropriate indicator.

b. **Endpoint**: The endpoint is typically detected by a color change due to the formation of iodine (I_2) or by a starch-iodine complex, which turns blue.

c. **Equivalence Point**: At the equivalence point, the moles of iodide ions added are stoichiometrically equivalent to the moles of the oxidizing agent present in the analyte.

3. Indicator Systems:

a. **Starch-Iodine Complex**: A common indicator used in iodometry is starch, which forms a blue complex with iodine.

b. **Color Change**: The endpoint is signaled by the disappearance of the blue color of the starch-iodine complex.

4. Standardization of Iodine Solution:

a. **Primary Standard**: Before use, the iodine solution is standardized against a primary standard, typically sodium thiosulfate ($Na_2S_2O_3$), which is weighed accurately and dissolved to a known concentration.

b. **Back Titration**: Alternatively, the iodine solution can be standardized by back-titrating it with a known concentration of sodium thiosulfate after reacting it with a known amount of a standard reducing agent.

5. Applications of Iodometry:

a. **Quantification of Oxidizing Agents**: Iodometry is used to determine the concentration of various oxidizing agents in samples, such as:

i. **Potassium Permanganate ($KMnO_4$)**: Used for quantitative analysis in water treatment, food industry, and environmental monitoring.
ii. **Chlorine (Cl_2)**: Used in the analysis of bleach and disinfectants.
iii. **Nitrites (NO_2^-)**: Used in food and environmental samples.

b. **Analysis of Pharmaceuticals**: It is employed in the pharmaceutical industry to determine the concentration of drugs containing oxidizing agents or impurities.

6. Advantages:

a. **Selective**: Iodometry is selective for substances that can oxidize iodide ions under acidic conditions.
b. **Sensitive**: It can detect low concentrations of oxidizing agents due to the highly visible endpoint with starch as an indicator.
c. **Versatile**: Iodometry can be adapted for various types of samples and analytes, making it a versatile technique in analytical chemistry.

APPLICATIONS OF IODOMETRY

Iodometry, a type of redox titration that uses iodide ions (I^-) as the titrant, finds diverse applications across different fields of analytical chemistry. Here are some key applications of iodometry in redox titrations:

1. Determination of Oxidizing Agents

a. **Application**: Iodometry is widely used to quantify oxidizing agents in various samples, including industrial, environmental, and pharmaceutical applications.
b. **Examples**:
   i. **Potassium Permanganate ($KMnO_4$)**: Used to determine its concentration in water treatment processes and industrial applications where $KMnO_4$ is used as an oxidizing agent.
   ii. **Chlorine (Cl_2)**: Used in the analysis of disinfectants and bleach solutions.

iii. **Nitrites (NO_2^-)**: Used in food industry to monitor nitrite levels in food products.

c. **Procedure**: The sample containing the oxidizing agent is titrated with iodide ions in acidic medium. The endpoint is detected using a starch-iodine indicator system, where the blue starch-iodine complex turns colorless upon completion of the reaction.

d. **Advantages**: Provides a reliable and quantitative method for assessing the concentration of oxidizing agents, ensuring product quality and regulatory compliance.

2. Analysis of Pharmaceuticals

a. **Application**: Iodometry is used in the pharmaceutical industry to determine the concentration of drugs containing oxidizing agents or to assess the purity of pharmaceutical formulations.

b. **Examples**:

i. **Determination of Drug Content**: Quantification of active pharmaceutical ingredients (APIs) that contain oxidizing agents, ensuring potency and efficacy.

ii. **Impurity Analysis**: Identification and quantification of impurities that may include oxidizing agents, ensuring product safety and quality.

c. **Procedure**: The drug sample is dissolved or extracted, and iodide ions are titrated against the sample under acidic conditions. The endpoint is determined using starch-iodine indicator or by back-titration with a standard reducing agent.

d. **Advantages**: Provides precise and sensitive analysis of pharmaceuticals, ensuring compliance with regulatory standards and quality assurance.

3. Environmental Monitoring

a. **Application**: Iodometry plays a crucial role in environmental monitoring to assess the levels of oxidizing agents and pollutants in water, air, and soil samples.

b. **Examples**:

   i. **Water Quality Assessment**: Measurement of chlorine residuals in drinking water and wastewater treatment processes.

   ii. **Pollutant Analysis**: Quantification of oxidizing pollutants such as heavy metals and organic contaminants.

c. **Procedure**: Samples are prepared and treated to release oxidizing agents, which are then titrated with iodide ions. The endpoint is determined using suitable indicators or by back-titration methods.

d. **Advantages**: Enables accurate monitoring of environmental pollutants, contributing to regulatory compliance and environmental management efforts.

4. Food and Beverage Industry

a. **Application**: Iodometry is used in the food and beverage industry for the analysis of oxidizing agents and antioxidants in food products.

b. **Examples**:

   i. **Analysis of Antioxidants**: Determination of antioxidant levels in food additives and natural products.

   ii. **Quality Control**: Assessment of oxidative stability and shelf-life of food products containing oxidizable compounds.

c. **Procedure**: Food samples are prepared and analyzed for oxidizing agents or antioxidants using iodometry. The titration process follows standard protocols with endpoint detection using starch-iodine complex or other indicators.

d. **Advantages**: Provides reliable data on the oxidative status of food products, ensuring consumer safety and product quality.

PRINCIPLES OF BROMATOMETRY

Bromatometry is a specific type of redox titration that utilizes bromine (Br_2) or bromide ions (Br^-) as the titrant. This technique is used primarily for the determination of substances that can be oxidized by bromine in acidic or alkaline conditions. Here are the key principles of bromatometry in redox titrations:

1. Oxidation by Bromine (Br_2):

a. **Bromine as Oxidizing Agent**: Bromine is a strong oxidizing agent capable of oxidizing many substances under suitable conditions.

b. **Reaction**: Bromine can oxidize substances that are easily reducible, similar to iodine in iodometry:

$$Br_2 + 2e^- \rightarrow 2Br^-$$

c. **Example**: The oxidation of sulfite ions (SO_3^{2-}) by bromine in acidic medium:

$$SO_3^{2-} + Br_2 + H_2O \rightarrow SO_4^{2-} + 2Br^- + 2H^+$$

2. Redox Reaction in Bromatometry:

a. **Titration Setup**: The sample containing the analyte (e.g., sulfite ions) is titrated with bromine or bromide ions.

b. **Endpoint**: The endpoint is typically detected by a suitable indicator, often a starch-iodine complex or a color change in the bromine solution itself.

c. **Equivalence Point**: At the equivalence point, the moles of bromine or bromide ions added are stoichiometrically equivalent to the moles of the oxidizable substance in the analyte.

3. Indicator Systems:

a. **Starch-Iodine Complex**: Similar to iodometry, a starch-iodine complex can be used as an indicator in bromatometry to detect the endpoint.

b. **Color Change**: The color change from blue (starch-iodine complex) to colorless indicates the endpoint of the titration.

4. Standardization of Bromine Solution:

a. **Primary Standard**: Before use, the bromine solution is standardized against a primary standard, such as sodium thiosulfate ($Na_2S_2O_3$), which is weighed accurately and dissolved to a known concentration.

b. **Back Titration**: Alternatively, the bromine solution can be standardized by back-titrating it with a known concentration of a standard reducing agent after reacting it with a known amount of a standard substance.

5. Applications of Bromatometry:

a. **Determination of Sulfur Dioxide in Wine**: Bromatometry is commonly used to determine the concentration of sulfur dioxide (SO_2) in wine, where SO_2 is released and titrated with bromine.

b. **Analysis of Reducing Sugars**: It can be used to quantify reducing sugars (e.g., glucose, fructose) in food products.

c. **Quantification of Bromine**: Bromatometry is used in industrial processes where bromine is used as a disinfectant or oxidizing agent.

6. Advantages:

a. **Selective**: Bromatometry is selective for substances that can be oxidized by bromine under appropriate conditions.

b. **Sensitive**: It can detect low concentrations of analytes due to the visible endpoint and suitable indicators.

c. **Versatile**: Bromatometry can be adapted for various types of samples and analytes, making it applicable in different fields of analytical chemistry.

APPLICATIONS OF BROMATOMETRY

Bromatometry, a specific type of redox titration that utilizes bromine (Br_2) or bromide ions (Br^-) as the titrant, finds various applications across different fields of analytical chemistry. Here are some key applications of bromatometry in redox titrations:

1. Determination of Sulfur Dioxide (SO_2) in Wine

a. **Application**: Bromatometry is widely used to determine the concentration of sulfur dioxide in wine and other beverages.

b. **Principle**: Sulfur dioxide in wine is released and reacts with bromine in an acidic medium:

$$SO_2 + Br_2 + H_2O \rightarrow SO_4^{2-} + 2Br^- + 2H^+$$

c. **Procedure**: The wine sample is titrated with bromine until the endpoint, often indicated by a starch-iodine complex turning from blue to colorless.

d. **Advantages**: Provides a reliable method for monitoring sulfur dioxide levels in wine, ensuring compliance with regulatory standards and maintaining product quality.

2. Analysis of Reducing Sugars in Food Products

a. **Application**: Bromatometry is used to quantify reducing sugars (e.g., glucose, fructose) in food products, such as honey, fruit juices, and syrups.

b. **Principle**: Reducing sugars react with bromine in an alkaline medium, producing brominated products:

$$\text{Glucose} + Br_2 + OH^- \rightarrow \text{Products} + 2Br^- + H_2O$$

c. **Procedure**: The food sample is hydrolyzed and treated with excess bromine. The remaining bromine is titrated with a standard solution of sodium thiosulfate until the endpoint is reached.

d. **Advantages**: Enables accurate determination of reducing sugar content in food products, critical for nutritional labeling and quality control.

3. Industrial Applications

a. **Application**: Bromatometry is used in various industrial processes where bromine is employed as an oxidizing agent or disinfectant.

b. **Examples**:

i. **Water Treatment**: Quantification of bromine residuals in drinking water and wastewater treatment.

ii. **Chemical Manufacturing**: Analysis of bromine-containing chemicals and intermediates.

c. **Procedure**: Samples containing bromine or bromine-containing compounds are titrated with iodide ions in the presence of an appropriate indicator to determine their concentration.

d. **Advantages**: Provides a robust method for monitoring bromine levels in industrial processes, ensuring efficiency and safety.

4. Pharmaceutical Analysis

a. **Application**: Bromatometry is utilized in the pharmaceutical industry to assess the content of bromine-containing compounds or impurities in drug formulations.

b. **Principle**: Bromine-containing substances are titrated with iodide ions under controlled conditions to determine their concentration.

c. **Procedure**: Pharmaceutical samples are dissolved or extracted, and bromine or bromine-containing compounds are titrated with iodide ions. The endpoint is determined using suitable indicators or by back-titration methods.

d. **Advantages**: Ensures the accuracy and compliance of pharmaceutical products with regulatory standards regarding the content of bromine or related compounds.

PRINCIPLES OF DICHROMETRY

Dichrometry is a specific type of redox titration that utilizes dichromate ions ($Cr_2O_7^{2-}$) as the titrant. This technique is particularly useful for determining substances that can be oxidized by dichromate ions in acidic medium. Here are the key principles of dichrometry in redox titrations:

1. Oxidation by Dichromate Ions ($Cr_2O_7^{2-}$):

a. **Dichromate as Oxidizing Agent**: Dichromate ions are strong oxidizing agents in acidic medium, capable of oxidizing a wide range of substances.
b. **Reaction**: Dichromate ions can be reduced to chromium(III) ions (Cr^{3+}) in acidic solution:

$$Cr_2O_7^{2-} + 14H^+ + 6e^- \rightarrow 2Cr^{3+} + 7H_2O$$

c. **Example**: The oxidation of ferrous ions (Fe^{2+}) by dichromate ions in acidic medium:

$$6Fe^{2+} + Cr_2O_7^{2-} + 14H^+ \rightarrow 2Cr^{3+} + 6Fe^{3+} + 7H_2O$$

2. Redox Reaction in Dichrometry:

a. **Titration Setup**: The analyte containing the reducing agent (e.g., ferrous ions) is titrated with dichromate ions in acidic medium.
b. **Endpoint**: The endpoint is typically detected by a visual indicator, such as a color change or by using an indicator that shows the formation of excess dichromate ions.
c. **Equivalence Point**: At the equivalence point, the moles of dichromate ions added are stoichiometrically equivalent to the moles of the reducing agent present in the analyte.

3. Indicator Systems:

a. **Internal Indicators**: In some cases, dichrometry can use internal indicators like the color change of the analyte solution itself as the endpoint indicator.
b. **External Indicators**: External indicators may also be used, such as diphenylamine sulfonic acid, which forms a blue color when excess dichromate is present.

4. Standardization of Dichromate Solution:

a. **Primary Standard**: Before use, the dichromate solution is standardized against a primary standard, such as ferrous ammonium sulfate

($Fe(NH_4)_2(SO_4)_2 \cdot 6H_2O$), which is weighed accurately and dissolved to a known concentration.

b. **Back Titration**: Alternatively, the dichromate solution can be standardized by back-titrating it with a known concentration of a standard reducing agent after reacting it with a known amount of a standard substance.

5. Applications of Dichrometry:

a. **Analysis of Iron in Ores**: Dichrometry is commonly used in metallurgical processes to determine the concentration of iron in ores and minerals.

b. **Water Analysis**: It is used in environmental monitoring to assess the levels of reducing agents and pollutants in water samples.

c. **Analysis of Organic Compounds**: Dichrometry is applied in organic chemistry for the quantitative analysis of organic compounds containing easily oxidizable functional groups.

6. Advantages:

a. **Selective**: Dichrometry is selective for substances that can be oxidized by dichromate ions under acidic conditions.

b. **Sensitive**: It can detect low concentrations of reducing agents due to the color change or suitable indicators used.

c. **Versatile**: Dichrometry can be adapted for various types of samples and analytes, making it applicable in different fields of analytical chemistry.

APPLICATIONS OF DICHROMETRY

Dichrometry, which utilizes dichromate ions ($Cr_2O_7^{2-}$) as the titrant in redox titrations, has several important applications across various fields of analytical chemistry. Here are some key applications:

1. Determination of Iron in Ores and Minerals

a. **Application**: Dichrometry is widely used to determine the concentration of iron in ores and mineral samples.

b. **Principle**: Iron(II) ions (Fe^{2+}) in the sample are oxidized by dichromate ions ($Cr_2O_7^{2-}$) in acidic medium:

$$6Fe^{2+} + Cr_2O_7^{2-} + 14H^+ \rightarrow 2Cr^{3+} + 6Fe^{3+} + 7H_2O$$

c. **Procedure**: The ore or mineral sample is dissolved in acid, and the iron content is titrated with a standardized dichromate solution until the endpoint, typically indicated by a color change.

d. **Advantages**: Provides a reliable method for determining iron content in geological samples, essential for mining and metallurgical industries.

2. Environmental Monitoring

a. **Application**: Dichrometry is used in environmental analysis to assess the levels of reducing agents and pollutants in water samples.

b. **Principle**: Various reducing agents in water samples, such as organic compounds or pollutants, can be oxidized by dichromate ions.

c. **Procedure**: Water samples are treated to release reducing agents, which are then titrated with a standardized dichromate solution. The endpoint is determined using appropriate indicators or by a visual change in color.

d. **Advantages**: Enables accurate monitoring of water quality and pollution levels, crucial for environmental protection and regulatory compliance.

3. Analysis of Organic Compounds

a. **Application**: Dichrometry is applied in organic chemistry for the quantitative analysis of organic compounds containing easily oxidizable functional groups.

b. **Principle**: Organic compounds with reducing functionalities, such as alcohols, aldehydes, and ketones, can be oxidized by dichromate ions.

c. **Procedure**: The organic compound is reacted with excess dichromate in acidic medium, and the remaining dichromate is titrated with a standardized reducing agent (e.g., ferrous ammonium sulfate) until the endpoint.

d. **Advantages**: Provides a method for determining the concentration of specific functional groups in organic compounds, important for pharmaceuticals, food chemistry, and industrial processes.

4. Industrial Applications

a. **Application**: Dichrometry finds applications in various industrial processes where the oxidation state of metals or organic compounds needs to be determined.

b. **Examples**:

  i. **Quality Control in Manufacturing**: Used to assess the purity and composition of chemicals and intermediates.

  ii. **Process Monitoring**: Employed to monitor chemical reactions and ensure process efficiency.

c. **Procedure**: Samples from industrial processes are analyzed using dichrometry to quantify specific substances or to assess the progress of chemical reactions.

d. **Advantages**: Supports quality assurance and process optimization in industries ranging from chemical manufacturing to pharmaceuticals.

TITRATION WITH POTASSIUM IODATE

Titration with potassium iodate (KIO_3) is a specific type of redox titration used primarily for the determination of reducing agents or substances that can be oxidized by iodate ions under acidic conditions. Here's an overview of titration with potassium iodate in redox titrations:

Principle of Titration with Potassium Iodate:

1. **Oxidation by Iodate Ions (IO_3^-)**:

   a. Potassium iodate (KIO_3) dissociates in water to form iodate ions (IO_3^-), which can act as strong oxidizing agents under acidic conditions:

$$IO_3^- + 5I^- + 6H^+ \rightarrow 3I_2 + 3H_2O$$

2. **Redox Reaction**:

    a. In the presence of reducing agents (e.g., thiosulfate ions, Fe^{2+}), iodate ions are reduced to iodine (I_2):

    $$IO_3^- + 5I^- + 6H^+ \rightarrow 3I_2 + 3H_2O$$

3. **Titration Procedure**:

    a. **Preparation**: The sample containing the reducing agent is prepared in acidic medium (typically sulfuric acid, H_2SO_4).

    b. **Titration**: A standardized potassium iodate solution is added gradually to the sample until the endpoint is reached.

    c. **Endpoint Detection**: The endpoint is typically detected using a starch-iodine indicator system. The blue color of the starch-iodine complex disappears when all the reducing agent has been oxidized by the iodate ions.

    d. **Calculation**: The amount of reducing agent present in the sample can be calculated based on the volume and concentration of the potassium iodate solution used in the titration.

Applications of Potassium Iodate Titration:

1. **Analysis of Reducing Agents**: Potassium iodate titration is used to quantify reducing agents in various samples, such as food products (e.g., Vitamin C content), pharmaceuticals, and environmental samples.
2. **Quality Control**: It is applied in industries to ensure the purity and potency of products containing reducing agents.
3. **Educational and Research Purposes**: Potassium iodate titration is used in educational laboratories and research settings to study redox reactions and oxidation-reduction principles.

Advantages:

1. **Selective**: Potassium iodate titration is selective for substances that can be oxidized by iodate ions under acidic conditions.

2. **Sensitive**: It can detect low concentrations of reducing agents due to the visible endpoint with starch-iodine complex.
3. **Versatile**: This method can be adapted for various types of samples and analytes, making it applicable in different fields of analytical chemistry.

Multiple Choice Questions (MCQs)

1. What is the primary purpose of redox titrations?
   a) To measure pH
   b) To determine the concentration of an unknown solution
   c) To measure temperature
   d) To analyze color change
2. Which of the following is a common redox titrant used in acidic medium?
   a) Sodium hydroxide
   b) Potassium permanganate
   c) Silver nitrate
   d) Sodium chloride
3. What is the role of a reducing agent in a redox titration?
   a) It gains electrons
   b) It loses electrons
   c) It acts as a solvent
   d) It changes color at the endpoint
4. Which indicator is commonly used in iodometric titrations?
   a) Methyl orange
   b) Phenolphthalein
   c) Starch
   d) Bromothymol blue
5. Potassium permanganate acts as an:
   a) Oxidizing agent

b) Reducing agent

c) Neutralizing agent

d) Buffer

6. What is the standard electrode potential of the Standard Hydrogen Electrode (SHE)?

a) 1.000 V

b) 0.000 V

c) 0.500 V

d) -0.500 V

7. In iodometry, what is the primary titrant used?

a) Iodine (I_2)

b) Potassium permanganate ($KMnO_4$)

c) Potassium dichromate ($K_2Cr_2O_7$)

d) Sodium thiosulfate ($Na_2S_2O_3$)

8. Cerimetry involves the use of which titrant?

a) Potassium iodate (KIO_3)

b) Potassium permanganate ($KMnO_4$)

c) Cerium(IV) sulfate ($Ce(SO_4)_2$)

d) Silver nitrate ($AgNO_3$)

9. Which method is commonly used to determine the endpoint in redox titrations?

a) pH meter

b) Conductivity meter

c) Color change

d) Temperature change

10. What color change is observed in the starch-iodine complex at the endpoint of an iodometric titration?

a) Blue to colorless

b) Red to blue

c) Yellow to green
d) Green to yellow

11. What is the role of potassium dichromate in redox titrations?
a) Reducing agent
b) Neutralizing agent
c) Oxidizing agent
d) Solvent

12. In cerimetry, cerium(IV) ions are reduced to:
a) Cerium(II) ions
b) Cerium(III) ions
c) Cerium(V) ions
d) Cerium(VI) ions

13. Which of the following is an application of bromatometry?
a) Determination of sulfur dioxide in wine
b) Analysis of iron in ores
c) Determination of vitamin C
d) Measurement of dissolved oxygen in water

14. What is the main advantage of using redox titrations?
a) High selectivity for specific ions
b) Simple and easy to perform
c) Requires no calibration
d) Provides colorless solutions

15. Which redox titration method uses sodium thiosulfate as a titrant?
a) Cerimetry
b) Iodometry
c) Dichrometry
d) Bromatometry

16. Which principle is applied in iodimetry for endpoint detection?
a) Formation of a blue complex

b) Change in pH
c) Formation of a red complex
d) Change in conductivity

17. In dichrometry, which ions are used as the titrant?
a) Permanganate ions
b) Dichromate ions
c) Iodate ions
d) Cerium ions

18. Titration with potassium iodate involves the oxidation of iodide ions to:
a) Iodine
b) Iodate ions
c) Iodine dioxide
d) Hypoiodite ions

19. Which application involves the use of iodometry?
a) Determination of iron in ores
b) Analysis of sulfur dioxide in wine
c) Determination of dissolved oxygen in water
d) Measurement of glucose in blood

20. In titration with potassium iodate, what is typically used to detect the endpoint?
a) pH meter
b) Conductivity meter
c) Starch-iodine indicator system
d) Temperature change

Short Answer Type Questions (Subjective)

1. What is the principle behind redox titrations?
2. Define oxidation and reduction in the context of redox reactions.
3. What role do oxidizing agents and reducing agents play in redox titrations?

4. Explain the significance of the equivalence point in redox titrations.
5. What is the Nernst equation used for in redox titrations?
6. Describe a direct redox titration with an example.
7. What is back titration, and when is it used?
8. Name two common redox titrants and their typical uses.
9. Why is potassium permanganate often used as an indicator in acidic medium?
10. How does starch act as an indicator in iodometric titrations?
11. What is the purpose of standardizing a titrant solution before titration?
12. Give an example of an application of redox titrations in environmental analysis.
13. How are redox indicators different from traditional acid-base indicators?
14. Describe the process of determining the iron content in ores using redox titration.
15. Explain how sodium thiosulfate is used in iodometric titrations.
16. What are the advantages of using cerium(IV) sulfate in cerimetry?
17. List two applications of iodimetry in pharmaceutical analysis.
18. What is the role of bromine in bromatometry?
19. How is dichrometry used to determine the concentration of iron in ores?
20. What is the principle of titration with potassium iodate?

Long Answer Type Questions (Subjective)

1. Discuss the principles and applications of redox titrations, including examples of common titrants and their uses.
2. Explain the concepts of oxidation and reduction in detail, including how these processes are utilized in redox titrations.
3. Describe the different types of redox titrations, providing examples and applications for each type.

4. What is cerimetry? Explain its principles, procedures, and applications in analytical chemistry.
5. Discuss iodimetry as a redox titration method. Include the principles, indicators used, and applications in various fields.
6. Explain iodometry in detail, including the principles of using iodide ions as a titrant and its applications.
7. Describe bromatometry as a redox titration technique. Discuss its principles, procedures, and key applications.
8. What is dichrometry? Explain the principles and applications of using dichromate ions in redox titrations.
9. Discuss the process and applications of titration with potassium iodate. Include the principles and procedures involved.
10. Compare and contrast iodimetry and iodometry, highlighting the key differences in their principles, procedures, and applications.

Answer Key

1. c) To determine the concentration of an unknown solution
2. b) Loss of electrons
3. b) Potassium permanganate
4. b) It loses electrons
5. c) Starch
6. a) Oxidizing agent
7. b) 0.000 V
8. d) Sodium thiosulfate ($Na_2S_2O_3$)
9. c) Cerium(IV) sulfate ($Ce(SO_4)_2$)
10. c) Color change (Procedures for Redox Titrations: Monitor the color change of the indicator or the solution itself.)
11. a) Blue to colorless
12. c) Oxidizing agent

13.b) Cerium(III) ions (Principles of Cerimetry: Cerium(IV) ions are reduced to cerium(III) ions (Ce^{3+}))

14.a) Determination of sulfur dioxide in wine

15.a) High selectivity for specific ions

16.b) Iodometry

17.a) Formation of a blue complex

18.b) Dichromate ions

19.a) Iodine

20.c) Determination of dissolved oxygen in water

CHAPTER – 13

CONDUCTOMETRY

Conductometry is a measurement technique in analytical chemistry that focuses on the electrical conductivity of a solution. Conductivity is the ability of a solution to conduct electric current, which depends on the presence of ions, their concentration, and mobility.

Principle

The principle of conductometry is based on Ohm's Law, which states that the electric current (I) passing through a conductor between two points is directly proportional to the voltage (V) across the two points and inversely proportional to the resistance (R). Mathematically, it's expressed as:

$$I = \frac{V}{R}$$

Conductometry measures the conductance (G), which is the reciprocal of resistance:

$$G = \frac{1}{R}$$

Conductance is measured in Siemens (S), and the electrical conductivity (κ) is given by:

$$\kappa = \frac{G \cdot l}{A}$$

where:

κ = Conductivity (S/cm)

G = Conductance (S)

l = Distance between electrodes (cm)

A = Area of electrodes (cm^2)

Conductivity and Concentration

The conductivity of a solution increases with the concentration of ions. In highly diluted solutions, conductivity increases linearly with concentration, but at higher concentrations, interactions between ions become significant, affecting the linearity.

Types of Conductometric Measurements

1. **Direct Conductometry**:
    a. Measures the conductance of the solution directly without any chemical reaction.
    b. Used to determine the purity of water or monitor the progress of a reaction where ion concentration changes.
2. **Indirect (Titrimetric) Conductometry**:
    a. Involves titration where the conductance of the solution is measured before and after adding a titrant.
    b. The conductance changes due to the formation or consumption of ions in the reaction.
    c. Used for determining the endpoint of titrations, such as acid-base or precipitation titrations.

Applications

1. **Determination of Water Purity**:
    a. Ultra-pure water has very low conductivity. Measuring the conductivity helps in assessing water purity.
2. **Monitoring Chemical Reactions**:
    a. Conductometry is used to monitor reactions where ionic species are formed or consumed, such as neutralization reactions.
3. **Determination of Salinity**:
    a. Used in environmental science to measure the salinity of water bodies.
4. **Pharmaceuticals**:
    a. Used to determine the ion concentration in pharmaceutical solutions.

5. **Food Industry**:
    a. Measures the salt content in food products.

Instrumentation

1. **Conductivity Cell**:
    a. Contains two electrodes, usually platinum, separated by a known distance.
    b. The cell constant (K) is determined by the geometry of the electrodes and is used to calculate conductivity.
2. **Conductometer**:
    a. Device that measures the conductance of the solution.
    b. Consists of a Wheatstone bridge circuit for measuring resistance.

Advantages

1. **Non-destructive**: Does not alter the sample.
2. **Rapid**: Provides quick results.
3. **Sensitive**: Detects small changes in ion concentration.
4. **Simple and Cost-effective**: Easy to use and relatively inexpensive.

Limitations

1. **Interference**: Presence of multiple ions can interfere with measurements.
2. **Temperature Dependency**: Conductivity is affected by temperature, requiring temperature control or compensation.
3. **Limited Specificity**: Cannot distinguish between different types of ions contributing to conductivity.

CONDUCTIVITY CELL

Definition

A conductivity cell is a device used in conductometry to measure the electrical conductivity of a solution. It consists of two electrodes, typically made of inert materials like platinum, placed at a fixed distance apart within a solution.

Construction

The conductivity cell comprises the following components:

1. **Electrodes**:
    a. Usually made of platinum or stainless steel to prevent corrosion and ensure longevity.
    b. The electrodes can be coated with platinum black to increase their surface area and improve the accuracy of measurements by minimizing polarization effects.
2. **Cell Body**:
    a. The electrodes are housed within a cell body, often made of glass or plastic, to provide structural support and electrical insulation.
    b. The cell body ensures that the electrodes are positioned at a fixed distance from each other.
3. **Connection Leads**:
    a. Wires or leads connect the electrodes to the conductivity meter or conductometer, enabling the measurement of conductance.

Cell Constant

The cell constant (K) is a crucial parameter of the conductivity cell, defined as the ratio of the distance between the electrodes (l) to the electrode surface area (A):

$$K = \frac{l}{A}$$

The cell constant is expressed in cm^{-1} and must be determined accurately to ensure precise conductivity measurements. It can be determined by measuring the conductivity of a standard solution with known conductivity.

Types of Conductivity Cells

1. **Two-Electrode Cell**:
    a. Consists of two electrodes placed parallel to each other.
    b. Simple in design but can suffer from polarization effects at high conductivities or low frequencies.
2. **Four-Electrode (or Four-Pole) Cell**:

a. Consists of two current-carrying electrodes and two potential-measuring electrodes.
b. Reduces polarization and electrode resistance effects, providing more accurate measurements, especially at high conductivities.

3. **Coaxial Cylindrical Cell**:
    a. Electrodes are in the form of coaxial cylinders, one inside the other.
    b. Provides uniform electric field distribution and is suitable for a wide range of conductivities.

Operation

1. **Calibration**:
    a. The conductivity cell must be calibrated using standard solutions with known conductivities.
    b. Calibration ensures accurate determination of the cell constant and reliable measurements.
2. **Measurement**:
    a. The cell is immersed in the solution to be measured.
    b. An alternating current (AC) voltage is applied across the electrodes to prevent electrolysis and polarization effects.
    c. The conductance (G) of the solution is measured, and the conductivity (κ) is calculated using the cell constant (K):

$$\kappa = G \cdot K$$

Factors Affecting Conductivity Cell Performance

1. **Temperature**:
    a. Conductivity is temperature-dependent; typically, it increases with temperature.
    b. Temperature control or compensation is necessary for accurate measurements.
2. **Electrode Fouling**:

a. Buildup of contaminants on the electrode surface can affect measurements.
b. Regular cleaning of electrodes is essential to maintain accuracy.

3. **Cell Geometry**:
    a. The distance between electrodes and their surface area affect the cell constant.
    b. Precise manufacturing and calibration are required to ensure consistent results.

Applications

1. **Water Quality Analysis**:
    a. Used to measure the purity and ionic content of water in environmental monitoring and water treatment plants.
2. **Chemical Manufacturing**:
    a. Monitors the concentration of ionic species in various chemical processes.
3. **Pharmaceutical Industry**:
    a. Measures the conductivity of pharmaceutical solutions to ensure quality and consistency.
4. **Food and Beverage Industry**:
    a. Determines the salt content and overall ionic strength of food and beverage products.

Maintenance and Care

1. **Cleaning**:
    a. Regularly clean the electrodes with appropriate cleaning solutions to remove any buildup or contaminants.
2. **Storage**:
    a. Store the conductivity cell in a clean, dry place when not in use to prevent damage and contamination.
3. **Calibration**:

a. Periodically recalibrate the cell using standard solutions to ensure ongoing accuracy.

CONDUCTOMETRIC TITRATIONS

Definition

Conductometric titration is an analytical technique where the change in the electrical conductivity of a solution is measured as a titrant is added. This method is used to determine the endpoint of the titration, which corresponds to the completion of a chemical reaction between the analyte and the titrant.

Principle

The principle of conductometric titration is based on the fact that the conductivity of a solution depends on the concentration and mobility of its ions. During the titration, the ionic composition of the solution changes as the titrant reacts with the analyte, leading to changes in the solution's conductivity. The endpoint is identified by analyzing these changes.

Types of Conductometric Titrations

1. **Strong Acid-Strong Base Titration**:
    a. Example: Hydrochloric acid (HCl) with sodium hydroxide (NaOH).
    b. As NaOH is added to HCl, H^+ and OH^- ions react to form water, decreasing the number of free ions and thus the conductivity until the equivalence point is reached. Beyond this point, the addition of excess NaOH increases the conductivity due to the presence of free OH^- ions.
2. **Weak Acid-Strong Base Titration**:
    a. Example: Acetic acid (CH_3COOH) with NaOH.
    b. Conductivity changes more gradually as weak acids partially ionize. The equivalence point is determined by the change in the slope of the conductivity curve.
3. **Strong Acid-Weak Base Titration**:
    a. Example: HCl with ammonia (NH_3).

b. Conductivity changes as HCl reacts with NH_3 to form NH_4^+ and Cl^- ions. The equivalence point is marked by a change in the conductivity curve's slope.

4. **Weak Acid-Weak Base Titration**:
   a. Example: CH_3COOH with NH_3.
   b. Conductivity changes less sharply due to partial ionization of both acid and base, requiring careful analysis to determine the equivalence point.
5. **Precipitation Titration**:
   a. Example: Silver nitrate ($AgNO_3$) with sodium chloride (NaCl).
   b. Conductivity decreases as Ag^+ reacts with Cl^- to form insoluble AgCl, removing free ions from the solution. Beyond the equivalence point, excess Ag^+ increases conductivity.
6. **Complexometric Titration**:
   a. Example: EDTA titration of metal ions.
   b. Conductivity changes as metal ions form complexes with EDTA, reducing the number of free ions. The endpoint is identified by a change in the conductivity curve.

Procedure

1. For other titrations, the equivalence point corresponds to a significant change in the curve's slope. **Preparation**:
   a. Prepare the analyte solution and titrant.
   b. Calibrate the conductivity meter and conductivity cell using standard solutions.
2. **Titration Setup**:
   a. Place the conductivity cell in the analyte solution.
   b. Ensure the solution is well-mixed and at a constant temperature to avoid conductivity fluctuations.

3. **Conductometric Measurement**:
    a. Start adding the titrant incrementally while continuously measuring the solution's conductivity.
    b. Record the conductivity after each addition of titrant.
4. **Plotting Conductivity Curve**:
    a. Plot the conductivity values against the volume of titrant added.
    b. The resulting curve will show distinct changes in slope corresponding to different stages of the titration.
5. **Determining the Endpoint**:
    a. Identify the equivalence point by analyzing the conductivity curve.
    b. For strong acid-strong base titrations, the

Advantages

1. **No Indicator Required**: Conductometric titration does not require a visual indicator, making it suitable for colored or turbid solutions.
2. **Sensitive**: Capable of detecting small changes in ion concentration, providing high precision.
3. **Applicable to Weak Acids/Bases**: Useful for titrations involving weak acids or bases where traditional indicators might not be effective.
4. **Automated Data Collection**: Conductivity meters can be interfaced with computers for automated data collection and analysis.

Limitations

1. **Temperature Sensitivity**: Conductivity is temperature-dependent, requiring precise temperature control or compensation.
2. **Interference from Other Ions**: Presence of other ions can affect conductivity measurements, potentially leading to inaccuracies.
3. **Calibration Requirement**: Regular calibration of the conductivity cell is necessary to maintain accuracy.

Applications

1. **Water Quality Analysis**:

a. Determining the concentration of ionic species in water samples.

2. **Pharmaceuticals**:

    a. Analyzing the composition of pharmaceutical solutions.

3. **Environmental Monitoring**:

    a. Monitoring pollution levels by measuring ionic content in environmental samples.

4. **Food Industry**:

    a. Measuring salt content and other ionic constituents in food products.

APPLICATIONS OF CONDUCTOMETRY

Conductometry is a versatile analytical technique used in various fields due to its ability to measure the ionic content and conductivity of solutions. Here are some detailed applications of conductometry:

1. Water Quality Analysis

a. Determination of Water Purity

i. **Ultra-pure Water**: Conductometry is used to ensure the purity of ultra-pure water in laboratories and industries. Ultra-pure water has very low conductivity, and any increase indicates contamination.

ii. **Potable Water**: The conductivity of drinking water is measured to monitor the levels of dissolved salts and minerals, ensuring it meets safety standards.

b. Monitoring Wastewater and Effluents

i. Conductometry helps in assessing the ionic content of wastewater and industrial effluents to ensure they are treated before being discharged into the environment. High conductivity may indicate high levels of pollutants.

c. Environmental Monitoring

i. Conductivity measurements in rivers, lakes, and groundwater help in monitoring pollution levels and the presence of dissolved salts and minerals.

2. Chemical Industry

a. Reaction Monitoring

i. Conductometry is used to monitor the progress of chemical reactions, especially those involving ionic species. For example, it can track neutralization reactions, precipitation reactions, and complex formation reactions.

b. Quality Control

i. The ionic content of raw materials and final products in the chemical industry can be assessed using conductometry to ensure quality and consistency.

3. Pharmaceutical Industry

a. Drug Formulation and Stability

i. Conductometry helps in the formulation and stability testing of pharmaceutical solutions. It ensures the correct ionic strength and pH are maintained for drug efficacy and safety.

b. Purity Testing

i. The purity of pharmaceutical ingredients and products can be verified by measuring their conductivity. Impurities and contaminants often affect the ionic content and conductivity.

4. Food and Beverage Industry

a. Salt Content Measurement

i. Conductometry is used to measure the salt content in food products, ensuring they meet regulatory standards and consumer preferences.

b. Quality Control

i. The ionic content and overall quality of beverages, such as mineral water, soft drinks, and dairy products, are monitored using conductometry.

5. Petrochemical Industry

a. Oil and Gas Exploration

i. Conductivity measurements help in identifying water-bearing zones and oil-bearing formations during drilling operations. The conductivity of drilling fluids can indicate the presence of hydrocarbons.

b. Process Control

i. Conductometry is used to monitor the ionic content of process streams in refineries and petrochemical plants, ensuring efficient and safe operations.

6. Agriculture

a. Soil Analysis

i. Soil conductivity measurements help in determining the soil salinity and fertility. High soil salinity can affect crop growth, and conductometry provides a quick and accurate assessment.

b. Irrigation Water Quality

i. The quality of irrigation water is monitored using conductometry to prevent soil salinization and ensure optimal crop yield.

7. Environmental Science

a. Pollution Monitoring

i. Conductometry helps in monitoring the ionic content of air, soil, and water to assess pollution levels and the impact of industrial activities on the environment.

b. Acid Rain Analysis

i. The conductivity of rainwater is measured to determine the presence and concentration of acidic components, such as sulfuric and nitric acids.

8. Biotechnology

a. Fermentation Processes

i. Conductometry is used to monitor the ionic content of fermentation media, ensuring optimal conditions for microbial growth and product formation.

b. Cell Culture Media

i. The ionic strength of cell culture media is critical for cell growth and productivity. Conductometry ensures the media are within the required specifications.

9. Academic and Research Laboratories

a. Fundamental Research

i. Conductometry is used in research to study ionic interactions, electrolyte behavior, and various chemical phenomena.

b. Teaching and Education

i. Conductometry experiments are commonly included in educational curricula to teach students about ionic conductivity, chemical reactions, and analytical techniques.

Multiple Choice Questions (MCQs)

1. What does conductometry measure?
   a) Mass of a solution
   b) Volume of a solution
   c) Electrical conductivity of a solution
   d) Temperature of a solution
2. What is the unit of conductance (G)?
   a) Ohm (Ω)
   b) Siemens (S)
   c) Volt (V)
   d) Ampere (A)
3. Which law is the principle of conductometry based on?
   a) Boyle's Law
   b) Charles's Law
   c) Ohm's Law

d) Avogadro's Law

4. In the formula $\kappa = G \cdot l/A$, what does κ represent?
    a) Conductance
    b) Resistance
    c) Voltage
    d) Conductivity
5. How does the conductivity of a solution change with increasing ion concentration at high concentrations?
    a) It increases linearly
    b) It remains constant
    c) It decreases
    d) It deviates from linearity due to ion interactions
6. Which type of conductometric measurement involves no chemical reaction?
    a) Direct conductometry
    b) Indirect conductometry
    c) Potentiometry
    d) Voltammetry
7. What is the role of a conductivity cell in conductometry?
    a) Measure pH
    b) Measure temperature
    c) Measure electrical conductivity
    d) Measure pressure
8. What is the cell constant (K) defined as?
    a) Ratio of voltage to current
    b) Ratio of distance between electrodes to electrode surface area
    c) Ratio of resistance to conductance
    d) Ratio of current to voltage
9. Which material is commonly used for electrodes in a conductivity cell?
    a) Copper

b) Aluminum

c) Platinum

d) Silver

10. In a conductometric titration, what indicates the endpoint?

a) Change in color

b) Change in pH

c) Change in conductivity

d) Change in temperature

11. Which type of conductometric titration involves a strong acid and a strong base?

a) Weak acid-strong base titration

b) Strong acid-weak base titration

c) Strong acid-strong base titration

d) Precipitation titration

12. In which industry is conductometry used to measure the salt content of products?

a) Pharmaceutical industry

b) Chemical industry

c) Food and beverage industry

d) Petrochemical industry

13. What is a major advantage of conductometric titration?

a) Requires a visual indicator

b) Only works with strong acids and bases

c) Can detect small changes in ion concentration

d) Requires extensive sample preparation

14. Which factor must be controlled during conductometric measurements due to its effect on conductivity?

a) Pressure

b) Temperature

c) Humidity

d) Light

15. How is the conductivity cell calibrated?

a) Using a visual indicator

b) Using standard solutions with known conductivity

c) Using temperature measurements

d) Using pH measurements

16. In which type of titration does the conductivity initially decrease and then increase after the equivalence point?

a) Strong acid-strong base titration

b) Weak acid-strong base titration

c) Precipitation titration

d) Complexometric titration

17. Which industry uses conductometry for monitoring ionic content during oil and gas exploration?

a) Pharmaceutical industry

b) Food and beverage industry

c) Petrochemical industry

d) Environmental science

18. Why is platinum often used for electrodes in conductivity cells?

a) It is inexpensive

b) It is inert and prevents corrosion

c) It is highly reactive

d) It changes color at the endpoint

19. Which application of conductometry is crucial for environmental monitoring?

a) Monitoring wastewater and effluents

b) Measuring soil salinity

c) Determining the salt content in food products

d) Monitoring the ionic content of pharmaceutical solutions

20. What is the main limitation of conductometry related to interference?

a) Requires a visual indicator

b) Presence of multiple ions can interfere with measurements

c) Conductivity is not affected by temperature

d) Cannot detect changes in ion concentration

Short Answer Type Questions (Subjective)

1. Define conductometry and explain its principle.
2. What is the unit of conductance and how is it measured?
3. Explain the relationship between conductivity (κ), conductance (G), distance between electrodes (l), and electrode area (A).
4. How does the concentration of ions affect the conductivity of a solution?
5. Differentiate between direct conductometry and indirect conductometry.
6. List three applications of conductometry in water quality analysis.
7. What materials are commonly used for electrodes in a conductivity cell and why?
8. Describe the cell constant (K) and how it is determined.
9. What are the advantages of using a four-electrode cell over a two-electrode cell?
10. Why is it important to calibrate the conductivity cell using standard solutions?
11. Explain the principle of conductometric titration.
12. Describe the changes in conductivity observed during a strong acid-strong base titration.
13. How is the equivalence point determined in a conductometric titration?
14. What are the limitations of conductometric measurements?
15. How does temperature affect conductivity measurements?
16. What are the maintenance steps required for a conductivity cell?

17.Explain the application of conductometry in the pharmaceutical industry.

18.How is conductometry used in the food and beverage industry?

19.What role does conductometry play in environmental monitoring?

20.Describe an example of a precipitation titration using conductometry.

Long Answer Type Questions (Subjective)

1. Discuss the principle, construction, and operation of a conductivity cell. Include the different types of cells and their specific applications.
2. Explain in detail the procedure for conducting a conductometric titration. Use a strong acid-strong base titration as an example to illustrate the steps involved and how the equivalence point is determined.
3. Describe the various factors affecting the performance of a conductivity cell and the steps taken to ensure accurate and reliable measurements.
4. Discuss the applications of conductometry in different industries, including water quality analysis, pharmaceuticals, food and beverage, and petrochemicals. Provide specific examples for each industry.
5. Explain the concept of the cell constant (K) in conductometry. How is it calculated, and why is it important for accurate conductivity measurements?
6. Describe the advantages and limitations of conductometric titration. How does this method compare with other titration techniques?
7. How is conductometry used to monitor chemical reactions? Provide examples of reactions where this technique is particularly useful.
8. Discuss the importance of calibration in conductometric measurements. Describe the steps involved in calibrating a conductivity cell using standard solutions.
9. Explain the role of conductometry in environmental science, particularly in monitoring pollution levels and assessing water quality. Provide examples of specific applications.

10.Discuss the use of conductometry in academic and research laboratories. How is this technique applied in fundamental research and education? Provide examples of typical experiments or studies.

Answer Key

1. (c) Electrical conductivity of a solution
2. (b) Siemens (S)
3. (c) Ohm's Law
4. (d) Conductivity
5. (d) It deviates from linearity due to ion interactions
6. (a) Direct conductometry
7. (c) Measure electrical conductivity
8. (b) Ratio of distance between electrodes to electrode surface
9. (c) Platinum
10. (c) Change in conductivity
11. (c) Strong acid-strong base
12. (c) Food and beverage industry
13. (c) Can detect small changes in ion concentration
14. (b) Temperature
15. (b) Using standard solutions with known conductivity
16. (a) Strong acid-strong base titration
17. (c) Petrochemical industry
18. (b) It is inert and prevents corrosion
19. (a) Monitoring wastewater and effluents
20. (b) Presence of multiple ions can interfere with measurements

CHAPTER – 14

POTENTIOMETRY

INTRODUCTION:

Potentiometry is an analytical method used to determine the concentration of a given ion in solution by measuring the electric potential (voltage) of a suitable electrochemical cell. This technique is based on the Nernst equation, which relates the potential of an electrochemical cell to the concentration of the ion of interest. Potentiometry is widely used in various fields, including chemistry, biochemistry, environmental science, and pharmacology.

Principles of Potentiometry

Electrochemical Cell

A typical potentiometric setup involves an electrochemical cell consisting of two electrodes:

1. **Reference Electrode:** This electrode has a known and stable potential, which does not change with the concentration of the analyte. Common reference electrodes include the saturated calomel electrode (SCE) and the silver/silver chloride (Ag/AgCl) electrode.
2. **Indicator Electrode (Ion-Selective Electrode):** This electrode responds to the activity of the specific ion being measured. Examples include glass electrodes for pH measurement, ion-selective electrodes for specific ions like fluoride or calcium, and metal electrodes for redox reactions.

Nernst Equation

The Nernst equation is fundamental to potentiometry and is given by:

$$E = E^\circ + \frac{RT}{nF} \ln a$$

where:

1. E is the measured cell potential.
2. E∘ is the standard electrode potential.
3. R is the universal gas constant (8.314 J/(mol·K)).
4. T is the temperature in Kelvin.
5. n is the number of electrons transferred in the half-reaction.
6. F is the Faraday constant (96485 C/mol).
7. a is the activity (effective concentration) of the ion.

Activity and Concentration

In dilute solutions, the activity of an ion is approximately equal to its concentration. However, in more concentrated solutions, the activity coefficient must be considered to account for interactions between ions.

Types of Potentiometric Measurements

1. **Direct Potentiometry:** This method involves measuring the potential directly with a suitable ion-selective electrode to determine the ion concentration.
2. **Potentiometric Titration:** This technique involves adding a titrant to the analyte solution and measuring the potential change. The endpoint of the titration is determined by the inflection point on the titration curve.

Ion-Selective Electrodes (ISEs)

Glass Electrodes

1. **pH Electrode:** The most common type of glass electrode used to measure hydrogen ion concentration (pH). It consists of a thin glass membrane that is selective to H^+ ions.
2. **Mechanism:** The glass membrane develops a potential difference proportional to the hydrogen ion activity in the solution.

Solid-State Electrodes

1. **Mechanism:** These electrodes use a solid ion-selective membrane, such as a crystalline material or a polymer, which selectively binds the ion of interest.

2. **Examples:** Fluoride-selective electrodes, chloride-selective electrodes.

Liquid Membrane Electrodes

1. **Mechanism:** These electrodes have a liquid ion-exchange membrane that selectively interacts with the ion of interest.
2. **Examples:** Calcium-selective electrodes, potassium-selective electrodes.

Enzyme Electrodes

1. **Mechanism:** These electrodes use an enzyme layer to selectively react with the analyte, producing a product that can be measured potentiometrically.
2. **Examples:** Glucose-selective electrodes (glucose oxidase).

Applications of Potentiometry

1. **pH Measurement:** Widely used in laboratories, industry, environmental monitoring, and healthcare.
2. **Ion Analysis:** Determination of various ions such as sodium, potassium, calcium, fluoride, chloride, and more.
3. **Water Quality Monitoring:** Measurement of ions and pollutants in water bodies.
4. **Clinical Diagnostics:** Monitoring electrolytes in blood, urine, and other bodily fluids.
5. **Food and Beverage Industry:** Quality control of products by measuring ion concentrations.

Advantages of Potentiometry

1. **High Selectivity:** Ion-selective electrodes provide selective measurements for specific ions.
2. **Non-destructive:** The sample remains largely unchanged during measurement.
3. **Real-time Monitoring:** Enables continuous and real-time analysis.
4. **Wide Range of Applications:** Useful in various fields from environmental science to medicine.

Limitations of Potentiometry

1. **Interference:** Other ions or substances in the solution can interfere with the measurement.
2. **Electrode Maintenance:** Electrodes require regular calibration and maintenance.
3. **Temperature Sensitivity:** The potential can be affected by changes in temperature.

ELECTROCHEMICAL CELL

An electrochemical cell in potentiometry consists of two electrodes: a reference electrode and an indicator (or working) electrode. The cell is designed to measure the potential difference (voltage) between these electrodes, which is related to the concentration of the ion of interest in the solution.

Components of an Electrochemical Cell

1. **Reference Electrode**
    a. **Function:** Maintains a constant and known potential regardless of the solution composition.
    b. **Common Types:**
        i. **Saturated Calomel Electrode (SCE):**
            1. Contains mercury in contact with a saturated solution of potassium chloride and mercury chloride (calomel).
            2. Potential is stable and well-defined.
        ii. **Silver/Silver Chloride Electrode (Ag/AgCl):**
            1. Contains a silver wire coated with silver chloride, immersed in a potassium chloride solution.
            2. Known for its stability and ease of use.
2. **Indicator Electrode**
    a. **Function:** Responds to the activity of the specific ion being measured.
    b. **Types:**

i. **Glass Electrodes:**

1. Typically used for measuring pH (hydrogen ion concentration).
2. Have a thin glass membrane that selectively binds hydrogen ions.

ii. **Ion-Selective Electrodes (ISEs):**

1. Designed for specific ions like fluoride, calcium, or potassium.
2. Have membranes that interact selectively with the target ion.

iii. **Metal Electrodes:**

1. Used for redox reactions (e.g., platinum electrodes).

Cell Setup

In a typical potentiometric setup:

1. The reference electrode is placed in the solution to provide a stable potential.
2. The indicator electrode is placed in the same solution to measure the potential that varies with the ion concentration.
3. A voltmeter is used to measure the potential difference between the reference and indicator electrodes.

STANDARD HYDROGEN ELECTRODE

The Standard Hydrogen Electrode (SHE) is a primary reference electrode used in electrochemistry. It provides a universal reference potential for measuring the electrode potentials of other electrodes. The SHE has a defined potential of 0.000 V under standard conditions, which include a hydrogen ion concentration of 1 M (pH 0), a temperature of 298 K (25°C), and a pressure of 1 atmosphere (101.3 kPa) of hydrogen gas.

Construction of the Standard Hydrogen Electrode

1. **Platinum Electrode:**
   a. A piece of platinum foil or wire is used as the electrode surface.

b. Platinum is chosen because it is chemically inert and provides a large surface area for the hydrogen gas to adsorb and desorb.

2. **Hydrogen Gas:**
   a. Pure hydrogen gas is bubbled around the platinum electrode.
   b. The gas must be at a pressure of 1 atmosphere.
3. **Electrolyte Solution:**
   a. The electrode is immersed in an acidic solution with a hydrogen ion concentration of 1 M.
   b. Commonly used acids include hydrochloric acid (HCl).
4. **Hydrogen Ion Equilibrium:**
   a. The equilibrium at the electrode surface can be represented by the half-reaction:

$$H_2(g) \rightleftharpoons 2H^+(aq) + 2e^-$$

Working of the Standard Hydrogen Electrode

1. **Electrode Reaction:**
   a. The hydrogen gas at 1 atm pressure is bubbled over the platinum electrode.
   b. The platinum surface catalyzes the equilibrium between hydrogen gas and hydrogen ions in the solution:

$$H_2(g) \rightleftharpoons 2H^+(aq) + 2e^-$$

2. **Measurement of Potential:**
   a. The potential of the SHE is defined as 0.000 V under standard conditions.
   b. When connected to another electrode in an electrochemical cell, the potential difference between the SHE and the other electrode can be measured using a high-impedance voltmeter.
   c. The SHE serves as a reference point to determine the standard electrode potentials of other half-cells.

3. **Use in Potentiometry:**
    a. In potentiometric measurements, the SHE can be used as the reference electrode.
    b. It provides a stable and known potential, allowing for accurate measurement of the potential of the indicator electrode.
    c. By connecting the SHE to an unknown half-cell, the electrode potential of the unknown half-cell can be determined relative to the SHE.

Applications of the Standard Hydrogen Electrode

1. **Standard Electrode Potentials:**
    a. The SHE is used to measure and tabulate the standard electrode potentials of various half-cells.
    b. These potentials are critical for understanding redox reactions and electrochemical processes.
2. **Calibration:**
    a. The SHE can calibrate other reference electrodes, ensuring accurate and consistent measurements in electrochemical experiments.
3. **Fundamental Research:**
    a. The SHE is used in fundamental research to study electrochemical phenomena and reaction mechanisms.

Advantages of the Standard Hydrogen Electrode

1. **Universal Reference:** Provides a universal reference potential of 0.000 V.
2. **Reproducibility:** Offers highly reproducible and stable potential measurements.
3. **Inert Electrode:** Platinum electrode is chemically inert and does not participate in the reaction.

Limitations of the Standard Hydrogen Electrode

1. **Handling of Hydrogen Gas:** Requires careful handling of hydrogen gas at 1 atm pressure, which can be hazardous.
2. **Maintenance:** The platinum electrode and electrolyte solution require regular maintenance and replenishment.
3. **Special Conditions:** Requires specific conditions (1 M H+ concentration, 1 atm H2 pressure) to maintain the standard potential.

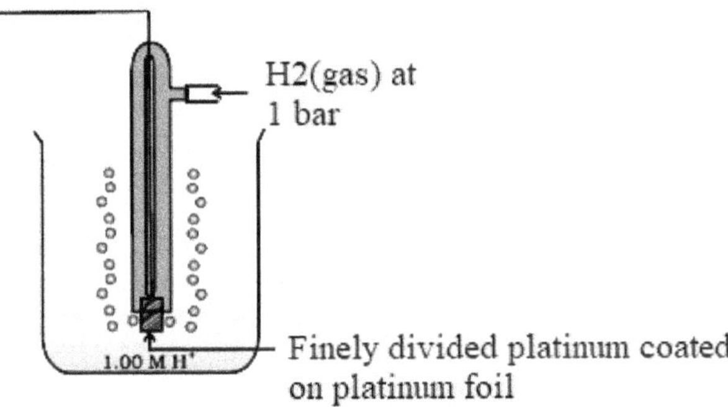

SILVER CHLORIDE ELECTRODE

The Silver/Silver Chloride (Ag/AgCl) electrode is a common reference electrode used in potentiometry and various electrochemical measurements. It is valued for its stable potential, ease of preparation, and reproducibility. The Ag/AgCl electrode consists of a silver wire coated with silver chloride and immersed in a chloride ion-containing solution, typically potassium chloride (KCl).

Construction of the Silver/Silver Chloride Electrode

1. **Silver Wire:**
   a. A silver wire (high purity) serves as the base material.
   b. The wire is cleaned thoroughly to remove any impurities or oxides on its surface.
2. **Coating with Silver Chloride:**

a. The cleaned silver wire is coated with a thin layer of silver chloride (AgCl).
b. This can be achieved by:
    i. **Electrolytic Method:** Immersing the silver wire in a chloride solution (e.g., HCl or KCl) and applying an electrical current to form the AgCl layer.
    ii. **Chemical Method:** Dipping the silver wire in a solution of sodium chloride (NaCl) or potassium chloride (KCl) and then exposing it to chlorine gas or immersing it in a hypochlorite solution.
c. The silver chloride coating should be uniform and adherent to ensure a stable and reproducible potential.

3. **Electrolyte Solution:**
    a. The electrode is immersed in a chloride ion-containing solution, typically potassium chloride (KCl).
    b. The concentration of the KCl solution can vary, with saturated KCl solution often used for high stability and low junction potential.
4. **Housing:**
    a. The Ag/AgCl electrode is housed in a suitable container, often a glass or plastic tube, with a porous junction (e.g., ceramic frit or fiber wick) to allow contact with the sample solution.
    b. The housing ensures the electrode is well-protected and provides a stable environment for the reference solution.

Working of the Silver/Silver Chloride Electrode

1. **Electrode Reaction:**
    a. The Ag/AgCl electrode works based on the equilibrium between the silver metal (Ag) and silver chloride (AgCl) in the presence of chloride ions (Cl^-).
    b. The half-reaction at the electrode surface is:

$$AgCl\ (s) + e^{-} \rightleftharpoons Ag\ (s) + Cl^{-}$$

2. **Electrode Potential:**
    a. The potential of the Ag/AgCl electrode is determined by the Nernst equation:

    $$E_{Ag/AgCl} = E^{\circ}_{Ag/AgCl} + \frac{RT}{F}\ln[Cl^{-}]$$

    b. Here, EAg/AgCl∘ is the standard electrode potential of the Ag/AgCl electrode, R is the gas constant, T is the temperature, and F is the Faraday constant.
    c. The electrode potential depends on the concentration of chloride ions in the electrolyte solution.
3. **Use in Potentiometry:**
    a. The Ag/AgCl electrode serves as a reference electrode, providing a stable and known potential.
    b. It is paired with an indicator electrode to form an electrochemical cell.
    c. The potential difference between the Ag/AgCl electrode and the indicator electrode is measured to determine the ion concentration in the sample solution.

Applications of the Silver/Silver Chloride Electrode

1. **pH Measurement:**
    a. Often used in combination with a glass pH electrode to measure the pH of solutions.
2. **Ion-Selective Measurements:**
    a. Used as a reference electrode in various ion-selective electrode (ISE) measurements for ions like sodium, potassium, and calcium.
3. **Electrochemical Studies:**
    a. Employed in electrochemical studies, including cyclic voltammetry, chronoamperometry, and potentiometric titrations.

Advantages of the Silver/Silver Chloride Electrode

1. **Stable and Reproducible Potential:** Provides a stable reference potential for accurate measurements.
2. **Ease of Preparation:** Relatively easy to prepare and maintain.
3. **Compatibility:** Compatible with a wide range of electrolyte solutions and sample matrices.
4. **Low Cost:** Generally inexpensive compared to other reference electrodes like the calomel electrode.

Limitations of the Silver/Silver Chloride Electrode

1. **Junction Potential:** Potential differences at the porous junction can introduce errors.
2. **Chloride Ion Sensitivity:** The electrode potential is dependent on the chloride ion concentration, which must be controlled.
3. **Temperature Dependence:** The potential can be affected by temperature changes, requiring compensation.

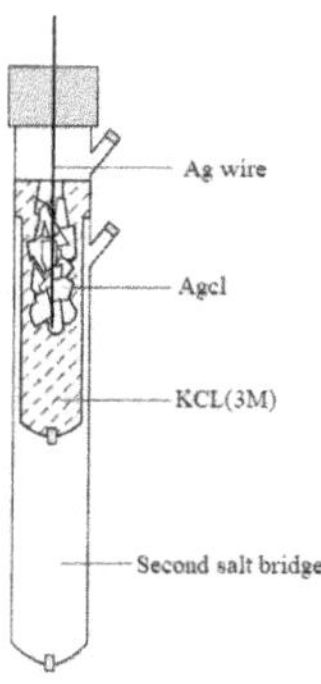

CALOMEL ELECTRODE

Metal electrodes are commonly used in potentiometry for measuring the potential of redox reactions. These electrodes are typically made from noble metals such as platinum, gold, or silver, which are chemically inert and capable of transferring electrons efficiently.

Construction of Metal Electrodes

1. **Electrode Material:**
    a. **Platinum (Pt):** Widely used due to its inertness and excellent conductivity.
    b. **Gold (Au):** Used for its chemical stability and inertness.
    c. **Silver (Ag):** Used in specific applications, often coated with silver chloride (Ag/AgCl).
2. **Electrode Design:**
    a. **Wire or Foil:**
        i. The metal is often fashioned into a wire or foil.
        ii. For platinum and gold electrodes, a thin wire or foil is typically used to increase surface area and sensitivity.
    b. **Disk or Rod:**
        i. Metal electrodes can also be constructed as a disk or rod, often embedded in an inert material like glass or epoxy for structural stability and ease of handling.
3. **Connection:**
    a. The metal electrode is connected to an electrical lead, usually encased in an insulating sheath to prevent interference.
    b. The exposed part of the electrode is polished to ensure a clean and active surface for the redox reactions.
4. **Protective Housing (Optional):**
    a. In some cases, the metal electrode is housed in a protective sheath, especially if it is used in harsh environments.

Working of Metal Electrodes in Potentiometry

1. **Electrode Reaction:**
    a. The metal electrode functions by participating in a redox reaction with the ions in the solution.
    b. For example, in a platinum electrode:

$$\text{Pt (s)} + \text{Red} \rightleftharpoons \text{Pt}^{n+} + \text{Ox} + ne^{-}$$

c. Here, "Red" and "Ox" represent the reduced and oxidized forms of the redox couple, respectively, and n is the number of electrons involved.

2. **Electrode Potential:**

a. The potential of the metal electrode is related to the concentration of the oxidized and reduced forms of the redox couple by the Nernst equation:

$$E = E^{\circ} + \frac{RT}{nF} \ln\left(\frac{[\text{Ox}]}{[\text{Red}]}\right)$$

b. E∘ is the standard electrode potential, R is the gas constant, T is the temperature, F is the Faraday constant, and n is the number of electrons transferred.

3. **Use in Potentiometry:**

a. Metal electrodes are paired with a reference electrode (such as an Ag/AgCl electrode) to form an electrochemical cell.

b. The potential difference between the metal electrode and the reference electrode is measured using a high-impedance voltmeter.

c. This potential difference is related to the concentration of the redox species in the solution, allowing for quantitative analysis.

Applications of Metal Electrodes

1. **Redox Titrations:**

a. Metal electrodes are used to detect the endpoint in redox titrations by measuring the potential change.

2. **Environmental Monitoring:**

a. Used to monitor redox potential (Eh) in natural waters, soils, and other environmental samples.

3. **Biochemical Analysis:**

a. Employed in studying redox-active biomolecules and enzymes.

4. **Electrochemical Studies:**

a. Used in various electrochemical techniques like cyclic voltammetry and chronoamperometry to study reaction kinetics and mechanisms.

Advantages of Metal Electrodes

1. **Chemical Inertness:** Noble metals like platinum and gold are chemically inert and resist corrosion.
2. **High Conductivity:** These metals have excellent electrical conductivity, allowing efficient electron transfer.
3. **Versatility:** Can be used in a wide range of redox reactions and environmental conditions.

Limitations of Metal Electrodes

1. **Cost:** Noble metals can be expensive, increasing the cost of the electrodes.
2. **Surface Fouling:** The electrode surface can become fouled by impurities or reaction products, requiring regular cleaning.
3. **Sensitivity to Interference:** The electrode potential can be influenced by other redox-active species in the solution.

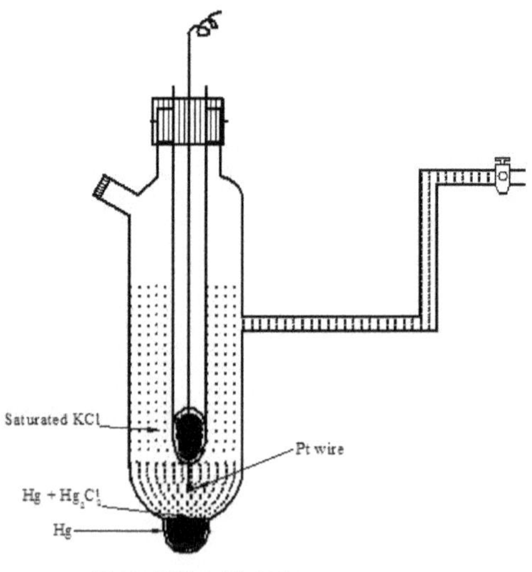

Standard Calomel Electrode

GLASS ELECTRODE

The glass electrode is a crucial component in potentiometric measurements, particularly for determining the pH of a solution. It is a type of ion-selective electrode that responds specifically to hydrogen ions (H^+) in the solution.

Construction of Glass Electrode

1. **Glass Membrane:**
   a. The core of the glass electrode is a thin-walled glass membrane, typically made from a special composition of silicate glass that is selectively permeable to hydrogen ions.
   b. The glass membrane has a high electrical resistance and is designed to allow hydrogen ions to exchange between the internal solution and the test solution.
2. **Internal Solution:**
   a. Inside the glass membrane is an internal solution of known and stable pH, usually a buffered solution containing a fixed concentration of hydrogen ions.
   b. Commonly used internal solutions include 0.1 M HCl or a buffer solution with a known pH.
3. **Internal Reference Electrode:**
   a. An internal reference electrode, often a silver/silver chloride (Ag/AgCl) electrode, is immersed in the internal solution.
   b. This electrode maintains a constant potential and is crucial for the stable operation of the glass electrode.
4. **External Reference Electrode:**
   a. The glass electrode is used in conjunction with an external reference electrode (e.g., Ag/AgCl or saturated calomel electrode) to complete the electrochemical cell.

5. **Electrode Body:**
    a. The entire assembly is housed in a durable, inert body made of materials like glass or plastic.
    b. The body often has a protective cap to prevent damage to the delicate glass membrane when not in use.
6. **Electrical Connection:**
    a. The internal reference electrode is connected to an electrical lead that transmits the potential difference to a high-impedance voltmeter or pH meter.

Working of the Glass Electrode in Potentiometry

1. **Electrode Potential Development:**
    a. When the glass electrode is immersed in a test solution, hydrogen ions from the test solution interact with the glass membrane.
    b. This interaction creates a potential difference (electromotive force, EMF) across the glass membrane, which is dependent on the hydrogen ion concentration (pH) of the test solution.
2. **Electrode Reaction:**
    a. The reaction at the glass membrane surface can be represented as:

    $$\mathrm{H}^{+}_{\text{test solution}} + \mathrm{H}^{+}_{\text{internal solution}} \rightleftharpoons \mathrm{H}^{+}_{\text{glass membrane}}$$

3. **Measurement of Potential:**
    a. The potential difference between the internal reference electrode and the external reference electrode is measured.
    b. This potential difference is related to the pH of the test solution by the Nernst equation:

    $$E = E^{\circ} + \frac{RT}{F} \ln[\mathrm{H}^{+}]$$

c. Here, E is the measured potential, E∘ is the standard potential, R is the gas constant, T is the temperature, FFF is the Faraday constant, and [H+] is the hydrogen ion concentration.

4. **Calibration:**
    a. The glass electrode must be calibrated using buffer solutions of known pH values before use.
    b. Calibration ensures accurate pH measurements by establishing the relationship between the measured potential and the pH.

Applications of Glass Electrodes

1. **pH Measurement:**
    a. Widely used for pH measurements in laboratories, industry, and environmental monitoring.
2. **Biochemical and Clinical Applications:**
    a. Used to measure pH in biological samples and clinical specimens.
3. **Food and Beverage Industry:**
    a. Used to monitor pH in food and beverage production for quality control.

Advantages of Glass Electrodes

1. **High Selectivity:** Specifically responsive to hydrogen ions, providing accurate pH measurements.
2. **Wide pH Range:** Can measure pH over a wide range, typically from pH 1 to pH 14.
3. **Durability:** The glass membrane is chemically resistant and durable.
4. **Reproducibility:** Provides consistent and reproducible measurements.

Limitations of Glass Electrodes

1. **Fragility:** The glass membrane is delicate and can be easily damaged.
2. **Calibration Requirement:** Requires regular calibration with standard buffer solutions.

3. **Temperature Sensitivity:** The potential can be affected by temperature changes, requiring temperature compensation.

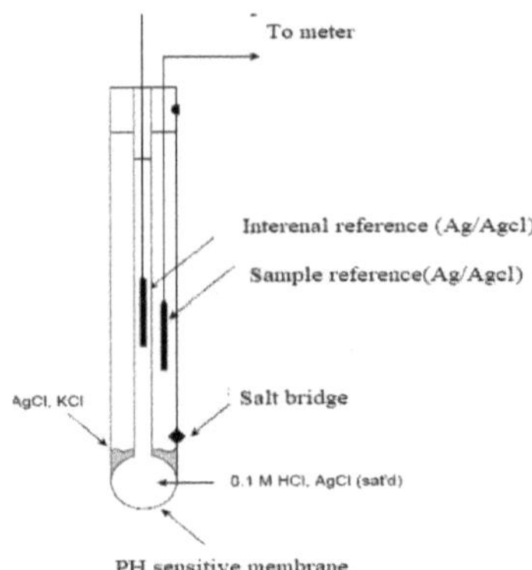

METHODS TO DETERMINE END POINT OF POTENTIOMETRIC TITRATION

Potentiometric titration is a technique where the potential difference between two electrodes is measured as a function of the titrant volume added. Determining the end point of a potentiometric titration is crucial for accurate analysis. Several methods can be used to identify the end point:

1. Graphical Method

The most common method involves plotting the potential (E) against the volume of titrant (V) and identifying the end point based on the shape of the titration curve.

a. **First Derivative Plot:**
    i. Plot dV/dE (change in potential per unit volume of titrant) against the volume of titrant.
    ii. The end point corresponds to the peak in the first derivative plot, where the slope of the E vs. V curve is the steepest.

b. **Second Derivative Plot:**
    i. Plot dV2/d2E (change in the first derivative) against the volume of titrant.

   ii. The end point is located where the second derivative crosses zero, which corresponds to the inflection point of the E vs. V curve.

2. Gran Plot

The Gran plot is a method used to determine the end point more accurately, especially in weak acid or base titrations.

a. **Acid-Base Titrations:**
   i. For an acid titrated with a strong base, plot $V \cdot 10-E/0.059$ against the volume of titrant added.
   ii. The end point is found by extrapolating the linear portion of the plot to intersect the volume axis.

b. **Redox Titrations:**
   i. Similar to acid-base titrations, but the y-axis may differ depending on the specific redox reaction involved.

3. Potential Jump Method

This method involves observing a significant change (jump) in the potential near the equivalence point.

a. **Sharp Change:**
   i. Near the end point, the potential typically changes sharply due to the rapid shift in the concentration of the titrated species.
   ii. The midpoint of this sharp change is taken as the end point.

4. Bipotentiometric Titration

a. **End Point Determination:**
   i. The end point is identified by a sudden change in the potential difference between the two electrodes.
   ii. This method is useful for titrations with no clear inflection point in a single electrode measurement.

5. Equivalence Point Determination Using pH Meter

For acid-base titrations, a pH meter can be used to monitor the pH change instead of potential.

a. **pH Curve:**

i. Plot pH against the volume of titrant.

ii. The end point is identified by the steepest part of the pH curve or the inflection point.

6. Differential Method

a. **Differential Plot:**

i. Plot the difference in potential (ΔE\Delta EΔE) against the volume of titrant.

ii. The end point is indicated by a maximum in the differential plot.

Example Procedure for Acid-Base Titration

1. **Setup:**
   a. Prepare the titration apparatus with a suitable reference electrode (e.g., Ag/AgCl) and an indicator electrode (e.g., glass electrode for pH measurement).
2. **Initial Measurement:**
   a. Measure the initial potential or pH of the solution before adding any titrant.
3. **Titration:**
   a. Add the titrant in small, measured increments.
   b. Record the potential or pH after each addition.
4. **Plotting:**
   a. Plot the potential or pH against the volume of titrant added.
   b. Alternatively, calculate and plot the first and second derivatives.
5. **End Point Identification:**
   a. Identify the end point using the graphical method (first or second derivative plot), Gran plot, or by observing the potential jump.

APPLICATIONS OF POTENTIOMETRY

Potentiometry is a versatile and widely used analytical technique with numerous applications across various fields. Here are some of the key applications:

1. pH Measurement

a. **Water Quality Monitoring:** Used to measure the pH of natural waters, wastewater, and drinking water to ensure safety and compliance with environmental regulations.

b. **Agriculture:** Helps in soil testing to determine soil pH, which is crucial for optimizing crop growth and nutrient availability.

c. **Food and Beverage Industry:** Monitors pH levels in the production of foods and beverages to ensure product quality and safety.

d. **Clinical and Biomedical Applications:** Measures the pH of biological fluids such as blood, urine, and saliva, which is important for diagnosing and monitoring various medical conditions.

2. Ion-Selective Electrode (ISE) Analysis

a. **Environmental Monitoring:** Detects and quantifies specific ions like nitrate, ammonium, and chloride in water and soil samples.

b. **Clinical Diagnostics:** Measures ion concentrations in blood, serum, and urine, including electrolytes like sodium, potassium, and calcium.

c. **Industrial Process Control:** Monitors ion concentrations in various industrial processes, such as the production of chemicals, pharmaceuticals, and semiconductors.

3. Redox Titrations

a. **Chemical Analysis:** Used for titrations involving redox reactions to determine the concentration of oxidizing or reducing agents.

b. **Environmental Testing:** Determines the levels of pollutants like heavy metals (e.g., chromium, lead) in water and soil samples through redox titrations.

c. **Pharmaceutical Analysis:** Quantifies active pharmaceutical ingredients and impurities in drug formulations through redox titrations.

4. **Potentiometric Titrations**
   a. **Acid-Base Titrations:** Determines the concentration of acidic or basic substances in various samples, such as food products, pharmaceuticals, and environmental samples.
   b. **Complexometric Titrations:** Measures the concentration of metal ions using complexometric titrations with chelating agents like EDTA.
   c. **Precipitation Titrations:** Quantifies ions that form insoluble precipitates, such as chloride, using silver nitrate titration.
5. **Electrochemical Studies**
   a. **Kinetics and Mechanisms:** Studies the kinetics and mechanisms of redox reactions and other electrochemical processes.
   b. **Corrosion Studies:** Investigates the corrosion behavior of metals and alloys by measuring their electrode potentials in various environments.
   c. **Battery and Fuel Cell Research:** Evaluates the performance of batteries and fuel cells by measuring the potentials of electrodes under different conditions.
6. **Quality Control and Assurance**
   a. **Manufacturing Industries:** Ensures product quality and consistency by monitoring the pH, ion concentration, and redox potential in various manufacturing processes.
   b. **Pharmaceutical Industry:** Conducts quality control tests on raw materials, intermediates, and finished products to ensure compliance with regulatory standards.
   c. **Food and Beverage Industry:** Maintains the quality and safety of food and beverage products by monitoring pH and ion concentrations during production.

7. Research and Development

a. **Chemical Research:** Develops new chemical compounds and materials by studying their electrochemical properties.
b. **Biological Research:** Investigates the electrochemical behavior of biomolecules, enzymes, and cells.
c. **Environmental Research:** Studies the impact of pollutants and environmental changes on the redox potential and pH of natural systems.

Multiple Choice Questions (MCQs)

1. What is potentiometry primarily used to determine?
    a) Temperature
    b) Pressure
    c) Ion concentration
    d) Mass
2. Which equation is fundamental to potentiometry?
    a) Arrhenius equation
    b) Nernst equation
    c) Michaelis-Menten equation
    d) Einstein equation
3. What is the role of a reference electrode in potentiometry?
    a) To measure temperature
    b) To maintain a constant and known potential
    c) To react with the analyte
    d) To change the pH of the solution
4. Which of the following is a common reference electrode used in potentiometry?
    a) Platinum electrode
    b) Gold electrode

c) Silver/Silver Chloride electrode

d) Copper electrode

5. What type of electrode responds to the activity of a specific ion being measured in potentiometry?

a) Reference electrode

b) Indicator electrode

c) Auxiliary electrode

d) Counter electrode

6. What is the primary function of a glass electrode?

a) Measure temperature

b) Measure pH

c) Measure pressure

d) Measure conductivity

7. Which ion does a glass electrode specifically respond to?

a) Sodium ion (Na+)

b) Chloride ion (Cl-)

c) Hydrogen ion (H+)

d) Calcium ion (Ca2+)

8. What type of titration involves measuring the potential change and determining the endpoint by the inflection point on the titration curve?

a) Direct potentiometry

b) Potentiometric titration

c) Gravimetric titration

d) Volumetric titration

9. Which of the following is an example of an ion-selective electrode?

a) Platinum electrode

b) pH electrode

c) Calomel electrode

d) Silver electrode

10. What is the standard potential of the Standard Hydrogen Electrode (SHE) under standard conditions?

a) 1.000 V

b) 0.500 V

c) 0.000 V

d) 0.250 V

11. Which electrode is often used in combination with a glass pH electrode?

a) Copper electrode

b) Silver/Silver Chloride electrode

c) Gold electrode

d) Platinum electrode

12. What is a common application of potentiometry in the food and beverage industry?

a) Measuring viscosity

b) Monitoring pH levels

c) Determining color

d) Measuring weight

13. Which ion-selective electrode is used for fluoride measurement?

a) Glass electrode

b) Silver electrode

c) Fluoride-selective electrode

d) Platinum electrode

14. What is the role of an internal reference electrode in a glass electrode?

a) To measure the external temperature

b) To provide a stable internal potential

c) To change the color of the solution

d) To increase the ion concentration

15. Which of the following is an advantage of potentiometry?

a) High interference from other ions

b) Non-destructive analysis

c) Complex equipment required

d) High maintenance cost

16. In the construction of the Silver/Silver Chloride electrode, which solution is used as the electrolyte?

a) Sodium chloride

b) Hydrochloric acid

c) Potassium chloride

d) Sulfuric acid

17. Which method in potentiometric titration involves plotting dE/dV against the volume of titrant?

a) Gran plot

b) Differential method

c) First derivative plot

d) Second derivative plot

18. What is a primary use of the Standard Hydrogen Electrode (SHE) in potentiometry?

a) Measuring temperature

b) Providing a universal reference potential

c) Measuring mass

d) Providing a standard pH value

19. Which electrode is used for redox reactions in potentiometry?

a) Glass electrode

b) Platinum electrode

c) Silver/Silver Chloride electrode

d) Reference electrode

20. What is the primary limitation of potentiometry regarding temperature?

a) Temperature stability

b) Temperature sensitivity

c) Temperature measurement

d) Temperature calibration

Short Answer Type Questions (Subjective)

1. Define potentiometry and describe its primary application.
2. What is the Nernst equation and how is it related to potentiometry?
3. List the components of a typical electrochemical cell used in potentiometry.
4. Explain the role of the reference electrode in potentiometry.
5. What are ion-selective electrodes and provide two examples?
6. Describe the function of a glass electrode in pH measurement.
7. What is the standard potential of the Standard Hydrogen Electrode (SHE)?
8. How is the potential of the Silver/Silver Chloride (Ag/AgCl) electrode determined?
9. What are metal electrodes commonly used for in potentiometry?
10. Explain how a glass electrode develops potential in a solution.
11. What is the significance of the activity coefficient in potentiometry?
12. Describe the procedure for calibrating a glass electrode.
13. What is the primary limitation of potentiometry with respect to temperature?
14. List three applications of potentiometry in clinical diagnostics.
15. How is the endpoint of a potentiometric titration determined using a first derivative plot?
16. Explain the principle of the potential jump method in potentiometric titrations.
17. What are the advantages of using ion-selective electrodes in potentiometry?
18. Describe how a Gran plot is used to determine the endpoint of a potentiometric titration.
19. What are the key advantages of using the Silver/Silver Chloride (Ag/AgCl) electrode?

20. Explain the concept of real-time monitoring in potentiometry and its importance.

Long answer type questions (subjective)

1. Describe the construction and working principles of the Standard Hydrogen Electrode (SHE). Include its applications and limitations.
2. Explain the construction and working of the Silver/Silver Chloride (Ag/AgCl) electrode. Discuss its advantages and limitations compared to other reference electrodes.
3. Discuss the various types of ion-selective electrodes (ISEs) used in potentiometry. Include examples and their specific applications.
4. Describe the methods used to determine the endpoint in potentiometric titrations. Discuss the graphical method, Gran plot, and potential jump method in detail.
5. Explain the applications of potentiometry in environmental monitoring. Include specific examples of ion analysis and pH measurement.
6. Discuss the role of potentiometry in the food and beverage industry. Include how pH and ion concentration measurements are used in quality control.
7. Describe the construction and working principle of a glass electrode used for pH measurement. Include the calibration process and factors affecting its accuracy.
8. Explain the principles of electrochemical cells used in potentiometry. Include the functions of reference and indicator electrodes, and how the potential difference is measured.
9. Discuss the applications of potentiometry in clinical diagnostics. Include specific examples of ion-selective measurements and their importance in healthcare.

10. Describe the limitations of potentiometry and how they can be addressed. Include interference from other ions, electrode maintenance, and temperature sensitivity.

Answer Key

1. c) Ion concentration
2. b) Nernst equation
3. b) To maintain a constant and known potential
4. c) Silver/Silver Chloride electrode
5. b) Indicator electrode
6. b) Measure pH
7. c) Hydrogen ion (H+)
8. b) Potentiometric titration
9. b) pH electrode
10. c) 0.000 V
11. b) Silver/Silver Chloride electrode
12. b) Monitoring pH levels
13. c) Fluoride-selective electrode
14. b) To provide a stable internal
15. b) Non-destructive analysis
16. c) Potassium chloride
17. c) First derivative plot
18. b) Providing a universal reference potential
19. b) Platinum electrode
20. b) Temperature sensitivity

CHAPTER – 15

POLAROGRAPHY

INTRODUCTION:

Polarography is an electrochemical technique used to study the behavior of substances in solution. It involves measuring the current that flows through an electrochemical cell as a function of an applied potential. Here's a detailed introduction to polarography:

Principles of Polarography:

1. **Electrochemical Cell Setup**: Polarography typically uses a three-electrode system consisting of a working electrode (often a dropping mercury electrode), a reference electrode (such as a saturated calomel electrode), and an auxiliary electrode (like a platinum wire). The working electrode is immersed in the solution under study.
2. **Mercury Drop Electrode**: The working electrode in polarography is often a dropping mercury electrode (DME). Mercury allows for the formation of drops of known surface area, ensuring reproducible results. The mercury surface is renewed periodically by dropping fresh mercury into the solution.
3. **Analytical Technique**: Polarography measures the current that flows between the working and auxiliary electrodes as the potential of the working electrode is varied linearly with time (linear sweep) or held constant (differential pulse). This current provides information about the concentration and electrochemical behavior of the analyte in solution.

Steps Involved in Polarography:

1. **Electrolyte Preparation**: Prepare the electrolyte solution containing the substance of interest. This solution must be stable and suitable for electrochemical analysis.

2. **Electrode Preparation**: Set up the electrochemical cell with the appropriate electrodes: working electrode (usually dropping mercury), reference electrode (e.g., calomel electrode), and auxiliary electrode (typically platinum).
3. **Measurement**: Apply a potential to the working electrode and measure the resulting current. The potential can be scanned linearly to produce a polarogram, which is a plot of current versus potential.
4. **Analysis**: Analyze the polarogram to determine key parameters such as the half-wave potential (E1/2), peak currents, and peak potentials. These parameters provide information about the redox behavior and concentration of the analyte.

Applications of Polarography:

1. **Quantitative Analysis**: Polarography is used for quantitative determination of substances in solution, particularly metal ions and organic compounds.
2. **Electrode Kinetics**: It provides insights into electrode kinetics and reaction mechanisms by studying the current-potential relationship.
3. **Environmental Monitoring**: Used in environmental monitoring to detect pollutants and trace metals in water samples.
4. **Biological Applications**: Applied in biological and pharmaceutical research to study biochemical reactions and pharmaceutical formulations.

Advantages and Limitations:

1. **Advantages**: High sensitivity, ability to analyze trace amounts, relatively simple instrumentation.
2. **Limitations**: Limited to electroactive substances, requires careful calibration and control of experimental conditions, and can be affected by electrode fouling.

PRINCIPLE OF POLAROGRAPHY

The principle of polarography revolves around the electrochemical behavior of substances in solution, particularly their reduction or oxidation processes at the surface of a working electrode. Here's a detailed explanation of the principle of polarography:

Electrochemical Behavior:

1. **Redox Reactions**: Polarography focuses on the study of redox (reduction-oxidation) reactions that occur at the interface between the working electrode and the solution. These reactions involve the transfer of electrons between the analyte species in solution and the electrode surface.
2. **Electrode Potential**: The potential applied to the working electrode is crucial. By varying this potential, either linearly or in steps, one can control the rate and direction of electron transfer reactions at the electrode surface.

Dropping Mercury Electrode (DME):

1. **Surface Renewal**: In polarography, the most commonly used working electrode is the dropping mercury electrode (DME). Mercury drops periodically renew the electrode's surface area, ensuring reproducibility and stability in measurements.
2. **Mercury Meniscus**: The mercury meniscus serves as the surface where the electrochemical reactions take place. As fresh mercury drops into the solution, it forms a new electrode surface, allowing continuous measurement without electrode passivation.

Polarographic Technique:

1. **Potential Sweep**: During a typical polarographic measurement, the potential applied to the working electrode is swept linearly or held at discrete steps while the resulting current is measured. This potential sweep allows for the characterization of the redox behavior of the analyte.
2. **Current Measurement**: The current flowing between the working and auxiliary electrodes is directly proportional to the rate of electrochemical reaction occurring at the electrode surface. This current is recorded as a function of the applied potential, producing a polarogram.

Half-Wave Potential (E1/2):

1. **Analytical Parameter**: One of the key parameters derived from polarography is the half-wave potential (E1/2). This is the potential at which half of the analyte molecules are oxidized and half are reduced, indicating the midpoint of the redox process.
2. **Peak Currents**: The polarogram also displays peak currents and peak potentials, which provide information about the concentration and electrochemical activity of the analyte in solution.

Applications:

1. **Quantitative Analysis**: Polarography is widely used for quantitative analysis of substances, particularly metals and organic compounds, in solution.
2. **Research and Development**: It is employed in research and development across various industries, including pharmaceuticals, environmental monitoring, and materials science, to study reaction mechanisms and electrochemical behavior.

Advantages and Limitations:

1. **Advantages**: High sensitivity, ability to analyze trace amounts, and relatively simple instrumentation compared to other electrochemical techniques.
2. **Limitations**: Limited to electroactive substances, potential interference from impurities or complex matrices in solution, and requires careful control of experimental conditions.

ILKOVIC EQUATION

The Ilkovič equation is a fundamental equation used in polarography to describe the relationship between the current (i) flowing through the working electrode and the applied potential (E). It helps in understanding the behavior of the electrochemical processes occurring during polarographic measurements.

Here's a detailed explanation of the Ilkovič equation and its significance in polarography:

Ilkovič Equation:

The Ilkovič equation is expressed as:

$$i = k \cdot n \cdot A \cdot D^{1/2} \cdot C \cdot v^{1/2}$$

Where:

1. **i**: Current (amperes, A)
2. **k**: Constant that depends on the specific electrochemical system
3. **n**: Number of electrons involved in the redox process
4. **A**: Electrode area (cm^2)
5. **D**: Diffusion coefficient of the electroactive species (cm^2/s)
6. **C**: Concentration of the electroactive species (mol/cm^3 or M)
7. **v**: Scan rate or sweep rate (V/s)

Detailed Components:

1. **Current (i)**: The current is directly measured during polarography and is influenced by the electrochemical reactions occurring at the electrode surface.
2. **Constant (k)**: This parameter incorporates several factors including the rate of electron transfer, surface area of the electrode, and the nature of the electroactive species.
3. **Number of Electrons (n)**: Represents the number of electrons transferred in the redox reaction at the electrode surface.
4. **Electrode Area (A)**: Refers to the active area of the working electrode where the electrochemical reaction takes place. In polarography, this is often controlled using a dropping mercury electrode (DME).
5. **Diffusion Coefficient (D)**: Describes how quickly the electroactive species diffuses through the solution towards the electrode surface. It depends on the properties of the analyte and the solvent.

6. **Concentration (C)**: The concentration of the electroactive species in solution. This parameter directly affects the current observed during polarography.
7. **Scan Rate (v)**: The rate at which the potential is scanned during polarographic measurements. It influences the rate of electrochemical reactions and hence the resulting current.

Significance and Applications:

1. **Quantitative Analysis**: The Ilkovič equation is crucial for quantifying the concentration of electroactive species in solution based on the measured current during polarography.
2. **Electrochemical Kinetics**: Helps in understanding the kinetics of electrode reactions, including the rate of electron transfer and diffusion of species to the electrode surface.
3. **Parameter Optimization**: By understanding how each parameter (such as concentration, electrode area, and scan rate) affects the current, researchers can optimize experimental conditions for accurate and reproducible measurements.

Limitations:

1. **Ideal Conditions**: The Ilkovič equation assumes ideal conditions, including uniform electrode surface, steady-state diffusion, and negligible interference from side reactions or impurities.
2. **Complex Systems**: In real-world applications, complex matrices or impurities in the solution can affect the accuracy of measurements, requiring careful calibration and validation.

MERCURY ELECTRODE

The dropping mercury electrode (DME) is a crucial component in polarography, serving as the working electrode where electrochemical reactions occur during measurements. Here's a detailed explanation of the construction and working principles of the dropping mercury electrode:

Construction of Dropping Mercury Electrode (DME):

1. **Mercury Reservoir**: The DME consists of a mercury reservoir connected to a fine capillary tube. The mercury reservoir allows controlled drops of mercury to form at the tip of the electrode.
2. **Capillary Tube**: The capillary tube regulates the flow of mercury drops into the solution. It ensures that drops of uniform size and shape are released at regular intervals.
3. **Electrode Holder**: The electrode is usually mounted on a holder that allows precise positioning and adjustment during experiments.
4. **Connection**: The electrode is connected to the external circuitry of the polarograph, allowing the measurement of current and the application of potential.

Working Principle of Dropping Mercury Electrode:

1. **Formation of Mercury Drops**: Initially, the mercury reservoir is filled with mercury. A constant potential is applied to the mercury reservoir, causing mercury drops to form at the tip of the capillary tube.
2. **Renewal of Electrode Surface**: As each drop of mercury forms and detaches, it exposes a fresh surface of mercury to the solution. This continuous renewal ensures a clean and reproducible electrode surface, minimizing electrode fouling and ensuring stable measurements over time.
3. **Electrochemical Reactions**: When a potential is applied between the dropping mercury electrode and the reference electrode (e.g., saturated calomel electrode), electrochemical reactions occur at the mercury-solution interface. These reactions involve the reduction or oxidation of electroactive species present in the solution.
4. **Measurement of Current**: The current flowing through the electrode due to these electrochemical reactions is measured. The current is directly proportional to the rate of electrochemical reaction, which in turn depends on the concentration and nature of the analyte species in the solution.

Advantages of Dropping Mercury Electrode:

1. **Reproducibility**: Provides a reproducible and stable electrode surface due to the continuous renewal of mercury drops.
2. **Wide Potential Range**: Can operate over a wide potential range, making it suitable for studying a variety of redox processes.
3. **High Sensitivity**: Offers high sensitivity in detecting electroactive species, allowing for the analysis of trace amounts.

Limitations:

1. **Mercury Handling**: Requires careful handling of mercury due to its toxicity and environmental concerns. Proper disposal and safety precautions are necessary.
2. **Limited to Electroactive Species**: Can only be used for substances that undergo electrochemical reactions at the mercury-solution interface.

Applications of Dropping Mercury Electrode:

1. **Quantitative Analysis**: Used for quantitative analysis of metals, organic compounds, and other electroactive species in solution.
2. **Kinetic Studies**: Enables the study of reaction kinetics and mechanisms at the electrode surface.
3. **Research and Development**: Widely employed in research and development across various fields including analytical chemistry, environmental monitoring, and electrochemistry.

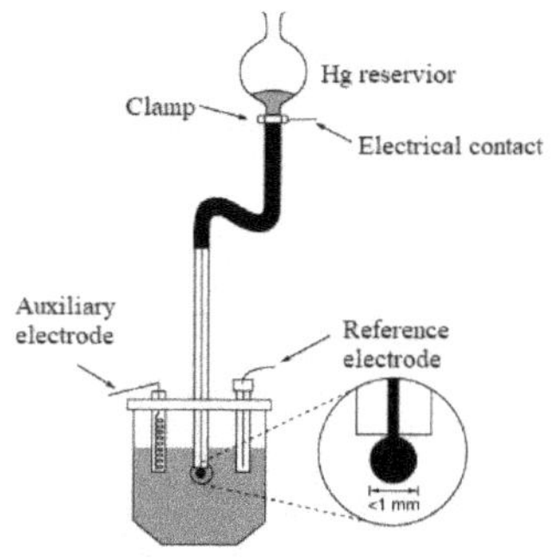

PLATINUM ELECTRODE

The dropping platinum electrode (DPE) serves as an alternative to the dropping mercury electrode (DME) in polarography, offering similar capabilities with the advantage of avoiding the use of mercury, which is toxic and requires careful handling and disposal. Here's a detailed explanation of the construction and working principles of the dropping platinum electrode:

Construction of Dropping Platinum Electrode (DPE):

1. **Platinum Wire**: The main component of the DPE is a fine platinum wire or electrode rod. Platinum is chosen for its inertness, stability, and conductivity in electrochemical applications.
2. **Capillary Tube**: Similar to the DME, the DPE includes a capillary tube or reservoir system connected to the platinum electrode. This tube controls the formation and release of drops of platinum into the solution.
3. **Electrode Holder**: The platinum electrode is typically mounted on a holder that allows precise positioning and adjustment during experiments.
4. **External Circuitry**: The electrode is connected to the external circuitry of the polarograph, facilitating the measurement of current and the application of potential.

Working Principle of Dropping Platinum Electrode:

1. **Formation of Platinum Drops**: Initially, the capillary tube connected to the platinum wire is filled with platinum. A constant potential is applied to the capillary, causing drops of platinum to form and detach from the electrode tip.
2. **Renewal of Electrode Surface**: As each drop of platinum forms and detaches, it exposes a fresh surface of platinum to the solution. This continuous renewal ensures a clean and reproducible electrode surface, similar to the DME.
3. **Electrochemical Reactions**: When a potential is applied between the dropping platinum electrode and the reference electrode (e.g., saturated

calomel electrode), electrochemical reactions occur at the platinum-solution interface. These reactions involve the reduction or oxidation of electroactive species present in the solution.

4. **Measurement of Current**: The resulting current flowing through the electrode due to these electrochemical reactions is measured. The current is directly related to the rate of electrochemical reaction, which depends on the concentration and nature of the analyte species in the solution.

Advantages of Dropping Platinum Electrode:

1. **Non-toxic**: Platinum electrodes avoid the toxicity associated with mercury, making them safer for laboratory use and environmentally friendly.
2. **Wide Potential Range**: Like the DME, platinum electrodes can operate over a wide potential range, allowing for the study of various redox processes.
3. **Reproducibility**: Offers reproducible measurements due to the controlled drop formation and renewal of the electrode surface.

Limitations:

1. **Cost**: Platinum is more expensive than mercury, which can increase the initial setup cost.
2. **Interference**: Platinum electrodes may be susceptible to surface contamination or reactions that interfere with measurements in certain environments.

Applications of Dropping Platinum Electrode:

1. **Analytical Chemistry**: Used for quantitative analysis of metals, organic compounds, and other electroactive species in solution.
2. **Environmental Monitoring**: Applied in environmental studies to detect and quantify pollutants and contaminants in water and soil samples.
3. **Research and Development**: Widely used in research to study reaction kinetics, electrochemical mechanisms, and the behavior of substances in solution.

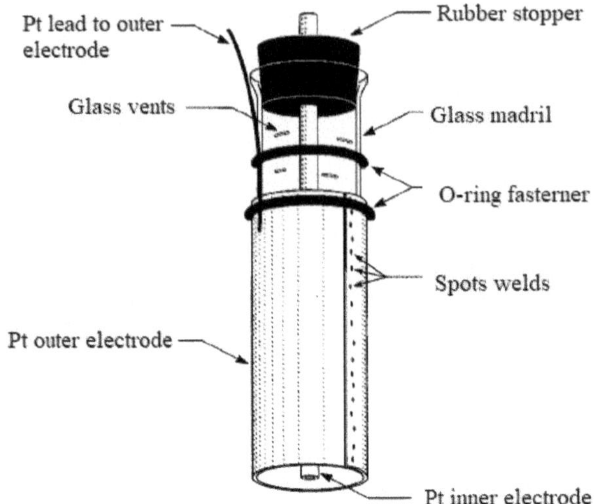

APPLICATIONS OF POLAROGRAPHY

Polarography, as an electroanalytical technique, finds diverse applications across various fields due to its ability to provide detailed information about electrochemical processes and substances in solution. Here's a detailed exploration of the applications of polarography:

Quantitative Analysis:

1. **Metal Ion Determination**: Polarography is extensively used for the quantitative determination of metal ions in solution. It offers high sensitivity and selectivity, making it suitable for detecting trace amounts of metals in environmental samples, biological fluids, and industrial processes.
2. **Organic Compound Analysis**: Polarography is also applied in the analysis of organic compounds that undergo electrochemical reactions, such as pharmaceuticals, pesticides, and organic pollutants. It allows for the determination of concentration levels and monitoring of chemical reactions.

Environmental Monitoring:

1. **Pollutant Detection**: Polarography plays a crucial role in environmental monitoring by detecting and quantifying pollutants in water, soil, and air samples. It can identify heavy metals, pesticides, and other contaminants that pose risks to ecosystems and human health.
2. **Water Quality Assessment**: It helps assess water quality parameters by measuring electroactive species indicative of contamination or changes in water composition. This information aids in environmental management and regulatory compliance.

Pharmaceutical and Biomedical Applications:

1. **Drug Analysis**: Polarography is utilized in pharmaceutical analysis to study the stability, degradation kinetics, and formulation of drugs. It provides insights into the electrochemical behavior of drug compounds, aiding in quality control and pharmacological research.
2. **Biological Fluid Analysis**: In biomedical research, polarography is employed to analyze biological fluids such as blood, urine, and cerebrospinal fluid. It can detect and quantify biomarkers, drugs, and metabolites present in these fluids, facilitating diagnostic and therapeutic monitoring.

Electrochemical Kinetics and Mechanisms:

1. **Reaction Kinetics**: Polarography allows researchers to study reaction kinetics and mechanisms at electrode surfaces. By analyzing current-potential relationships, it provides information about reaction rates, activation energies, and electrode processes.
2. **Electrode Surface Modifications**: It is used to investigate electrode modifications and coatings, enhancing electrode performance and selectivity in electrochemical sensors and devices.

Industrial Applications:

1. **Process Control**: Polarography is applied in industrial processes for real-time monitoring and control of electrochemical reactions and product

quality. It ensures consistent production standards and facilitates process optimization.

2. **Corrosion Studies**: It helps in studying corrosion mechanisms and evaluating corrosion inhibitors by monitoring changes in electrochemical parameters over time.

Other Applications:

1. **Food and Beverage Industry**: Used to analyze additives, contaminants, and quality parameters in food and beverage products.
2. **Materials Science**: Applied in materials research to study electrochemical properties, surface coatings, and corrosion resistance of materials.

Advantages of Polarography:

1. **High Sensitivity**: Capable of detecting trace amounts of analytes.
2. **Selective**: Able to distinguish between different electroactive species.
3. **Quantitative**: Provides accurate measurement of concentrations.
4. **Versatile**: Applicable to a wide range of substances and sample types.

Limitations:

1. **Electroactive Species**: Limited to substances that undergo electrochemical reactions.
2. **Instrumentation**: Requires specialized equipment and expertise for operation and data analysis.
3. **Interferences**: Susceptible to interferences from impurities or complex matrices in samples.

Multiple Choice Questions

1. What is polarography primarily used to study?
    a) Magnetic properties
    b) Electrochemical behavior of substances in solution
    c) Thermal conductivity

d) Optical properties

2. Which electrode is commonly used as the working electrode in polarography?
   a) Platinum wire
   b) Glass electrode
   c) Dropping mercury electrode
   d) Gold electrode
3. What does the term 'polarogram' refer to in polarography?
   a) A plot of current versus temperature
   b) A plot of current versus potential
   c) A plot of potential versus time
   d) A plot of resistance versus current
4. What is the primary function of the reference electrode in a polarographic setup?
   a) To generate current
   b) To measure resistance
   c) To maintain a constant potential
   d) To measure temperature
5. Which parameter is obtained from a polarogram and indicates the midpoint of the redox process?
   a) Peak potential
   b) Diffusion coefficient
   c) Half-wave potential (E1/2)
   d) Capillary rise
6. In the Ilkovič equation, what does the term 'D' stand for?
   a) Diameter of the electrode
   b) Diffusion coefficient of the electroactive species
   c) Density of the solution
   d) Dilution factor

7. What is a significant advantage of using a dropping mercury electrode (DME) in polarography?
   a) High cost
   b) Continuous renewal of the electrode surface
   c) Limited potential range
   d) Toxicity issues
8. Which substance is commonly used as a reference electrode in polarographic measurements?
   a) Silver/silver chloride electrode
   b) Glass electrode
   c) Platinum electrode
   d) Saturated calomel electrode
9. Why is the dropping mercury electrode (DME) preferred for polarographic analysis?
   a) It is inexpensive
   b) It provides a large electrode surface area
   c) It allows for the formation of reproducible mercury drops
   d) It does not require any maintenance
10. Which parameter in the Ilkovič equation represents the concentration of the electroactive species?
   a) A
   b) n
   c) C
   d) v
11. What is the typical auxiliary electrode used in a polarographic cell setup?
   a) Glass electrode
   b) Silver electrode
   c) Platinum wire
   d) Graphite rod

12. What does the term 'half-wave potential' (E1/2) indicate in polarography?

a) The start of the redox process
b) The potential at which half of the analyte is reduced or oxidized
c) The end of the redox process
d) The diffusion rate of the analyte

13. Which of the following is a limitation of polarography?

a) High sensitivity
b) Requires careful calibration and control of experimental conditions
c) Ability to analyze trace amounts
d) Simple instrumentation

14. What type of analysis can polarography be used for in the field of environmental monitoring?

a) Thermal analysis
b) Spectroscopic analysis
c) Detection of pollutants and trace metals in water samples
d) Structural analysis

15. How does the dropping mercury electrode ensure reproducibility in measurements?

a) By using a constant current source
b) By renewing the mercury surface periodically
c) By increasing the temperature of the solution
d) By using a platinum wire

16. Which application is NOT commonly associated with polarography?

a) Quantitative analysis of metal ions
b) Study of electrode kinetics
c) Determination of optical properties
d) Environmental monitoring

17. What is the primary disadvantage of using a dropping mercury electrode?

a) High cost

b) Toxicity and environmental concerns

c) Low sensitivity

d) Limited potential range

18. What type of electrode is used to avoid the toxicity issues associated with mercury in polarography?

a) Gold electrode

b) Dropping platinum electrode

c) Glass electrode

d) Carbon electrode

19. In polarography, what is the function of the auxiliary electrode?

a) To measure the current

b) To apply potential

c) To maintain a constant potential

d) To complete the circuit and allow current flow

20. What is the Ilkovič equation used for in polarography?

a) To calculate the resistance of the solution

b) To describe the relationship between current and applied potential

c) To measure the temperature of the solution

d) To analyze the optical properties of the solution

Short Answer Type Questions (Subjective)

1. What is polarography, and what does it measure?
2. Name the three electrodes commonly used in a polarographic setup.
3. Explain the role of the dropping mercury electrode (DME) in polarography.
4. What is a polarogram?
5. How is the half-wave potential (E1/2) determined in polarography?
6. Describe the primary application of polarography in quantitative analysis.
7. What is the Ilkovič equation, and what does it describe?
8. List the main components of the Ilkovič equation.

9. Explain the significance of the diffusion coefficient (D) in the Ilkovič equation.
10. What are the advantages of using a dropping mercury electrode in polarography?
11. How does polarography aid in environmental monitoring?
12. What is the principle behind the continuous renewal of the electrode surface in DME?
13. Describe the construction of a dropping mercury electrode.
14. Explain how polarography is used in pharmaceutical analysis.
15. What is the primary advantage of using a dropping platinum electrode over a dropping mercury electrode?
16. What are the main limitations of polarography?
17. How does polarography help in studying electrochemical kinetics?
18. Mention one industrial application of polarography.
19. Explain the concept of electrode passivation and how it is prevented in DME.
20. What role does the reference electrode play in a polarographic cell setup?

Long Answer Type Questions (Subjective)

1. Discuss the working principles of polarography and its electrochemical cell setup.
2. Explain the Ilkovič equation in detail, including its components and significance in polarographic measurements.
3. Describe the steps involved in a polarographic analysis, from electrolyte preparation to data analysis.
4. Compare and contrast the dropping mercury electrode (DME) and the dropping platinum electrode (DPE) in terms of construction, working principle, advantages, and limitations.

5. How does polarography contribute to environmental monitoring and pollutant detection? Provide examples.
6. Explain the role of polarography in pharmaceutical and biomedical applications, with specific examples.
7. Discuss the various applications of polarography in industrial processes and materials science.
8. What are the advantages and limitations of polarography as an analytical technique? How can the limitations be addressed?
9. Describe the process of preparing and conducting a polarographic analysis for the determination of metal ions in solution.
10. How does polarography help in studying reaction kinetics and mechanisms at electrode surfaces? Provide a detailed explanation with examples.

Answer Key

1. b) Electrochemical behavior of substances in solution
2. c) Dropping mercury electrode
3. b) A plot of current versus potential
4. c) To maintain a constant potential
5. c) Half-wave potential (E1/2)
6. b) Diffusion coefficient of the electroactive species
7. b) Continuous renewal of the electrode surface
8. d) Saturated calomel electrode
9. c) It allows for the formation of reproducible mercury drops
10. c) C
11. c) Platinum wire
12. b) The potential at which half of the analyte is reduced or oxidized
13. b) Requires careful calibration and control of experimental conditions
14. c) Detection of pollutants and trace metals in water samples
15. b) By renewing the mercury surface periodically

16. c) Determination of optical properties
17. b) Toxicity and environmental concerns
18. b) Dropping platinum electrode
19. d) To complete the circuit and allow current flow
20. b) To describe the relationship between current and applied potential

www.ingramcontent.com/pod-product-compliance
Lightning Source LLC
LaVergne TN
LVHW021135160826
845679LV00023B/1915